T0406691

International Political Economy Series

Series Editor
Timothy M. Shaw
Visiting Professor
University of Massachusetts
Boston, USA

Emeritus Professor, University of London, UK

The global political economy is in flux as a series of cumulative crises impacts its organization and governance. The IPE series has tracked its development in both analysis and structure over the last three decades. It has always had a concentration on the global South. Now the South increasingly challenges the North as the centre of development, also reflected in a growing number of submissions and publications on indebted Eurozone economies in Southern Europe. An indispensable resource for scholars and researchers, the series examines a variety of capitalisms and connections by focusing on emerging economies, companies and sectors, debates and policies. It informs diverse policy communities as the established trans-Atlantic North declines and 'the rest', especially the BRICS, rise.

More information about this series at
http://www.palgrave.com/gp/series/13996

Fulya Apaydin

Technology, Institutions and Labor

Manufacturing Automobiles in Argentina and Turkey

palgrave
macmillan

Fulya Apaydin
Institut Barcelona d'Estudis Internacionals
Barcelona, Spain

International Political Economy Series
ISBN 978-3-319-77103-8   ISBN 978-3-319-77104-5   (Ebook)
https://doi.org/10.1007/978-3-319-77104-5

Library of Congress Control Number: 2018935931

Cover image © Rob Friedman/iStockphoto.com

Printed on acid-free paper

This Palgrave Macmillan imprint is published by the registered company Springer International Publishing AG part of Springer Nature.
The registered company address is: Gewerbestrasse 11, 6330 Cham, Switzerland

To my family

PREFACE AND ACKNOWLEDGMENTS

Technological disruptions change the world of work. The first industrial revolution in the nineteenth century initiated a process where the pace of this change constantly gains speed with each innovation adopted by the market. The launch of the first steam engine, the birth of Fordism and later Toyotism, and the recent spread of automated production technologies thanks to computerized systems have each demanded a different set of skills on the part of the workers. The response of labor in the face of these pressures is far from being uniform across the globe, however. This is because disruptive technologies reorganize production in previously unforeseen ways. Moreover, most employees lack the time and resources to acquire new skills much demanded by this transformed work environment. In most cases, workers who are steeped in old systems find themselves redundant unless they quickly adapt to this fast pace of upgrading.

Yet, the increasing threat of exclusion from the labor market could be very taxing on the society. To avoid potential unrest getting out of control, the government is motivated to intervene, manage the transition and ensure that labor unrest does not escalate. This is because a high number of unemployed individuals threaten the political and economic stability in any given setting. In the most extreme case, persistent economic exclusion may trigger the growth of radical political movements that lure supporters to the ranks of extremist populism. However, the capacity of politicians to contain the disruptive implications of technological advances is limited, often due to institutional constraints.

This book reveals that the transformative impact of technological disruptions on worker skills is contingent on the political dynamics.

Specifically, it shows that political institutions are highly relevant in understanding how labor responses to market-induced pressures are governed in developing areas. Based on a comparison of worker experiences employed by the same multinational company in Turkey and Argentina, the book demonstrates that unitary systems enjoy several institutional advantages in controlling labor unrest, while federal systems characterized by political rivalries are more conducive to escalation of industrial conflict. Importantly, the following chapters reveal that vocational education programs are highly relevant in understanding how labor unrest is governed in developing areas. This is because the content of these training programs shapes ordinary workers' attitudes toward new technologies. To reveal these dynamics, this manuscript traces diverse trajectories of manufacturing worker consent in the Global South by comparing vocational education and training reform processes in federal and unitary systems. The recent experiences of developing countries that had a disruptive shift in production systems offer important lessons for others that are going through a similar change driven by innovations in robotics and computerized production systems today.

* * *

Writing this book was not easy. But the people I met while working on this project made the process more pleasant and enjoyable. During the past years that led up to this manuscript, I benefited tremendously from the intellectual and financial support of numerous institutions and individuals. The field research for this study was made possible by numerous grants from Brown University Graduate School. The writing stage has been supported by a generous grant from Josephine De Kármán Fellowship Trust.

My greatest intellectual debt is to my mentors Melani C. Cammett and Richard O. Snyder. The completion of this project stands as a solid evidence of their generous advice, encouragement and wisdom, for which I am forever grateful. I also benefited immeasurably from the sharp questions, insightful comments and genuine encouragement of Jose Itzigsohn, whom I would like to acknowledge with great respect.

I consider myself very lucky to have received comments and generous feedback from many others during my time at Brown University. Jorge Alves, Maria Angelica Bautista, Gavril Bilev, Catherine Corliss, Mila Dragojevic, Eli Feiman, Patrick Heller, Pauline Jones, Eduardo Moncada, Feryaz Ocakli, Cecilia Perla, Heather Silber, Barbara Stallings, Rebecca

Weitz-Shapiro and late Alan Zuckerman kept me alert with their construc-
tive criticism and questions at various stages of this project. My under-
graduate professors at Bogazici University, Mine Eder, Zeynep Gambetti,
Kemal Kirişçi, Taha Parla and Hakan Yilmaz contributed to my intellectual
development from miles away, and I sincerely thank them for their support
and early encouragement.

Embarking on a fieldwork for this study would not have been possible
without the kind help of many individuals and institutions. In Turkey,
Cem Erciyes, Birim Özer and Oğuz Tunçyürek helped me reach important contacts and sources of information. Evrensel Daily Archive
Department allowed me to go through their big stack of newspapers without any hesitation. Ministry of Education Head Office workers in Bursa
and Istanbul kindly allowed me to go through their well-organized and
archived meeting minutes. In Argentina, Tulia Falleti, Valeria Brusco and
Martin Maldonado made it much easier to have access to key interviewees
by putting me in touch with people from their network. In addition, the
National Ministry of Labor workers in Buenos Aires and Ministry of Labor
officers of Córdoba Province helped me a great deal to understand the
intricacies of labor relations in Argentina. In Turkey and Argentina, FIAT
Auto Inc. and Koç Holding kindly opened their doors to observe production processes and conduct interviews on the shopfloor. Most importantly,
I am grateful to the workers of these factories for generously sharing their
training experiences and insights with me.

In revising the manuscript, I also benefited greatly from the intellectual
environment at my home institution at Institut Barcelona d'Estudis
Internacionals and also from a visit to Princeton University, which was
made possible thanks to Jose Castillejo mobility grant from the Spanish
Ministry of Education. For earlier comments and questions on different
parts of this manuscript, I would like to sincerely thank Miriam Bradley,
Lesley-Ann Daniels, Juan Diez-Medrano, Aina Gallego, Elisabeth
Johansson-Nogues, Jacint Jordana and Yannis Karagiannis. At Princeton
University, Killian Clarke, Gozde Guran, Tommaso Pavone, Manuel Vogt
and the participants of the qualitative research seminar series provided
very useful feedback.

In preparing the final manuscript, I would like to thank the team at
Palgrave for their excellent guidance. For his encouragement, support and
guidance, I am truly grateful to the IPE series editor Timothy Shaw. In
addition, the anonymous reviewer's sharp and insightful feedback on the

manuscript has been very helpful as I worked on the final revisions. Christina Brian has been a pleasure to work with from start to finish and her attention to detail only made this project better. I would also like to thank many others and the entire team at Palgrave for their kind help at every step of preparing this book.

My family has been the greatest source of support as I worked on this project. For their unending love and encouragement, I cannot thank my parents Nuriye and Vedat Apaydin and my sister Muge Apaydin enough. They have supported me in immeasurable ways throughout my studies as I tried to put my findings into perspective. Finally, I am grateful to Matthias vom Hau for his enduring love, care and friendship. In addition to reading every page of this book and sharing his intellectual wisdom, he witnessed my joys and pains as I continue to explore the world of social sciences. I consider myself very lucky that we embarked on an exciting journey together. Along the way, our wonderful children joined us. Therefore, it is to my growing family that I dedicate this work.

Barcelona, Spain   Fulya Apaydin

CONTENTS

LIST OF ACRONYMS

AKP	Adalet ve Kalkinma Partisi (Justice and Development Party)
ANAP	Anavatan Partisi (Motherland Party)
AP	Adalet Partisi (Justice Party)
BIRLESIK-METAL	Birlesik Metal Iscileri Sendikasi (United Metalworkers Union)
BTSO	Bursa Sanayi ve Ticaret Odasi
CGT	Confederacion General de Trabajo (General Workers Confederation)
CHP	Cumhuriyet Halk Partisi (Republican People's Party)
CIM	Camara Industria de Metalurgicos (Chamber of Metallurgy Industrialists)
CME	Coordinated Market Economy
CNAOP	Comision Nacional de Aprendizaje y Orientacion Profesional (National Commission for Learning and Professional Orientation)
CNC	Computed Numerically Controlled
COPIC	Federal Council for Production, Investment and Growth
DYP	Dogru Yol Partisi (True Path Party)
EMER	Expansion y Mejoramiento de Educacion Rural (Expansion and Improvement of Rural Education)

EMETA	Expansion y Mejoramiento de la Ensenanza Tecnica Agropecuaria (Expansion and Improvement of Technical Training for Agriculture)
FDI	Foreign Direct Investment
HME	Hierarchized Market Economy
ISI	Import Substitution Industrialization
LME	Liberal Market Economy
MESS	Metal Esya Sanayicileri Sendikasi (Union of Metal Goods Producers)
MNC	Multinational Corporation
MUSIAD	Association of Individual Industrialists and Businessmen (Mustakil Sanayici ve Isadamlari Dernegi)
OEM	Original Equipment Manufacturer
PJ	Partido Justicialista (Peronist Party)
PRONAPAS	Programas de Apoyo a la Reconversion Productiva (Support Program for Production Re-conversion)
SMATA	Sindicato de Mecanicos y Afines del Transporte Automotor (Union of Mechanics and Related Trades of the Automotive Industry)
SME	Small and Medium Enterprises
TGSD	Turkiye Giyim Sanayicileri Dernegi (Turkish Apparel Industrialists Association)
TOBB	Turkiye Odalar ve Borsalar Birligi (Turkish Chambers Association)
TQM	Total Quality Management
TURK-IS	Turkiye Isci Sendikalari Konfederasyonu (Turkish Workers Union Confederation)
TURKMETAL	Turkiye Metal Sanayi Iscileri Sendikasi (Turkish Metal Workers Union)
TUSIAD	Turkiye Sanayici ve Isadamlari Dernegi (Turkish Association of Industrialists and Businessmen)
UCR	Union Civica Radical (Radical Civic Union)
UIC	Union Industrial Córdoba (Industrial Union of Córdoba)
UOM	Union Obrera Metalurgica (Union of Metallurgical Workers)
VoC	Varieties of Capitalism

LIST OF FIGURES

LIST OF ILLUSTRATIONS

LIST OF TABLES

CHAPTER 1

Introduction: The Politics of Changing Hearts and Minds

As early as the 1980s, most developing countries in the Global South—including Turkey and Argentina—began to abandon protectionist economic measures in favor of economic liberalization. While Turgut Ozal in Turkey championed free-markets in the aftermath of the 1980 coup, Carlos Menem heralded from Argentina promoting a similar agenda, 13 years after the military intervention of 1976. Weary workers in both countries faced rising pressures to acquire a new set of skills and adapt to changing workplace organizations to keep their jobs. In the automobile industry, managers demanded rapid and seamless worker adaptation to flexible and lean production systems inspired by Toyotism. However, as rising productivity did not translate into rising wages and workers increasingly lost their autonomy on the shopfloor, conflicts in the workplace began to increase. Around the world, tensions induced by industrial upgrading were most visible in the form of extended protests, strikes and walkouts (such as in Argentina, Brazil, India, South Africa), while elsewhere (such as in Turkey, Chile) similar disputes lost their heat quickly, and workers went back to the production line, albeit grudgingly.

In developing capitalist economies, a switch to Toyotism marks a radical break with the older production systems (i.e. Fordism) because it introduces new management technologies. Shopfloor practices of Toyotism combine lean manufacturing with employee participation (via proposal schemes) to lower production costs and optimize just-in-time

© The Author(s) 2018
F. Apaydin, *Technology, Institutions and Labor*, International Political Economy Series, https://doi.org/10.1007/978-3-319-77104-5_1

1

production.[1] This demands a multitasking worker who voluntarily engages in brainstorming, data collection, cause and effect analysis and proposal making (Hutchins 1985, 44). Historically, the birth of Toyotism was initiated by managers who faced increasing pressures to control growing worker unrest in Japan in the aftermath of World War II (WWII) (Silver 2003, 42). To avoid frequent interruptions on the shopfloor, the managers combined these new technologies with handsome benefits (such as lifetime employment opportunities) to a core group of workers (Silver 2003, 42). The success of this management system soon reached international fame, and rapidly spread around the globe like a wildfire.

Targeting the expanding consumer base in middle income countries, most automobile companies with production sites in developing areas followed similar business plans to reduce costs, enhance quality and maximize efficiency. To meet market demands, personnel managers avoided high labor turnover rates and focused on eliminating interruptions on the production line.[2] Across most of these companies, securing the consent of the workforce was designated as "the best practice" to prevent labor contention. Despite these measures, labor commitment to new industrial practices exhibited notable discrepancies ranging from outright rejection to enthusiastic approval of new techniques even across different factories of the same corporation: not all workers felt equally motivated to abandon old habits in favor of new ones.

In Turkey and Argentina, auto-workers employed by a global multinational corporation (MNC) (FIAT) also resisted proposed changes at the outset. However, while labor opposition was quickly eliminated and FIAT employees rapidly endorsed Toyotism in Turkey, their counterparts in Argentina stayed in opposition for longer. This book is motivated by this puzzling behavior. Tracing a broader set of policies adopted by politicians in governing labor unrest, it offers a nuanced account by putting the analytic lens on politics of industrial upgrading in a comparative perspective. Specifically, the following chapters show that vocational education and training programs are highly relevant in understanding how labor unrest is governed in developing areas. This is because the content of these training programs shapes ordinary workers' attitudes toward new technologies and influences whether they will turn into unrepentant luddites or flexible bees. While much ink has been spilled on the ideal recipe for creating competitive national industries in advanced industrialized countries (Piore and Sabel 1984; Schmitz and Musyck 1994; Porter 1998, 2000) and the importance of skills, not all training programs have a positive impact on workers' future income earnings. More importantly, by overlooking how some vocational modules deprive employees of their hard-skills in the long run, these works rarely establish any connection between training programs and labor unrest, especially in the Global South.

Existing accounts on training workers in developing contexts often present a very bleak picture, citing historical barriers to developing an active industrial policy.[3] These include colonial legacies and state building trajectories (Schneider 2015), rent-seeking and a divided business community (Schneider and Karcher 2010) and/or political institutions such as electoral and party systems (Schneider and Soskice 2009). However, these accounts do not tell us a very important part of the story: the mechanism through which labor preferences evolve from staunch opposition to enthusiastic approval of new production technologies. Cases presented in the following chapters address this blind spot by critically unpacking the institutional background of vocational education and training reform—a key mechanism behind labor preference formation—and problematizing diverse trajectories of manufacturing worker consent. As we shall see, in developing settings, synchronizing blue-collar preferences with innovations in production techniques is a process where political dynamics play a key role in shaping labor responses.

WHERE MARX MEETS INSTITUTIONS: AN INTERDISCIPLINARY THEORETICAL FRAMEWORK

To develop these points, the following chapters take an interdisciplinary approach and combine insights from the writings of Karl Marx with those from an institutionalist, political economy perspective. There are at least two reasons why this is necessary for a clearer analysis. First, much of the existing works in the political economy tradition following the footsteps of "marginal revolution" explain capital accumulation not in terms of surplus value extraction, but rather, in terms of utility function—defined as the extra price individuals are willing to pay to increase the pleasure (often gained from consumption) (Rapley 2017). This turn away from David Ricardo's labor theory of value—and also Marx's elaboration of the concept—has fundamentally transformed the development economists' focus, pushing many to exclusively problematize the micro-level, individual behavior to explain divergent outcomes ranging from firm performance to industrial relations and labor union strategies. This narrow angle in most economic models further makes very ambitious universal claims, masking important variations across time and space (Rodrik 2015).

Nevertheless, many of these models are oversimplified—and empirically unverified—imaginations that disregard how employers and employees interact, especially in developing settings. Turning a blind eye to mechanisms of surplus value creation and extraction does not simply make these dynamics irrelevant or go away. While labor theory of value is not without its critics on the grounds that it over-estimates the contribution of manufacturing at the expense of service and finance to value creation, this comment does not adequately capture the experience of the Global South. As we shall see, across much of the developing world, capital accumulation depends on the repression of wages through a mixture of absolute and relative surplus labor extraction tactics (Selwyn 2014, 267). This is different than advanced capitalist settings where technological innovations and/or other mechanisms—such as highly sophisticated financial instruments—may accelerate the accumulation of capital in faster ways (until the next crisis). Yet, in many countries of the Global South, such dynamics are conspicuously absent: financial markets are often underdeveloped and game-changing technological innovations are either limited or non-existent. Rather, these settings stand as attractive zones of investment largely due to cheaper labor costs.

At the same time, however insightful as he might have been, Marx's theoretical framework also has its limitations. This brings us to the second motivation that guides this book's interdisciplinary focus. In *Das Capital*, Marx thoroughly maps out the mechanisms of surplus extraction, including exploitation and dynamics that lead to class conflict. However, in the original writings, there is very little emphasis on how institutions—and especially political institutions and the state—intervene in these processes. To be fair, Marx never set out to unpack the relationship between the state and capitalist development: his writings on the subject are scattered over a few essays including *The Class Struggles in France, the 18th Brumaire of Louis Bonaparte* and *The Civil War in France* (Miliband 1965, 278), and in those works, the state is conceptualized as a bourgeois construct that only intervenes to sustain the interest of the capitalist class (i.e. those who own private property).[4] In that sense, Marx would not be surprised to see false consciousness—or the manufacturing of consent, in Burawoy's (1979) terms—culminated through an extensive network of public schools and education professionals that defend capitalist development as the best option for the society.

However, the same framework is unable to explain why some states are better at promoting these ideas (and controlling labor unrest) as opposed to others. For Marx, capitalist states are essentially the same:

Property and all that makes up the content of law and the state is, with some modifications, the same in the United States as in Prussia; the republic in America is thus only a purely political form as is the monarchy in Prussia. (Marx quoted in Miliband 1965, 281)

This is most famously re-stated in the *Communist Manifesto* where Marx and Engels note that the state "is but a committee for managing the common affairs of the whole bourgeoisie" (Marx and Engels 1978, 475).

It is true that debates over the state among the Marxist scholars in the twentieth century added important modifications to this reading, and highlighted further nuances of state-class relations in greater precision. Moving beyond economic determinism, these works highlight the relational dimension of state vis-à-vis class and formulate state capacity as a two-way street (vom Hau 2015, 133) where policies formulated by the state affect the balance of class power, by creating bias in favor of certain classes (Hirsch and Viertel 1977; Offe 1984; Jessop 1990; vom Hau 2015). According to these perspectives, state institutions are not simply instruments in the hands of hegemonic capitalists but rather emerge as a compromise after decades of struggles between the state and social forces (Jessop 1990, 2007). Yet, as we shall see, the recent experiences of Turkey and Argentina point at dynamics that Marxist frameworks cannot identify with accuracy and precision. In both cases, the contemporary ability of the state to intervene on behalf of the propertied class has been constrained by political institutions (and the territorial organization of political power) which have been established decades (or even centuries) earlier, under very different state and class configurations. The implications of this historical discrepancy are rarely problematized by studies in the Marxist tradition.

Turkey and Argentina are very similar in terms of the level of their capitalist development: both are situated in the semi-periphery with moderate levels of industrialization and employ similar technologies of surplus extraction that primarily depend on the repression of wages. Production is not fully automated in most sectors, and the manufacturing industry largely depends on the employment of a sizeable blue-collar labor force. Yet, when faced with similar challenges—such as the arrival of Toyotism in a liberalized market economy following the import substitution industrialization (ISI) period—the Turkish and the Argentine states did not follow the same route to control emerging labor unrest. While Turkish state officials worked hand in hand with employers, their counterparts in Argentina did not take on a similar role. There, neither the state bureaucrats nor politicians acted as natural allies of businessmen. Contrasting experiences like this remain a puzzle for Marxist perspectives since many institutional nuances that surround these exchanges are—rather hastily—disregarded.[5] In that sense, a major value added of this study is to reveal—through the lens of vocational education—how the implementation of capitalist value extraction techniques in the Global South are contingent on political institutions that enable or constrain the state to intervene on behalf of the employers, and manage labor unrest.

An Uneasy Business: The Challenge of Transforming Skills in Developing Countries

In the second half of the twentieth century, due to the limitations of an ISI-based model that encouraged production for domestic consumption in relatively small markets, the implementation of the formula "mass production, mass consumption" reached its limit in the Latin American and Middle Eastern contexts.[6] In response, politicians concocted a unique mix of populist and authoritarian policies to maximize surplus labor extraction after dropping ISI from their developmentalist agenda.[7] During this process, squeezing wages without redistributive compensation further contributed to the polarization of business and labor relations. Angry workers and firm management frequently clashed, and in some settings, labor unions systematically faced violence and endured repression in the hands of right-wing governments. By the early 1980s, this instability posed major challenges to capital accumulation and reinvestment in many countries, including Turkey and Argentina.

To address these problems, governments in both contexts encouraged the development of high-value-added industries—most notably automobiles—and adopted ambitious agendas to create new export markets for these producers (Duruiz 1998; Miozzo 2000, 657). These included providing incentive schemes to automobile producers in the form of subsidies, tax breaks and other tangible benefits. Policy makers also expected these measures to stimulate an upgrading of production around the principles of flexible, just-in-time production as widely popularized by the Toyota Motor Corporation.

Though proponents contend that systematic exposure to Toyotism reduces industrial conflict in the long run, not all workplaces have a smooth experience with implementing these practices. For one thing, higher profits are not reflected in worker wages and the new system excludes material rewards as a source of worker motivation. Moreover, while workers are encouraged to make cost-cutting proposals, their shop-floor autonomy is limited because workers cannot implement original solutions without the approval of their supervisors (Kelemen 2003, 135). Thus, technological upgrading calls for a more comprehensive strategy: in order to sustain productivity in a flexible work environment, the hearts and minds of the workers need to be committed as well. Thus, in breaking with the past, a radically different training policy is a must.

A NEW CHALLENGE

Following the diffusion of Toyotism, labor unrest in the automobile industry did not disappear once multinational companies decide to apply a "spatial fix" and moved production to developing settings with little potential for labor militancy. In a much-cited book, Beverly Silver suggests that where capital went, conflict also followed (Silver 2003). According to Silver, the primary mechanism driving labor unrest is the lack of protective benefits that accompany these new technologies. Whereas Toyotist revolution in Japan created a core group of automobile workers who enjoyed job security and other attractive benefits, multinational companies in the Global South adopted this technology without offering similar protections. For Silver, this explains the global resurgence of labor activism in the post-Fordist era.

While this may be indeed true for some of the cases (such as South Korea and Brazil) and also in Argentina, Turkey stands out as an exception to this pattern. This is curious because Turkish workers neither had job security nor were offered extensive social protection as Toyotism penetrated deeper into the production process.[8] Yet, while workers in Argentina took the contentious route, their counterparts in Turkey grew increasingly complacent and quiet. This outlier behavior begs further inquiry into the limits of Silver's explanation. A promising clue lies in unpacking vocational education and training modules, which are very influential in the formation of worker preferences.

According to most economists, vocational training is one of the primary mechanisms through which capitalist development thrives because it enhances manual and intellectual capacity of individuals to increase their earnings. Arguably, skills and worldviews acquired at the beginning of one's career influence the productivity and efficiency of a worker in later stages. At the same time, across much of the developing world, the issue of financing vocational education is a thorny problem: firms are generally reluctant to cover the costs of early training since this would drive down profits while public budgets are often limited to finance these expenses. As businesses try to stay afloat in an ever-growing competition to increase productivity while reducing costs, they increasingly rely on tactics inspired by Toyotism to extract surplus and increase firm earnings.

Since the early nineteenth century, surplus labor extraction techniques evolved with each wave of disruptive technologies and periods of crisis.[9] As elaborated by Karl Marx, surplus labor extraction refers to the appropriation of value created by a worker's labor input, in addition to the basic minimum value a worker has to create in order to survive.[10] Capital accumulation mainly depends on the systematic accrual and reinvestment of this extra value.[11] However, capitalist development since the times of Marx experienced two major moments that further transformed the nineteenth-century forms of profit-making.[12] With the emergence of Fordism in the early 1900s, followed by Toyotism in the 1970s, surplus extraction in the manufacturing industry picked up speed (Harvey 2016, 43), first through the use of manual labor in a fast-moving assembly-line, and later through the use of manual and intellectual labor in a radically reorganized shopfloor.[13]

Manual labor refers to the use of physical strength in order to perform a value-generating action. Before the global diffusion of Toyotism in the 1980s, manual labor stood as the primary means of surplus labor extraction in the automobile industry. Skills required for employing manual labor demand some prior training for executing tasks on the line. Under Fordism's hierarchical structure, workers were expected to fulfill the orders of their supervisors, and did not face any pressure to participate in finding cost-cutting solutions. Rather, with each repetitive action on the band, workers were expected to master simple tasks and produce more in a shorter timeframe. Under this system, the pace of a moving band on the shopfloor is the key mechanism to increase profits.[14]

Before the arrival of Toyotism, national governments in Turkey and Argentina played a key role in coordinating skill formation through a network of vocational schools and centers. At that time, the curricula exclusively focused on the acquisition of manual skills. Until the introduction of flexibility, lean production and just-in-time principles, the concept of skilled worker excluded an emphasis on using one's intellectual labor. Thus, schools had no motivation to include modules on developing soft-skills (such as empathy, team-work, willingness to collaborate, proposal making, commitment to the company) of the future workforce.

However, the arrival of Toyotism introduced notable changes. The rise of Toyotist practices is roughly associated with the stagnation in the rate of capital accumulation during the 1970s in advanced industrialized countries because of at least two reasons. First, existing market institutions were unable to accommodate changing demand composition of consumers, and second, governments were having a difficult time to create new markets for domestic producers. Profits in the manufacturing industry were in sharp decline. Faced by these challenges, companies were ready to embrace promising strategies to reverse the trend. Toyotism offered a quick and easy fix.

Unlike vertical integration, Toyotism best functions in horizontally integrated firms. Under this arrangement, different production units enjoy some degree of autonomy and their ability to act independently is not constrained by strict firm hierarchies. The elimination of vertical integration subsequently requires an effective combination of manual and intellectual labor where workers are expected to help their team members in overcoming production challenges through proposal schemes. Successful implementation of this technique is expected to add a new impetus to increase the rate of surplus extraction.[15]

At the same time, Toyotism does not require highly skilled workers. Very commonly, blue-collars on the shopfloor are not required to have a deep understanding of the tools they operate with. Rather, this new system depends on quick learners who feel comfortable with performing multiple duties across different units. Under lean production, technical trainings on the shopfloor—if any—are short, superficial and intense. When workers are rotated from one station to another—say, from paint-shop to engine— previously acquired skills gradually erode under the mounting expectations of new supervisors. With a few exceptions, most of these workers are not very attractive for poaching by rival firms that seek specialized knowledge. A constant component of Toyotism is an emphasis on behavioral skills. Managers put so much value on discipline, order and commitment to increase profits that these workers are frequently exposed to new tricks and tactics to modify their behavior. In some cases, an over-exposure to these modules facilitates loss of acquired skills as workers try to master new tools and responsibilities in a maze of rotations. Very importantly, these trainings neither increase the market value of workers nor improve their future earnings prospects as predicted by most economists.

The deskilling of workers under a capitalist production system was seen inevitable by Harry Braverman (1974) and early followers of labor process theory. Unlike critical management scholars who distinguish between strategies of the management and owners of capital in controlling labor unrest, Braverman's framework does not mark such a distinction. Rather, it sees an unavoidable path to deskilling as capital seeks to maximize profits. However, later subscribers to this approach mark a "managerialist distinction" and argue that corporate Chief Executive Officers (CEOs) and their teams enjoy sufficient autonomy to control labor independent of the preferences of capital owners. When that is the case, they resort to tactics other than scientific management and manipulation of human relations on the shopfloor (Alvesson and Willmott 1992; Hassard et al. 2001, 348). In that sense, deskilling is not driven by the natural laws of capitalist production, but takes place by way of human intervention. While some suggest that deskilling—as envisioned by Braverman's hypothesis—did not take place (Tanner et al. 1992), the replacement of hard-skills with soft-skills picked up further speed after modified versions of Toyotism were firmly embedded in many factories across the globe. In many ways, Toyotism provides a unique opportunity to craft new strategies to transform skills— and to control and contain potential labor unrest.

Given the management's high expectations, lack of job security, limited autonomy and declining wages, Toyotism's new workplace is a highly stressful environment for workers. Under these circumstances, a seemingly small conflict between employees and the management could easily escalate into a much bigger one. This bears important risks such as bringing the production to a total halt—sometimes indefinitely. Firm-based behavioral trainings are precisely calibrated to prevent such incidents. However, these tactics are also limited in eliminating the risk of worker mobilization because of their short-term focus. Explaining the principles of 5S, Kaizen, total quality improvement and other similar modules to seasoned workers on the shopfloor only informs them of management expectations. The commitment that comes out of a firm-based exposure to these ideas is a temporary one. This is especially problematic in MNCs that are weakly embedded in local networks.

Interruptions due to management-worker tension bear additional risks for securing a seamless, high quality and on-demand delivery of orders. Transforming the hearts and minds of employees to avoid such risks requires long-term strategies that contain and eliminate potential labor unrest. Early exposure to the indispensability of Toyotist principles—ideally before one begins his/her career—combined with repeated trainings on the shopfloor is one powerful tactic recently adopted by multinational firms in developing contexts. Firms communicate their expectations to vocational education and apprentice training centers, and lobby intensely to modify the curricula to fit their human capital needs. In this way, skill formation programs turn into a major transmission belt for manufacturing labor consent, favoring firm expectations. However, especially in countries like Turkey and Argentina, the diversity of political and economic institutions plays a key role in these processes, leading to varying levels of labor consent in favor of production strategies inspired by Toyotism.

MAKING SENSE OF DIVERGENT WORKER RESPONSES

Acquiring new skills to excel at work is generally welcomed as positive by most researchers and policy makers adamantly promote as the *sine-qua-non* of improving one's future earning potential. None of these debates conceptualize it as a mechanism of social control.

A widely discussed theory of skills was formulated by the Nobel laureate economist Gary Becker, who—like many other economists—assumes that vocational training programs are essentially to the benefit of the workers.[16] For Becker, on-the-job trainings are the key determinants of human capital formation, and this is an issue of common concern for the employer and the employee. Therefore, the model exclusively focuses on the shopfloor, and predicts that under conditions of perfect equilibrium in the labor market, rational blue-collars will be willing to cover the costs of training because, in the long run, this will pay-off in higher wages, seniority privileges and bonuses.[17]

However, market imperfections are everywhere, and perhaps even more so in developing capitalist economies. Becker's model assumes that private goods, such as industry-specific skills, will always be sponsored by private actors and/or interest groups. Yet, in most developing economies, it is not uncommon to see public actors financing the provision of private goods. Even in the context of some advanced industrialized settings, Becker's model excludes industry-specific trainings offered beyond the factory premises (e.g. at a public institution, and/or the union). In some countries (e.g. Germany, France, Italy) the state channels large sums of money to maintain and improve vocational schools and training centers.

Second, Becker's theory conceptualizes vocational training as an intrinsically valuable asset that will improve the material well-being of the worker over the long run. This assumption underlies both general and firm-specific skills: in both cases, expected returns are positive, albeit of different magnitude. However, recent findings on everyday experiences of blue-collar workers challenge these assumptions. As flexible and lean production turned into a global norm and an emphasis on soft-skills gained greater attention, the outcome was polarization: while highly skilled workers acquired additional talent and increased their future earnings, low-skill employees were increasingly deskilled (Brown and Campbell 2001). Those in developing economies were no exception. Under additional market imperfections, business-labor cooperation has not been a harmonious one as wages are continuously pressured downwards.

With an attempt to modify Becker's theory, Acemoglu (1997) and Acemoglu and Pischke (1998, 1999) introduce a new model that seeks to incorporate such market imperfections into account.[18] Highlighting the German model of apprentice training, where firms cover the costs in addition to the state, they argue that this case poses the biggest puzzle vis-à-vis Becker's model. In order to explain this anomaly, Acemoglu and Pischke introduce "imperfection in labor markets," and argue that under imperfectly competitive markets, firms cover the initial training costs until the firm acquires *relative* monopsony power in the market. In this way, Acemoglu and Pischke suggest that firms are the key actors capable of resolving collective action dilemmas because of their underlying private interest.

Yet, just like Becker, Acemoglu and Pischke are primarily occupied with explaining firm behavior without adequate attention to the political context. While this framework explains why firms would have incentives to invest in training programs, Acemoglu and Pischke do not problematize the role of public institutions in sustaining the apprentice training system in Germany. Instead, this is taken into account as a market imperfection. However, the question of why the state mobilizes a broad array of resources and invests large sums into private skill formation is an equally relevant—and perhaps a bigger—puzzle.

Furthermore, like most models in economics, Acemoglu and Pischke's model assumes employees and producers to be players devoid of a capacity for collective action. However, in the majority of cases, these actors are also organized under professional associations. Across the formal sector and especially in big automobile plants, workers are often unionized, which potentially gives them some form of bargaining power on training-related issues. Moreover, by excluding unions from their model, Acemoglu and Pischke do not explain why some unions agree to share part of training costs with businesses while others staunchly oppose such schemes.

In a recent challenge to Acemoglu and Pischke, Dustmann and Schoenberg (2008) modify this model by introducing the unions into the picture and argue that when unions sign collective wage agreements for extended periods of time, they agree on a lower wage in return for company-based trainings. According to this framework, collaboration between the firms and labor unions is possible as long as stakeholders follow the principle of *tit-for-tat*, which would ensure labor compliance under Toyotism. Yet, while Dustmann and Schoenberg's model highlights the role of unions in the provision of skills, it does not explain why unions should accept wage compression in return for training when there are repetitive shocks that lead to losses in union membership due to frequent lay-offs. At least in the case of Turkey and Argentina, economic liberalization policies and export-oriented production was accompanied by major market shocks, and labor earnings experienced severe downturns. In both countries, frequent worker lay-offs in the automobile industry were not uncommon and with each wave of dismissals, unions lost a share of dues-paying members.

Like many economists, Dustmann and Schoenberg also assume that training provided by the firm improves technical skills of the unionized workers, enabling them to gain further expertise. However, Toyotism asks employees to stretch beyond technical skills and requires them to invest in behavioral skills for faster surplus extraction. Under this system, firms have to make repeated investments to ensure worker commitment, so that employees can contribute to cost-cutting proposals even when they are shuffled around to other departments in the factory.[19] At the same time, over-emphasis on building soft-skills happens at the expense of useful investment in higher or firm-specific technical skills.

Overall, the models of Becker, Acemoglu-Pischke and Dustmann-Schoenberg offer partial explanations of why and how businesses and unions cooperate on training schemes. These economists—perhaps very optimistically—expect vocational education and training schemes to have a positive impact on worker earnings. More importantly, these models are all muted in the face of state-labor interaction during challenges induced by technological disruptions. By treating vocational education and training programs as inherently beneficial to workers, these accounts fail to see negative externalities generated by some programs—such as deskilling—and thereby miss the implications of these processes on labor responses and mobilization patterns.

Unlike economists who focus on the rational incentives of firms, unions and individuals, sociologists that problematize cross-national and/or local variation in skill formation focus on social relations and constraints, arguing that material interests of economic stakeholders operate under certain parameters that shape resulting skill formation schemes (Blossfeld 1992; Granovetter and Swedberg 1992; Hodkinson et al. 1996; Rees et al. 1997). According to these studies, formulating investment in skills as a by-product of rational calculations that involves business and labor is an inaccurate representation of what actually takes place on the ground because its fundamental assumptions disregard the effect of social limitations (e.g. social background, class identity, organizational constraints) on the preferences of stakeholders.[20] "Just as an egg remains an egg, irrespective of how it is cooked, so an individual's background restricts the career opportunities available to him or her" write Rees et.al. (Rees et al. 1997, 490), assuming that timing, duration and content of investment in skills would be subject to change only if there is a radical transformation in the social limitations that constrain these actors.

Approaches that highlight social constraints assume that collective action depends primarily on favorable social conditions that enable actors to participate in these schemes. However, the question of how a favorable environment comes about remains a big question. In general, scholars that single out social constraints place very little emphasis on the question of agency in collective action. A hidden assumption behind these models is: if workers have limited means to oppose new production schemes and trainings, then they would readily accept them.

By contrast, industrial sociologists invoke worker agency. In an earlier landmark study, Burawoy (1979) finds that workers adapt to the reorganization of production by routinizing the details of new arrangements through inventing competitive games as they complete their tasks on the shopfloor. In Burawoy's experience, one important dynamic that drives this is a workplace culture where manifestations of masculinity translate into competitive behavior. Others contextualize the experiences of workers by highlighting labor networks (Seidman 1994; Anner 2003, 2011), suggesting that blue-collars actually have substantial knowledge over the details of the production processes. Importantly, transnational ties among blue-collars facilitate information exchange among these solidarity networks and influence how workers position themselves vis-à-vis new management strategies (Anner 2011).

In many ways, the capacity of workers to contest business strategies rests on their associational and structural power (Wright 2000). According to this distinction, structural power of labor is influenced by the relative position of workers in the overall economic system (e.g. workers who can disrupt an entire supply chain thanks to their critical position on the production line enjoy substantial structural power to challenge capital) (Wright 2000, 962). On the other hand, workers' associational power is strongly influenced by the capacity of workers to initiate and sustain collective action, for example, through trade unions (Wright 2000, 962). Power-based approaches suggest that the configuration of these two coordinates best explain conditions under which labor mobilization takes place.

Others who have a more skeptical view of labor-power turn to unpack management strategies and suggest that facilitating worker commitment in firms primarily depends on the strategies of supervisors and managers (Tuckman and Whittall 2002; Vallas 2003; Rothstein 2006). These studies are built on the premise that managers do not fully inform the workers about the implications of industrial upgrading and therefore, blue-collar consent to these technologies is usually uninformed thanks to managerial tactics and tricks. While workers may enjoy associational rights, formal institutions do not always guarantee associational power of the blue-collars, especially when managers systematically intervene. For example, Vallas (2003) finds that when corporate executives refrain from an exclusively technical managerial style, they are better equipped to convince workers to endorse new forms of shopfloor reorganization. Comparing worker responses to industrial upgrading across Mexican and US factories of the same MNC, Rothstein (2006, 2016) reaches a similar conclusion. Puzzled by varying levels of voluntary participation practices adopted at two different factories of General Motors in the USA and Mexico, Rothstein concludes that local factory managers have imposed different control parameters on workers on the shopfloor, despite the fact that general guidelines of lean production remained the same (Rothstein 2006, 171–172).[21]

Though these snapshots provide extensive details on the shopfloor interaction between employers, unions and employees, they offer partial accounts of why similar managerial tactics adopted by the same multinational company generate contrasting reactions from the workers that seemingly enjoy similar levels of structural power. Shopfloor surveillance schemes in multinational production are indeed relevant and management is generally very alert toward blue-collar non-compliance. However, worker attitudes toward new production technologies are not simply a by-product of shopfloor exchanges. The training background of the employees and the political context in which they operate also matter in shaping labor capacity to effectively mobilize.

Recently, a growing body of research in this field points that political institutions and interests—which are shaped over the course of history—play a major role in the unfolding of worker mobilization pathways. For example, structures of partisan competition (Martin and Swank 2012) may yield varying labor regulations (Kus and Ozel 2010) and contrasting institutional legacies (Cohen 1989; Cook 1998), which in turn may constrain or facilitate collective worker response to industrial upgrading. Similarly, political institutions may shape national industrial cultures and repertoires of resistance (Hofstede 1983; Francis 1995; Black 1999, 2001), creating varying mobilization outcomes. Indeed, the process of governing worker responses in Turkey and Argentina reveals that efforts to consolidate Toyotism are largely driven by political dynamics, where local officials play an important role.

Bringing Politics Back In

In some countries going through industrial upgrading, local officials play a notable role in overseeing the transformation of shopfloor relations (Carrillo 1995; Jonas 1996; Montero 2001a, b; Schrank 2011; Chen 2014). The comparative advantage of these actors lies in opportunities to collect and analyze information relatively faster, thanks to their physical proximity to producers and workers. Arguably, an ability to effectively assess industrial problems within their district provides them the means for devising new strategies when responding to an ongoing strife. These strategies are not only limited to networking, negotiating and providing material incentives but also include organizational resources—such as vocational education and training programs—to influence the early formation of labor preferences.

Yet, local officials are bound by political institutions and historical legacies that shape them. For example, assuming that voter interests determine the policy choices regarding the acquisition of skills, Iversen and Soskice (2001) and Iversen and Stephens (2008) find that electoral systems (or systems of interest representation) aggregate policy preferences of the voters in distinct patterns, which explains the resulting type of vocational education schemes sponsored by top-level decision makers. In advanced industrialized countries, majoritarian systems encourage private provision of skills while proportional representation incentivizes public institutions for coordinating skill formation.[22] However, this finding does not replicate well in the Global South: proportional representation has not always created favorable conditions for the diffusion of public vocational education in many developing countries. Understanding why this is the case requires deeper probing into historical dynamics.

The evolution of political institutions as we know them is a long, protracted process and full of unexpected turns. Today, Germany stands as the poster-child of a harmonious state-business-union cooperation that consistently yields high skills thanks to an exemplary apprentice training system. Surprisingly, however, the initial stages of this process were led by a very conservative and authoritarian government that had no such plan in mind in the late nineteenth century: the 1897 law that sets the stage for apprentice training was intended to protect traditional artisans against a rapidly growing industrial working class (Thelen 2004, 7). German industrialization took place under an authoritarian state where traditional artisanal organizations survived. These organizations were very important in apprentice training. So, when modern labor unions finally emerged on the horizon, thanks to rapid spread of industrialization, the competition over skill formation systems was not sharply divided over class lines in Germany. Rather, unionized workers competed against traditional master-artisans over apprenticeship programs and skills (Thelen 2004, 21). Thelen suggests that in the aftermath of WWI, modern unions had many reasons to collaborate with firms against artisanal organizations who sought to monopolize skill formation pathways. It was in this context that the early seeds of a corporatist alliance between German unions and businesses were sown. This path is very different than that in the UK where industrialization destroyed traditional artisanal organizations and early labor organizations were repressed. Under these circumstances, skilled workers united together to defend themselves and control the market on their skills (Thelen 2004, 21). This led to a situation where skill formation was contested across the class divide: as workers organized in defense of their skills, employers repeatedly attacked them (Thelen 2004, 21). The growing conflict over skill formation in the UK prevented the formation of a corporatist alliance as the apprentice system deteriorated and firm-based training was on the decline. These dynamics prevented the emergence of a German-style vocational education system in the UK in the subsequent decades.

Overall, the historical evolution of the German apprentice system into its current form was one that involved a lot of institutional layering. This was largely driven by the changing configuration of political interests during the long course of the twentieth century (Thelen 2004; Culpepper and Thelen 2008). Through a comparative political analysis of vocational education institutions, Thelen highlights the historical roots of the incentive structures of key actors, and shows how a federal arrangement in Germany provided unexpected avenues for the political incorporation of labor—a process that eventually led to an extensive network of vocational training institutions around the country. A crucial factor that drives the emergence of vocational institutions (or the lack thereof) is the conditions under which state intervention takes place. In countries where the state played a key role cutting back on incentives, (e.g. like England—a unitary setting—where traditional artisanal organizations had either been destroyed or never fully developed) there was minimal competition over access to workers with specific skills, and the resulting training programs put the emphasis on the acquisition of general skills. On the other hand, in countries with no such experience, resulting competition between different groups (i.e. artisans vs. industrial producers in Germany) over skills was mediated through political incorporation of labor under a federal scheme, creating a vocational education system that eventually accommodated the concerns of both parties (Thelen 2004).

Though Thelen's book does not explicitly designate Germany's apprentice system as a tool for governing labor unrest, the book makes frequent reference to conflicts between industrial employees and craft workers over the course of negotiations on skills in a decentralized setting. Unlike the experience of developing countries today, these conflicts were overcome despite Germany's federal political structure, thanks to an intense competition between artisanal organizations and labor unions over skills. However, across most federal settings in the Global South—including Argentina—similar historical competitions did not result in lasting corporatist arrangements. There, contestation over training policy in the manufacturing industry has been largely divided across class lines. Under these circumstances, the territorial organization of political power (e.g. federal vs. unitary systems) in the Global South led to different outcomes in shaping preferences over vocational education and training.

THE ARGUMENT: ORGANIZATION OF POLITICAL POWER AND WORKER RESPONSE TO INDUSTRIAL UPGRADING

How does the geographic dispersal or concentration of political power influence strategies for governing labor unrest in the Global South? I argue that mobilizing a comprehensive transformation in worker attitudes is contingent on whether local officials agree to comply with the preferences of the central government on strategies of conflict mediation and/ or prevention. In countries like Turkey and Argentina, the diffusion of just-in-time production around the principles of Toyotism initially generated a major labor unrest. However, governing this unrest unfolded in different ways. At least two major dynamics played a key role in these processes: (1) career motivations of local officials, and (2) the availability of institutional resources to manage skill formation processes.

At the beginning of the 1990s, shopfloor training modules were insufficient to win the hearts and minds of skeptical workers in favor of just-in-time, flexible and lean production. In order to have labor on board, automobile producers turned to local politicians for help. In unitary Turkey, local officials were key to building an exclusionary yet powerful network that brought educators, producers and labor associations together, and initiated a major reform in vocational schools. In Bursa, local governors cooperated with the central administration and played a key role in transforming the hearts and minds with a long-term plan. Specifically, these officials coordinated information exchange between business and vocational schools through an institutional platform, and ensured student exposure to the expectations of a new production system from a very early age. In that sense, state officials at both levels in unitary Turkey worked in favor of employer interests.

On the other hand, in Córdoba, the process was riddled with conflicts between supporters of rival political parties. During this period, politicians in Córdoba disagreed with the federal government on a number of economic reform issues, including decentralization of education and flexibilization of the labor force. This unfavorable climate further intensified existing political rifts between the federal government that demanded an immediate elimination of conflict to avoid capital flight, and the provincial government that ignored these demands. The local governor was too busy trying to save his political career than spending time to build industrial peace and invest in long-term programs to win workers. Thus, the federal system in Argentina created fractions within the state apparatus, pitting pro-business federal officials against their subnational counterparts who were not convinced by this exclusionary alliance in favor of multinational automobile producers. In the midst of this political fight, workers found an opportunity to stay in opposition for a much longer period.

This argument stands in contrast to the economists who expect that, in the medium term, political differences would be irrelevant to economic reforms because the market mechanisms are expected to adjust prices, eliminating any resort to politically motivated rivalries between the stakeholders. Rather, the findings in subsequent chapters support existing evidence that highlight the role of political differences in shaping economic policies in capitalist systems (Boix 1997, 2000; Garrett 1998; Wibbels 2005). In particular, when local and central politicians have competing economic agendas in a federal setting, resulting conflicts could be highly disruptive for business and labor cooperation at the subnational level.

My argument strongly resonates with Wibbels' earlier finding on how partisan harmony is a prerequisite for economic reform in federal environments. Based on a subnational comparison of Argentine provinces during the 1990s, Wibbels observes strong opposition to the economic reform agenda of the federal government especially in provinces where governors heavily relied on the public sector for political support and clientelist relations dominated exchanges between politicians and their constituency. In fact, Córdoba is discussed at length as a negative case to demonstrate how partisan discrepancy between the *Union Civica Radical* (UCR)-led local government and the *Partido Justicialista* (PJ)-led federal government was the source of a long and protracted opposition to Menem's economic reform agenda.

While public sector reform was undeniably a major point of contestation between local and federal governments in Argentina (Murillo 2001; Falleti 2010) the experiences of automobile workers in Córdoba further show us that private interest groups, such as unions and business associations, are also affected by partisan discord over issue areas that are—seemingly—of no immediate concern to them (such as decentralization of education and privatization). As I elaborate further in Chap. 4, what is really surprising—at least in the case of Córdoba—is the prolonged mobilization and opposition by private actors (such as automobile workers) who are not directly embedded in the arguably clientelistic networks of the local government (in this case, the UCR in Córdoba). In fact, these workers were affiliated with unions that had historically very strong links to the incumbent PJ, yet, here they were, occupying factories,

blocking roads and exhibiting a broad array of militant tactics in opposition to the deal promoted by the federal government. Consequently,
there were serious delays in transitioning to a new production regime
due to politically induced conflicts. The case of Córdoba thus reveals
how federal institutions could constrain local politicians while allowing
more room for labor opposition.

A NOTE ON CASE SELECTION AND METHODOLOGY

This book analyzes the impact of government structure on labor response
to industrial upgrading with a special focus on the automobile sector in
Turkey and Argentina. To explain these divergent responses, I build on
the principles of Rohlfing's (2008) *case-study-based nested analysis*
(Rohlfing 2008). This method is different from Lieberman's (2005)
regression-based nested analysis framework where the researcher is almost
always advised to start with a large-N quantitative analysis before moving
on to trace the causal mechanism by closely probing carefully selected
cases. By contrast, Rohlfing suggests that this approach may give way to
flaws in data analysis when key variables of interest are not appropriately
specified. Alternatively, he proposes to start with a small-N analysis as a
first step to identify whether a variable of interest is systematic or non-
systematic in a causal model.

In line with this orientation, I start with a controlled comparison of two
subnational units in two different countries to increase the explanatory
leverage to be derived from a mixed-methods framework. In selecting
these two cases, I follow Mill's method of difference, and control for corporate strategies and shopfloor dynamics—two oft-cited factors in existing
studies as potential *explanans* for the duration of labor conflict. This pairing strategy also controls for additional confounders that are relevant:
both factories are situated in countries that switched from import-
substituted industrialization to an export-led growth model in the early
1980s following military interventions. In the early 1990s, both governments put substantial emphasis on the automobile industry, adopted policies that designated this sector as the locomotive of development and
offered handsome subsidies to domestic and international investors.
Moreover, following a switch to export-led industrialization and economic
liberalization, both countries experienced major economic crises around
the same time periods (in 1994 and 2000), respectively.

To further control for shopfloor-related factors, the following chapters focus on two factories of the same MNC based in Bursa (Turkey) and Córdoba (Argentina). This is important because manufacturing in the developing world—including Turkey and Argentina—is increasingly concentrated in local clusters largely due to pressures from incoming MNCs (Cammett 2006). Thus, to unpack why labor response to new skill formation policies varies in federal and unitary systems, I focus on the contrasting experiences of workers employed in two factories of the same multinational automobile company (FIAT) located in two provinces that accommodate a dense network of automobile MNCs and their local providers.

This way of matching cases follows the principles of J.S. Mill's methods of systematic comparison. In order to control for the role of capital and business-specific strategies across the cities, I narrow the universe of cases by focusing on the skill formation practices in locations where the same multinational company has production sites.[23] Focusing on human capital formation policies around a single MNC in industrializing countries reduces the number of analyzable regions to four in three countries, setting the boundaries of a small-N comparison.[24] Because I am interested in understanding the variation in post-Fordist transitions after the 1990s, I exclude those provinces that have factories launched after 2000.[25] This leaves me three factories located in three cities across three countries: Betim (Brazil), Córdoba (Argentina) and Bursa (Turkey). However, because the size of the factory in Brazil is considerably bigger than Córdoba and Bursa, and due to limitations of resources for carrying research in Brazil, I exclude Betim from the analysis. This way of filtering cases reduces the noise level and allows pairing of Turkey and Argentina based on the principle of most similar systems design, controlling for relevant macro-economic factors in addition to firm-related variables. Moreover, by focusing on the implications of industrial upgrading in automobile production across two different places, the analysis follows the footsteps of studies that focus on a single sector with a cross-national perspective.[26] But most importantly, this way of pairing cases also sharpens the variation in political factors once we control for the role of capital and allow us to focus on the implications of federal and unitary regimes on skill formation and labor mobilization.

The results from this qualitative comparison reveal that a multi-government setting is more conducive to prolonged worker protests especially when partisan conflicts and political rivalries between the central and regional governments dominate the scene. Following the presentation of qualitative findings, I then test the external validity of these results by situating Turkey and Argentina in a broader sample with data from 37 middle income and lower-middle income countries covering the period between 1990 and 2012. This cross-validation test allows us to partially address two commonly encountered problems in observational, small-N studies: omitted variable bias and model overfitting. Employing correlated random effects and fixed effects models, this part tests three relevant hypotheses and indeed finds that federal systems significantly enhance the maneuvering capacity of labor by prolonging industrial conflict.

Focusing on carefully matched industrializing countries in two different geographic regions—one in Latin America and one in the Middle East—is a relatively underexploited method in comparative politics. Studies using a subnational strategy generally focus on federal systems and usually make comparisons selecting provinces within a single country.[27] In small-N cross-national studies, federal and unitary systems are treated as different categories and are rarely matched. On the other hand, large-N studies barely focus on the system of government as a variable of interest and do not problematize this distinction in explaining labor responses to unfavorable economic reform agendas.

However, this is an important yet largely underemphasized variable that plays a major role in resulting skill formation policies and labor responses to industrial upgrading, especially in developing areas. As discussed earlier, federal systems accommodate multiple governments ruling over a single territory, which increases the likelihood of disagreements among politicians operating at the federal and subnational levels. This enables labor unions to maintain their contentious position by means of exploiting rivalries in a multi-level political competition. On the other hand, the maneuvering capacity of labor is very limited in unitary systems where local officials rarely dispute demands of the central government. These findings further speak to a growing body of scholarship that highlights how political institutions that surround the exchanges between firms, unions and workers influence industrial conflict and development pathways (Gunderson and Melino 1990; Rubin and Smith 1991; Tuman 1994; Murillo 2001; Murillo and Ronconi 2004; Crowley 2004; Hurst 2004; Aleman 2009; Kim and Gandhi 2010; Robertson and Teitelbaum 2011; Lee et al. 2014). In that sense, moving the spotlight on institutional factors complements and goes beyond explanations that exclusively rest on shopfloor dynamics, macro-economic factors and/or exclusively rational calculations of actors involved in an industrial strife.

THE ROAD AHEAD

The remainder of this book is organized as follows. Chapter 2 begins with a discussion on the significance of the automobiles sector in industrial development across the semi-periphery, then maps out the position of Turkey and Argentina in global production chains, and explains the political significance of skill formation by focusing on the changes brought about by a transition from assembly-line, Fordist production to a more flexible system built on the principles of just-in-time delivery as inspired by the Toyota Corporation. This chapter expands the discussion on how new skill formation programs are essential ingredients of surplus extraction and capital accumulation processes, and reveals the entry points of actors into local channels of industrial development policy coordination. At the same time, Chap. 2 also highlights the added value of comparing cases in different geographic regions by situating them within broader debates on the *varieties of capitalism*, and engages in a critical debate with scholars (e.g. Schneider and Soskice 2009; Schneider 2013) who recently embarked on a task of conceptualizing capitalist development beyond advanced industrialized countries. As I discuss the opportunities available to, and limitations that constrain politicians, I elaborate how the system of government influences the scope, content and duration of vocational training programs after Fordism.

The subsequent chapters add empirical flesh to these theoretical debates. Chapter 3 details the process that led to the development of a comprehensive transformation in skill formation schemes in Bursa under a unitary system of government. Automobile producers in this province collaborated with the local governor for adding new modules to vocational education and training programs. This was possible thanks to the absence of a broader political conflict between different levels of government in a unitary setting. Resulting arrangements facilitated mobilization of local resources for coordinating new policy frameworks, leading to contained and shorter industrial conflicts. The political proximity between politicians and automobile producers further contributed to the dissemination of behavioral training techniques across other producers in the province. Not only did public schools modify their curricula with an emphasis on soft-skills, but labor unions also actively promoted the participation of their members in seminars and trainings collaboratively organized by the business organizations.

Shifting the focus across the Atlantic, Chap. 4 explores how a different arrangement emerged in Córdoba. This experience shows us how firm-based arrangements without broader public support for skill formation prevail especially when economic and political stakeholders are divided into partisan camps. In contrast to FIAT-Bursa, FIAT-Córdoba managers were caught under the fire between the federal and local governments. Because local politicians lacked resources to effectively finance the proposed changes in vocational schools, the federal government intervened. But the resulting arrangements were far from consolidating a frictionless worker commitment to Toyotism, and frequent and longer instances of shopfloor conflict over reorganizing production characterized the industrial relations at this factory.

Chapter 5 situates these findings in a broader sample and presents findings on how federalism has a notable impact on labor mobilization outcomes in developing countries since the 1990s. Based on panel data analysis, this section shows that federal systems are more conducive to prolonged labor mobilization in contrast to their unitary counterparts. The discussion documents empirical support for this argument based on a sample of 37 middle income and lower-middle income countries for the period between 1990 and 2012. These findings offer important clues to further unpack how the system of government influences labor response to skill formation and industrial upgrading in Turkey and Argentina.

The final chapter synthesizes the theory and the argument and situates the findings in a broader debate on skill formation policies in countries beyond the two qualitative cases. It discusses the implications of the findings and highlights two follow-up questions that open up new avenues of research, which are: (1) How well does the argument travel to other economic sectors? Does the arrival of new technologies unfold similarly across the manufacturing sector beyond automobiles? and (2) How do political institutions shape the responses of informal labor in the face of rapidly changing production technologies?

NOTES

1. Lean production techniques seek to maximize efficiency by reducing waste/externalities in the production process.
2. Labor turnover rate is measured by dividing the number of employers who left their position in a given year by the average number of employees per year. A high turnover rate signals problems with retaining skills and efficiency in production (Glebbeek and Bax 2004).

3. Active industrial policy in developing economies is characterized by a close partnership between business and the government, where "the former needs to be highly transparent and willing to share information on a regular basis and the government introduces incentive schemes and performance standards to improve industrial output and efficiency" (Schneider 2015, 11).

4. In fact, intervention on behalf of capitalists is what Marx would expect to observe even under a Bonapartist state, where he grants it some autonomy and situates it somewhat above the direct control of the dominant class. See Miliband 1965.

5. For a recent exception, see Yeldan 1995.

6. Arguably, Brazil is a partial exception to this pattern. There, the firms were able to exploit Fordist opportunities in a relatively large domestic market, together with the help of state institutions. See Evans 1995.

7. These means include, but not limited to, restriction of labor rights, squeezing wages, banning strikes and repeated attacks on organized labor groups.

8. See Article 17 of the Labor Law No. 1475 in Turkey.

9. It must be noted that surplus extraction across a given industry is relative: the rate of surplus extraction is not the same when a large corporation reaps the larger share, accumulating "super-profits" while others—such as second tier parts suppliers which I briefly discuss in Chap. 2—are unable to do the same.

10. See Marx (1990 [1976]), pp. 320–329 for a discussion on the creation of surplus value. According to Marx, there are two main forms of surplus extraction: absolute and relative. Absolute surplus value refers to extra value that is generated by increasing the hours worked per working day. On the other hand, relative surplus value is generated by "cutting down wages and [thereby]…reducing the necessary labor time in proportion to the surplus labor time" (http://www.marxists.org/encyclopedia/terms/a/b.htm#absolute), accessed on 10 October 2009. Other strategies include techniques of immiseration (i.e. pushing wages down) and super-exploitation (e.g. paying wages below subsistence requirements) (Selwyn 2014). Yeldan (1995) suggests that these coercive aspects better characterize surplus extraction techniques in developing economies given active involvement of the state.

11. According to Marx, there are at least three ways in which capital accumulation occurs: first is primitive accumulation through appropriating resources (i.e. land, goods), second by the appropriation of extra value created by the worker, and third is through exchange of goods in trade.

12. Even though surplus labor extraction is a fundamental component of capital accumulation, it is not the only mechanism that sustains it. As much as capital accumulation depends on the surplus value appropriated from the

worker, it also needs new markets for consumption, trading goods and reinvesting capital. We can best imagine this process through a symbolic scale with two legs: market creation and value extraction. Capitalist crises are more likely to erupt when the balance is tipped toward either side. In addition to negotiating the terms of domestic market interactions, advanced industrialized countries also strive to create new trade prospects by facilitating access to export markets for domestic firms. In this way, politicians play a key role in fine-tuning capital accumulation mechanisms not only by institutionalizing surplus labor extraction methods, but also by enabling firm access to new markets. Together with supporting market institutions (i.e. labor law, anti-trust laws, welfare measures) state and social actors seek to prevent crises (i.e. sharp rise in unemployment, inflation, market failure) from fundamentally disrupting capital accumulation—an important lesson learned after the US market crash in 1929 (Jessop 2002, 61).

13. While some students of Marx suggest that capitalism is bounded by the falling rate of profit, more recent accounts suggest that Marx did not make such an ambitious claim (see Harvey 2016). As it stands, there is very little empirical evidence that singles out falling rate of profit as the sure-cause behind crises of capitalism (Harvey 2016, 39–43). While it is true that rate of capital accumulation slows down at times of a major meltdown, technological innovations that involve greater use of labor in relation to capital—once they become widespread in use—could sustain productivity (Marx quoted in Harvey 2016, 42). For example, data from the US Bureau of Labor Statistics reveal that the output per worker in the manufacturing industry has been consistently on the rise, except for periods of recession (see https://data.bls.gov/pdq/SurveyOutputServlet). Research on the Japanese automobile industry similarly shows that productivity has grown rapidly beginning from as early as the 1960s. See for example, https://sloanreview.mit.edu/article/manufacturing-innovation-lessons-from-the-japanese-auto-industry/. In both settings, the rate of wage increases was much slower compared with the rate of increase in productivity. While increasing productivity is not necessarily the best measure of surplus extraction, at the heart of Toyotism sits a dedicated and docile worker who is expected to prioritize the company's performance and work without a (fair) compensation if necessary. The fact that the rate of wage increase falls below the rate of output per worker provides suggestive evidence on how the rate of surplus extraction has increased over time.

14. Nevertheless, that does not mean training was completely neglected by governments under Fordism. The more the workers are trained, the higher the efficiency would be (i.e. the risks for workplace accidents are reduced, and probability of faulty production is minimized). Thus, exposing work-

ers to vocational education and training programs not only facilitates specialization but also enables *faster* surplus labor extraction by minimizing the costs through ensuring the efficient use of manual labor.

15. Some scholars imply that post-Fordism essentially marks the beginnings of a post-materialist era in production. For example, Hardt and Negri (2001, 2005) and Lazzarato (1996) from the post-modern school note that the significance of manual labor has been in decline especially with increasing automation and use of computerized systems. According to this school, immaterial labor is the new defining feature of our times. Immaterial labor is defined as a specific form that does not require the use of manual power in production; rather, it is characterized by the use of a different type of physical power (i.e. mental thinking, intellectual activities) that yield products that are *immaterial* in character (e.g. information, services). Taking a bolder step, Hardt and Negri give car production as an example to the gradual disappearance of manual labor with the increasing use of machinery on the shopfloor. As we shall see, this observation is not very accurate in developing contexts. There, the use of manual labor is highly prevalent in the manufacturing industry and most importantly, in high-value-added sectors—such as automobiles—production runs on a combination of automation and manual labor. Long before Hardt and Negri's work appeared on the horizon, Hirst and Zeitlin (1992) complained about oversimplified depictions of transition from Fordism to post-Fordism as an exclusively market and technology driven process—at least in the context of advanced industrialized countries. In a famous essay published in *Economy and Society*, these authors are highly critical of the "technological determinism" adopted by many scholars, including Marxists, and propose that the reality involves a great deal of complexity, with hybrid models adopted by different firms, sectors and national economies. Nevertheless, unlike advanced industrialized settings where the pace of technological change in the automobile industry was more gradual, producers in the Global South—mostly local subsidiaries of global MNCs—rapidly had to introduce standardized business plans drafted in company headquarters elsewhere. Importantly, these processes were bounded by the institutional context in which they unfolded.

16. In his classical 1962 article, Becker defined investment in human capital as "activities that influence the future real income through the imbedding of resources in real people" (Becker 1962, 9).

17. According to most economists, individuals seek to maximize their material well-being (or utility) in economic transactions; they possess full knowledge of market conditions; and they act rationally to achieve their preferences in the light of this knowledge (Martinelli and Smelser 1990, 29).

18. For related firm-based accounts of vocational training also see Katz and Ziderman 1990, Chang and Wang 1996, Acemoglu 1997.

19. For example, some companies and big holdings emphasize flexibility so much so that they shift groups of workers employed in different sub-sectors when there are severe external shocks. For example, Koc Holding in Turkey shifted a group of workers from their Ford Factory, which produces cars, to Arcelik LG (owned by the same group), which produces air conditioning equipment ("Ford Iscileri Arcelik LG'de calisacak" (Ford workers will be employed at Arcelik LG), Sabah, 9 April 2009. Available at: http://www.sabah.com.tr/2009/04/09/haber,EFC9FA8ADE4941888093A0 DA31A1844A.html, accessed on 1 May 2009)

20. Some studies with a neo-Marxist perspective take this assumption further and argue that vocational education is a "class-based solution invented by capitalist businessmen and industrial managers to consolidate their power over the emerging corporate capitalist economies" (Spring 1972; Violas 1978 quoted in Benavot 1983). Based on this framework, Braverman (1974) implies that new vocational training programs disempowered the working class and left it without control over skill formation systems. These scholars claim that the learning capacity of individuals—which is generally taken as a given by the economists—is actually shaped by the class relations and relative access to resources. One of the earliest studies in this framework by Boudon (1974) suggests that there are two types of social effects that influence skill development: primary and secondary effects. Primary effects are environmental stimuli that shape cognitive abilities and learning motivation in children conditioned by different class backgrounds (Müller and Jacob 2008, 130). Relatedly, secondary effects include "class differences in the choices individuals make in their educational careers, given the same performance in schools" (Müller and Jacob 2008, 130). Boudon argues that primary and secondary effects accumulate over time, sharpening class-based inequalities as the level of education increases. Yet, these studies remain quiet on how differences in the skill composition due to class-based inequalities aggregate and translate into national and/or cross-national variation in the skill formation *systems*.

21. Rothstein looks at a particular shopfloor policy (e.g. Andon system) that requires the use of manual labor by the workers, and excludes a broader focus on intellectual participation schemes, which follow relatively standardized managerial control systems. Andon system is a practice by which workers could stop the assembly-line during production to address problems to guarantee quality (Rothstein 2006, 153). On a related note, this practice was no longer in use at FIAT factories due to time loss and delays in meeting production deadlines.

22. According to Iversen and Soskice (2001), partisan composition of governing coalitions is critical for understanding redistribution policy. A government's approach to redistribution is highly likely to shape the skill formation system to be endorsed by the ruling coalition. Because electoral systems play an important role in deciding on the political composition of the executive, they are the key to understanding whether the government will channel large sums of money into public vocational education and training programs.

23. This is a Europe-based automobile corporation that specializes in cars for the middle income group.

24. These provinces are Minas Gerais-Betim (Brazil); Minas Gerais-Sete Lagoas (Brazil); Córdoba (Argentina); Bursa (Turkey).

25. This includes Sete Lagoas (Brazil) established in 2000.

26. Some works in this tradition include Dunning 2008; Cammett 2007a, b; Caliskan 2010; Karl 1997; Paige 1997; Bates 1981.

27. For an overview of subnational comparative methods, see Snyder 2001. Recent political analyses that apply subnational methods to analyze empirical evidence from federal systems include Gibson and Calvo 2000; Heller 2000; Varshney 2001; Snyder 2001; Jones Luong 2002; Chavez 2003; Wibbels 2005; Hiskey 2005; Calvo and Micozzi 2005; Hecock 2006; Urdal 2008; Weitz-Shapiro 2014. For recent examples of subnational comparisons based on single non-federal systems see Putnam et al. 1993; Locke 1997; Moncada 2009.

BIBLIOGRAPHY

Acemoglu, D. 1997. Training and Innovation in an Imperfect Labor Market. *The Review of Economic Studies* 64: 445–464.

Acemoglu, D., and J.S. Pischke. 1998. Why Do Firms Train? Theory and Evidence. *Quarterly Journal of Economics* 113: 79–119.

———. 1999. Beyond Becker: Training in Imperfect Labor Markets. *The Economic Journal* 109: F112–F142.

Aleman, J. 2009. The Politics of Tripartite Cooperation in New Democracies: A Multi-level Analysis. *International Political Science Review* 30 (2): 141–162.

Alvesson, M., and H. Willmott. 1992. On the Idea of Emancipation in Management and Organization Studies. *Academy of Management Review* 17: 432–464.

Anner, M. 2011. *Solidarity Transformed: Labor Responses to Globalization and Crisis in Latin America*. Ithaca: ILR Press, an Imprint of Cornell University Press.

———. 2003. Industrial Structure, the State, and Ideology: Shaping Labor Transnationalism in the Brazilian Auto Industry. *Social Science History* 27 (4): 603–634.

Bates, R. 1981. *Markets and States in Tropical Africa: The Political Basis of Agricultural Policies.* Berkeley: University of California Press.

Becker, G.S. 1962. Investment in Human Capital. *The Journal of Political Economy* 70: 9–49.

Benavot, A. 1983. The Rise and Decline of Vocational Education. *Sociology of Education* 56: 63–76.

Black, B. 1999. National Culture and Labour-market Flexibility. *The International Journal of Human Resource Management* 10 (4): 592–605.

———. 2001. National Culture and Industrial Relations and Pay Structures. *Labour* 15 (2): 257–277.

Blossfeld, H.P. 1992. Is the German Dual System a Model for a Modern Vocational Training System? *International Journal of Comparative Sociology* 33: 170–181.

Boix, C. 1997. Political Parties and the Supply Side of the Economy: The Provision of Physical and Human Capital in Advanced Economies. *American Journal of Political Science* 41 (3): 814–845.

———. 2000. "Partisan Governments, the International Economy and Macroeconomic Policies in OECD Countries" 1964–93. *World Politics* 53: 38–73.

Boudon, R. 1974. *Education, Opportunity and Social Inequality.* New York: Wiley.

Braverman, H. 1974. *Labor and Monopoly Capital.* New York: Monthly Review Press.

Brown, C., and B. Campbell. 2001. Technical Change, Wages, and Employment in Semiconductor Manufacturing. *ILR Review* 54 (2): 450–465.

Burawoy, M. 1979. *Manufacturing Consent: Changes in the Labor Process Under Monopoly Capitalism.* Chicago: The University of Chicago Press.

Caliskan, K. 2010. *Market Threads: How Cotton Farmers and Traders Create a Global Commodity.* Princeton: Princeton University Press.

Calvo, E., and J.P. Micozzi. 2005. The Governor's Backyard: A Seat-vote Model of Electoral Reform for Subnational Multiparty Races. *The Journal of Politics* 67: 1050–1074.

Cammett, M. 2006. Development and the Changing Dynamics of Global Production: Global Value Chains and Industrial Clusters in Apparel Manufacturing. *Competition and Change* 10: 23–48.

———. 2007a. *Globalization and Business Politics in Arab North Africa.* New York: Cambridge University Press.

———. 2007b. Business-government Relations and Industrial Change: The Politics of Upgrading in Morocco and Tunisia. *World Development* 35: 1889–1903.

Carrillo, J. 1995. Flexible Production in the Auto Sector: Industrial Reorganization at Ford Mexico. *World Development* 23: 87–101.

Chang, C., and Y. Wang. 1996. Human Capital Investment Under Asymmetric Information: The Pigovian Conjecture Revisited. *Journal of Labor Economics* 14: 505–519.

Chavez, R.B. 2003. The Construction of the Rule of Law in Argentina: A Tale of Two Provinces. *Comparative Politics* 35: 417–437.

Chen, L. 2014. Varieties of Global Capital and the Paradox of Local Upgrading in China. *Politics and Society* 42 (2): 223–252.

Cohen, Youssef. 1989. *The Manipulation of Consent: The State and Working-Class Consciousness in Brazil*. Pittsburgh: University of Pittsburgh Press.

Cook, Maria Lorena. 1998. Toward Flexible Industrial Relations? Neo-Liberalism, Democracy, and Labor Reform in Latin America. *Industrial Relations: A Journal of Economy and Society* 37 (3): 311–336.

Crowley, S. 2004. Explaining Labor Weakness in Post-Communist Europe: Historical Legacies and Comparative Perspective. *East European Politics & Societies* 18 (3): 394–429.

Culpepper, P., and K. Thelen. 2008. Institutions and Collective Actors in the Provision of Training: Historical and Cross-national Comparisons. In *Skill Formation: Interdisciplinary and Cross-National Perspectives*, ed. K.U. Mayer and H. Solga. New York: Cambridge University Press.

Dunning, T. 2008. *Crude Democracy: Natural Resource Wealth and Political Regimes*. New York: Cambridge University Press.

Duruiz, L. 1998. Globalization Efforts of Turkish Car Industry. *Actes du GERPISA*: 42–54.

Dustmann, C., and U. Schoenberg. 2008. Why Does German Apprentice System Work? In *Skill Formation: Interdisciplinary and Cross-national Perspectives*, ed. K.U. Mayer and H. Solga. New York: Cambridge University Press.

Evans, P. 1995. *Embedded Autonomy: States and Industrial Transformation*. Princeton: Princeton University Press.

Falleti, T.G. 2010. *Decentralization and Subnational Politics in Latin America*. New York: Cambridge University Press.

Francis, J.L. 1995. Training Across Cultures. *Human Resource Development Quarterly* 6 (1): 101–107.

Garrett, G. 1998. *Partisan Politics in the Global Economy*. New York: Cambridge University Press.

Gibson, E.L., and E. Calvo. 2000. Federalism and Low-Maintenance Constituencies: Territorial Dimensions of Economic Reform in Argentina. *Studies in Comparative International Development* 35: 32–55.

Glebbeek, A., and E. Bax. 2004. Is High Employee Turnover Really Harmful? An Empirical Test Using Company Records. *Academy of Management Journal* 47 (2): 277–286.

Granovetter, M., and R. Swedberg. 1992. *The Sociology of Economic Life*. Boulder: Westview Press.

Gunderson, M., and A. Melino. 1990. The Effects of Public Policy on Strike Duration. *Journal of Labor Economics* 8 (3): 295–316.

Hardt, M., and A. Negri. 2001. Adventures of the Multitude: Response of the Authors. *Rethinking Marxism* 13: 236–243.

———. 2005. *Multitude*. New York: Vintage.

Harvey, D. 2016. Crisis Theory and the Falling Rate of Profit. In *The Great Financial Meltdown*, ed. Turan Subasat. Cheltenham: Edward Elgar.

Hassard, J., J. Hogan, and M. Rowlinson. 2001. From Labor Process Theory to Critical Management Studies. *Administrative Theory & Praxis* 23 (3): 339–362.

Hecock, D.R. 2006. Electoral Competition, Globalization, and Subnational Education Spending in Mexico, 1999–2004. *American Journal of Political Science* 50: 950–961.

Heller, P. 2000. Degrees of Democracy: Some Comparative Lessons from India. *World Politics* 52: 484–519.

Hirsch, J., and J. Viertel. 1977. Elements of a Materialist Theory of the State. *International Journal of Politics* 7 (2): 9–82.

Hirst, P., and J. Zeitlin. 1992. Flexible Specialization vs. Post-Fordism: Theory, Evidence and Policy Implications. In *Pathways to Industrialization and Regional Development*, ed. M. Storper and A.J. Scott. London: Routledge.

Hiskey, J. 2005. The Political Economy of Subnational Economic Recovery in Mexico. *Latin American Research Review* 40: 30–55.

Hodkinson, P., A. Sparkes, and H. Hodkinson. 1996. *Triumphs and Tears: Young People, Markets and the Transition From School to Work*. London: David Fulton.

Hofstede, G. 1983. National Cultures in Four Dimensions: A Research-Based Theory of Cultural Differences Among Nations. *International Studies of Management & Organization* 13 (1/2) (April 1): 46–74.

Hurst, W. 2004. Understanding Contentious Collective Action by Chinese Laid-Off Workers: The Importance of Regional Political Economy. *Studies in Comparative International Development* 39: 94–120.

Hutchins, D. 1985. *Quality Circles Handbook*. London: Pitman Publishing.

Iversen, T., and D. Soskice. 2001. An Asset Theory of Social Policy Preferences. *American Political Science Review* 95: 875–893.

Iversen, T., and J.D. Stephens. 2008. Partisan Politics, the Welfare State, and Three Worlds of Human Capital Formation. *Comparative Political Studies* 41: 600–637.

Jessop, B. 1990. *State Theory: Putting the Capitalist State in Its Place*. University Park: Pennsylvania State University Press.

———. 1992. Fordism and Post-fordism; a Critical Formulation. In *Pathways to Industrialization and Regional Development*, ed. M. Storper and A.J. Scott. London: Routledge.

———. 2002. *The Future of the Capitalist State*. Cambridge: Polity.

———. 2007. *State Power: A Strategic-Relational Approach*. Cambridge: Polity.

Jonas, A. 1996. Local Labor Control Regimes: Uneven Development and the Social Regulation of Production. *Regional Studies* 30 (4): 323–338.

Jones-Luong, P. 2002. *Institutional Change and Political Continuity in post-Soviet Central Asia: Power, Perceptions, and Pacts.* New York: Cambridge University Press.

Kang, D.C. 2002. *Crony Capitalism: Corruption and Development in South Korea and the Philippines.* Cambridge: Cambridge University Press.

Karl, T.L. 1997. *The Paradox of Plenty: Oil Booms and Petro-states.* Berkeley: University of California Press.

Katz, E., and A. Ziderman. 1990. Investment in General Training: The Role of Information and Labor Mobility. *The Economic Journal* 100: 1147–1158.

Kelemen, M. 2003. *Managing Quality.* London: Sage Publications.

Kim, W., and J. Gandhi. 2010. Coopting Workers Under Dictatorship. *The Journal of Politics* 72 (03): 646–658.

Kus, B., and I. Ozel. 2010. United We Restrain, Divided We Rule: Neoliberal Reforms and Labor Unions in Turkey and Mexico. *European Journal of Turkish Studies. Social Sciences on Contemporary Turkey* (11) (October 21). http://ejts.revues.org/4291.

Lazzarato, M. 1996. Immaterial labor. In *Radical Thought in Italy: A Potential Politics,* ed. P. Virno and M. Hardt. Minneapolis: University of Minnesota Press.

Lee, H., G. Biglaiser, and J. Staats. 2014. The Effects of Political Risk on Different Entry Modes of Foreign Direct Investment. *International Interactions* 40 (5): 683–710.

Lieberman, E.S. 2005. Nested Analysis as a Mixed-Method Strategy for Comparative Research. *American Political Science Review* 99 (03): 435–452.

Locke, R. 1997. *Remaking the Italian Economy.* Ithaca: Cornell University Press.

Martin, C.J., and D. Swank. 2012. *The Political Construction of Business Interests.* New York: Cambridge University Press.

Martinelli, A., and N.J. Smelser. 1990. Economic Sociology: Historical Threads and Analytical Issues. *Current Sociology* 38 (2): 1–49.

Marx, K., and F. Engels. 1978. The Communist Manifesto. In *The Marx–Engels Reader,* ed. R. Tucker. New York: W.W. Norton Company.

Marx, K. 1990 [1976]. *Capital, Volume I.* London: Penguin Books.

Miliband, R. 1965. Marx and the State. *Socialist Register* 2 (1): 278–296.

Miozzo, M. 2000. Transnational Corporations, Industrial Policy and the 'War of Incentives': The Case of the Argentine Automobile Industry. *Development and Change* 31: 651–680.

Moncada, E. 2009. Toward Democratic Policing in Colombia? Institutional Accountability Through Lateral Reform. *Comparative Politics* 41: 431–449.

Montero, A.P. 2001a. Making and Remaking 'Good Government' in Brazil: Subnational Industrial Policy in Minas Gerais. *Latin American Politics and Society* 43 (2): 49–80.

———. 2001b. After Decentralization: Patterns of Intergovernmental Conflict in Argentina, Brazil, Spain, and Mexico. *Publius* 31: 43–64.

Müller, W., and M. Jacob. 2008. Qualifications and Returns to Training Across the Life Course. In *Skill Formation: Interdisciplinary and Cross-national Perspectives*, ed. K.U. Mayer and H. Solga. New York: Cambridge University Press.

Murillo, M.V. 2001. *Labor Unions, Partisan Coalitions, and Market Reforms in Latin America*. Cambridge: Cambridge University Press.

Murillo, M.V., and L. Ronconi. 2004. Teachers' Strikes in Argentina: Partisan Alignments and Public-sector Labor Relations. *Studies in Comparative International Development* 39 (1): 77–98.

Offe, C. 1984. *Contradictions of the Welfare State*. Boston: MIT Press.

Paige, J. 1997. *Coffee and Power: Revolution and the Rise of Democracy in Central America*. Cambridge, MA: Harvard University Press.

Piore, M., and C. Sabel. 1984. *The Second Industrial Divide*. New York: Basic Books.

Porter, M.E. 1998. Clusters and the New Economics of Competition. *Harvard Business Review* (November–December): 77–90.

———. 2000. Location, Competition, and Economic Development: Local Clusters in a Global Economy. *Economic Development Quarterly* 14 (1): 15–34.

Putnam, R., R. Leonardi, and R.Y. Nanetti. 1993. *Making Democracy Work: Civic Traditions in Modern Italy*. Princeton: Princeton University Press.

Rapley, J. 2017. *Twilight of the Money Gods*. London: Simon and Schuster.

Rees, G., R. Fevre, C.J. Furlong, and S. Gorard. 1997. History, Place and the Learning Society: Towards a Sociology of Lifetime Learning. *Journal of Education Policy* 12 (6): 485–197.

Robertson, G.B., and E. Teitelbaum. 2011. Foreign Direct Investment, Regime Type, and Labor Protest in Developing Countries. *American Journal of Political Science* 55 (3): 665–677.

Rodrik, D. 2015. *Economics Rules*. Oxford: Oxford University Press.

Rohlfing, I. 2008. What You See and What You Get: Pitfalls and Principles of Nested Analysis in Comparative Research. *Comparative Political Studies* 41 (11): 1492–1514.

Rothstein, J.S. 2006. Selective Participation: Controlling Workers' Input at General Motors. *Research in the Sociology of Work* 16: 151–175.

———. 2016. *When Good Jobs Go Bad: Globalization, De-unionization, and Declining Job Quality in the North American Auto Industry*. New Brunswick: Rutgers University Press.

Rubin, B.A., and B.T. Smith. 1991. Strike Durations in the United States. *Sociological Quarterly 32* (1): 85–101.

Schmitz, H., and B. Musyck. 1994. Industrial Districts in Europe: Policy Lessons for Developing Countries? *World Development* 22: 889–910.

Schneider, B.R. 2013. *Hierarchical Capitalism in Latin America: Business, Labor, and the Challenges of Equitable Development.* New York: Cambridge University Press.

———. 2015. *Designing Industrial Policy in Latin America.* Basingstoke: Palgrave Macmillan.

Schneider, B.R., and S. Karcher. 2010. Complementarities and Continuities in the Political Economy of Labor Markets in Latin America. *Socio-Economic Review* 8 (4): 623–651.

Schneider, B.R., and D. Soskice. 2009. Inequality in Developed Countries and Latin America: Coordinated, Liberal and Hierarchical Systems. *Economy and Society* 38: 17–52.

Schrank, A. 2011. Co-producing Workplace Transformation: The Dominican Republic in Comparative Perspective. *Socio Economic Review* 9 (3): 419–445.

Seidman, G. 1994. *Manufacturing Militance: Workers' Movements in Brazil and South Africa, 1970–1985.* Berkeley: University of California Press.

Selwyn, B. 2014. Commodity Chains, Creative Destruction and Global Inequality: A Class Analysis. *Journal of Economic Geography* 15 (2): 253–274.

Silver, B. 2003. *Forces of Labor.* New York: Cambridge University Press.

Snyder, R. 2001. *Politics After Neoliberalism.* Cambridge: Cambridge University Press.

Spring, J. 1972. *Education and the Rise of the Corporate State.* Boston: Beacon Press.

Tanner, J., D. Scott, and B. O'Grady. 1992. Immanence Changes Everything: A Critical Comment on the Labor Process and Class Consciousness. *Sociology* 26: 439–454.

Thelen, K. 2004. *How Institutions Evolve: The Political Economy of Skills in Germany, Britain, the United States, and Japan.* Cambridge: Cambridge University Press.

Tuckman, A., and M. Whittall. 2002. Affirmation, Games and Insecurity: Cultivating Consent Within a New Workplace Regime. *Capital & Class* 26 (1): 65–93.

Tuman, J.P. 1994. Organized Labor Under Military Rule: The Nigerian Labor Movement, 1985–1992. *Studies in Comparative International Development* 29 (3): 26–44.

Urdal, H. 2008. Population, Resources, and Political Violence: A Subnational Study of India, 1956–2002. *Journal of Conflict Resolution* 52: 590–617.

Vallas, S.P. 2003. Why Teamwork Fails: Obstacles to Workplace Change in Four Manufacturing Plants. *American Sociological Review* 68: 223–250.

Varshney, A. 2001. *Ethnic Conflict and Civic Life: Hindus and Muslims in India*. New Haven: Yale University Press.

Violas, P. 1978. *The Training of the Urban Working Class: A History of 20th Century American Education*. Chicago: Rand McNally.

Vom Hau, M. 2015. State Theory: Four Analytical Traditions. In *The Oxford Handbook of Transformations of the State*, ed. S. Leibfried et al. Oxford: Oxford University Press.

Weitz-Shapiro, R. 2014. *Curbing Clientelism in Argentina: Politics, Poverty, and Social Policy*. New York: Cambridge University Press.

Wibbels, E. 2005. *Federalism and the Market: Intergovernmental Conflict and Economic Reform in the Developing World*. New York: Cambridge University Press.

Wright, E.O. 2000. Working-Class Power, Capitalist-Class Interests, and Class Compromise. *American Journal of Sociology* 105 (4): 957–1002.

Yeldan, E. 1995. Surplus Creation and Extraction Under Structural Adjustment: Turkey, 1980–1992. *Review of Radical Political Economics* 27 (2): 38–71.

CHAPTER 2

Automobiles, Skill Formation and Development

In the aftermath of the 2008 global financial crisis, fearing a major labor unrest and a total breakdown of the industry, prominent automobile producers in the USA approached the federal government in search of financial support to save their businesses. The *operation bailout* immediately caught public attention, and critiques harshly attacked the government for using taxpayer money to cover private debts of crisis-stricken entrepreneurs. Jokes followed. "The three big domestic automakers are now saying they are working jointly on a new hybrid car" commented Jay Leno. "It runs on a combination of state and federal bailout money."[1]Despite critiques, under the leadership of the state, big corporations like GM, Ford and Chrysler were able to work with the largest union in the sector UAW to save a teetering auto industry from collapsing.[2] Soon, the US bailout plan inspired German and French governments who drafted similar plans in collaboration with large automobile producers and labor unions.

On the other hand, the response of some national governments in the developing world included additional measures. For example, in Turkey, officials focused on creating alternative means for infrastructural support (e.g. state-sponsored training programs, temporary work suspension with insurance coverage, postponing credit repayments) in order to keep the businesses afloat.[3] One consequence of these efforts was a growing emphasis on public training programs intended to develop skills of blue-collar

© The Author(s) 2018   39
F. Apaydin, *Technology, Institutions and Labor*, International Political
Economy Series, https://Doi.org/10.1007/978-3-319-77104-5_2

workers. An important motivation behind these schemes focused on controlling potential escalation of labor unrest.

It is true that advanced industrialized countries and developing economies do not exactly share similar industrial development trajectories.[4] Despite cross-national differences in state response to market crises, such snippets from advanced industrialized countries and late-developers have two important points in common: (1) without state intervention, the automobile industry can hardly survive in the face of capitalist market crises and (2) without some form of mediation by the state, businesses in the developing world lack adequate resources to advance their investment agendas. However, national governments are not the only actors that run to the needs of automobile producers during hard times. In addition to top-level officials, the last few decades witnessed the growing prominence of local actors in developing economies. These actors were—formally or informally—delegated the task of coordinating resources to make sure production stays afloat, industrial peace is consolidated and ensure surplus extraction remains profitable to meet overall growth targets in local industrial zones.

Local industrial zones refer to interlinked industrial clusters that are closely monitored and regulated by local government agencies. The scope of this concept is not just limited to economic activity based in urban regions (Sellers 2002), and covers production in suburban areas within a subnational political unit (e.g. provinces) as well. In that sense, a focus on local industrial zones offers a more useful tool to go beyond studies that only examine capital accumulation patterns in cities and urban centers (e.g. Sassen 1994, 2001; Sellers 2002; Scott 2009). Though industrial activity in developing economies tend to concentrate around major cities, changing production technologies in Turkey and Argentina gave rise to the emergence of new producers beyond the city who occupy lower echelons in the supply chain by producing semi-finished goods and/or providing raw materials. In some provinces, new industrial zones beyond the city centers multiplied, creating densely concentrated production networks to speed up the accumulation of capital.[5]

This chapter discusses how politics in these areas came to the forefront in debates over transforming skills by focusing on automobile production. In doing so, it starts with the changing dynamics of new surplus labor extraction and capital accumulation techniques (such as the combination of manual and intellectual labor under Toyotism). In countries like Turkey and Argentina, pressures to build human capital, manage resources and adapt to fast-changing technological upgrading brought political dynamics to the forefront. This gave way to the diffusion of different surplus extraction techniques, where exchanges between the local and central government played a key role.[6]

The exclusive focus is on automobiles, because until very recently, this has been *the* leading sector in shaping production relations in the twentieth century—first under the Fordist, and later under post-Fordist systems. These mechanisms that shape capital accumulation, investment and redistribution often generate conflict of interest between labor unions and businesses who do not always agree on the terms of reorganizing production. Global competition to attract foreign capital has greatly intensified in developing areas, and technological change brought about by automation via robotics and computerized systems has led to the reorganization of shopfloor production since early 1990s. In most of these areas, rising productivity is no longer linked with rising wages, and workers increasingly find themselves at odds with the management.

From Karl Polanyi's (2001 [1944]) *The Great Transformation* to Peter Hall and David Soskice's (2001) *Varieties of Capitalism*, the role of the state in resolving market-induced conflicts under capitalist development in advanced industrialized countries is quite well documented. But the implications of the interaction between local and central state actors in industrial processes across the developing world beg a more systematic inquiry. In countries like Turkey and Argentina, transition from Fordist to post-Fordist production models unfolded in diverse ways. The arrival of new technologies in Turkey and Argentina introduced very similar challenges to workers in the automobile industry. In both cases, workers were required to complete a greater number of tasks in lesser time, sustain top-level performance when rotating across different units, frequently collaborate with their peers on cost-cutting and quality improvement, be flexible in the face of production reorganization and refrain from demanding pay-rise in return for their extra efforts.

Despite these shared expectations on the corporate end, the duration of worker resistance in the face of mounting tasks and diminishing wages showed notable variation: FIAT's Córdoba workers in federal Argentina opposed the new terms for a much longer period between 1996 and 1997, demonstrated little interest in quality improvement workshops, contested the proposal schemes and questioned rotation across different workstations. On the other hand, FIAT management in unitary Turkey did not experience a major problem with getting the workers on board: there, a major industrial conflict triggered by the transformation of production in

1998 surprisingly cooled off rapidly, and workers were much faster in adapting to novel practices.

The key to understanding this variation lies in tracing the political dynamics of labor control for smoother surplus labor extraction and capital accumulation. To that end, this chapter is organized into four parts. First I begin by discussing dynamics of capital accumulation and then present three different models of surplus labor extraction on a historical time line. This part lays out how—in addition to technological upgrading—innovations in techniques of labor force control transformed capital accumulation in different ways, calling for a closer coordination of human capital formation schemes between the local and central government. This section also justifies the significance of skill formation in capitalist development, and explains why it is the core focus of my argument. Next, I show how these new techniques operate on the shopfloor, based on an overview of automobile production processes. This is followed by the debate on the link between state, skill formation and markets in advanced industrialized countries through a critical reading of the *Varieties of Capitalism* approach. The categories (i.e. liberal or coordinated or hierarchical market economies) introduced by this body of work appear incomplete, because technologies of labor control vary. This critique sets the ground for analyzing the political dynamics during the transition from Fordism to post-Fordism, which I elaborate in the final section.

CAPITAL ACCUMULATION AND THREE KEY MOMENTS OF SURPLUS LABOR EXTRACTION

Ever since Henry Ford designed a system for producing Model T every three minutes on a production band in 1904, the world has been a different place. The mass production of a highly sophisticated machine not only changed the entire urban and rural landscape (Kay 1997), but it also marked a new era in capitalist development. Though Henry Ford is portrayed as the genius behind this revolution, the US government also played a central role in supporting this critical industry that came to symbolize industrialization, technological advancement and consumerism (Studer-Noguez 2002, 20–21). In fact, the role of state support in automobile production was not only limited to the USA during the first half of the twentieth century: almost every government in today's advanced industrialized countries either played a direct role in building a national automobile industry, or supported private entrepreneurs in order to secure a place in the competition for industrialization.[7]

Fordist automobile production and subsequent technological advancements radically revolutionized the existing capital accumulation patterns after the textile mill. During the 1800s, surplus labor extraction took place mainly through partial control of the manual labor power. For example, workers in Lancashire textile mills toiled for long hours, but the producers did not have absolute control over the surplus extraction process; the pace of production depended on the workers (Marx (1976) in Burawoy 1984, 252).[8] However, with transfer to Fordist assembly-line in the 1900s, the moving band established greater control over manual labor, allowing the employer to calculate the precise amount of extra-value to be taken-off from a worker's input.[9] Because the automobile worker had no control over the speed of the moving band, s/he had to make sure to catch up with the production pace preset by the manager. This enabled more and controlled surplus value creation in a shorter time frame by pegging the employee to the band, and gradually turned the worker into a natural extension of the production machinery. Perhaps no other movie than Charlie Chaplin's *Modern Times* (1936) better shows how Fordist assembly-line transforms the worker into a mere cog in the wheel.[10] In a famous scene, Chaplin's signature character, the Tramp, is unable to keep up with the increasing speed of the moving band and keeps falling behind his peers. His supervisor scorns at him, pushing the Tramp to work faster, and eventually Chaplin's character jumps on the moving band and begins to roll around cogs and wheels of the factory. Unable to stand against the pressure, and under the absolute control of the band, the Tramp is eventually transformed into a part of the production machinery.

However, what Chaplin's *Modern Times* does not exactly show is the role of the state in coordinating the institutions for sustaining control over the use of manual labor. What we do not see in the movie are varying interactions between the state and the factory owner on how to recruit, train and keep the workforce. For instance, if Chaplin had to make this movie on Germany, rather than England or the USA, we could have seen a completely different picture on the mechanisms that ensured control over manual labor, perhaps with a scene in vocational training centers, a zoom into shopfloor organizations and a peek at worker councils. Similarly, the experience of industrial workers with surplus extraction and control in late-developers during this period is different from advanced industrialized countries, shaped by broader contextual variables (most notably, the political environment) that coordinate capital accumulation processes.

Over time, the implementation of Fordist surplus extraction principles gradually went through a transformation across the globe under the impact of growing firm competition.[11] The emergence of new rivals on the scene and the rise of new producers such as VW, FIAT, Renault and Citroen in Europe were initial challenges to the dominance of three Fordist principles, namely, product standardization, use of special purpose equipment, and the elimination of skilled labor in direct production (Tolliday and Zeitlin 1986, 2–3). These producers essentially modified the implementation of scientific management techniques on the shopfloor and pushed for technological improvements. Still, the use of manual power was the key mechanism through which surplus extraction took place in the manufacturing industry between 1900 and 1970 (see Table 2.1). In other words, until the 1970s, control over manual labor on the factory shop-floor was a fundamental component of raising profits. During this period, producers were primarily concerned with employing workers who could keep up with the pace of the moving band, and comply with the orders of their supervisors.[12]

However, these processes went through another round of restructuring after the late 1970s and early 1980s. During this period, surplus extraction techniques using novel technologies inspired by Toyotism introduced new mechanisms of control over intellectual labor of the workers through quality trainings, proposal systems and teamwork (Rothstein 2006; Womack et al. 2007). The additional requirements of post-Fordist production imposed new limitations on the available pool of human resources. Very importantly, making the most out of this system required a social embedding of post-Fordism beyond the factory, aligning worker preferences

Table 2.1 Surplus labor extraction patterns in the manufacturing industry after the industrial revolution

	Dominant forms of surplus labor extraction		
	Pre-Fordist (1800s)	*Fordist (1900–1970)*	*Post-Fordist (1970-...)*
Method	Partially controlled manual labor	Fully controlled manual labor	Control over manual *and* intellectual labor

with those of business and thereby transform skill formation schemes along the lines of a new production regime. In some emerging market economies, politicians played a key role in this process.

Given these market-induced pressures, how do governments get involved in coordinating the skill formation schemes in developing settings? In order to understand this, the next section maps out how intellectual labor complements manual labor at all levels of production in the automobile factories. Looking at the changing role of workers in supplier-producer networks better reveals under what circumstances producers step out of the shopfloor and seek cooperation with local officials to change vocational education schemes. This also sets the ground for explaining how politics gets in the way of industrial competition and transforming skills.

Supplier-Producer Networks: Surplus Labor Extraction in Automobile Production

Contemporary automobile production runs on a coordination of complex web of activities between auto-parts suppliers and car producers. Essentially, there are two tiers of suppliers to the main plant: the first tier produces semi-finished or finished components that are technologically more sophisticated, such as electric wires, audio, break and computer systems.[13] The second tier producers operate in multiple sectors and supply textile, rubber, glass, plastic, paint and metal-based products to be used in production at the main plant and the first tier suppliers. The majority of second tier suppliers are small and medium sized enterprises with relatively low concentration of capital, while the first tier is a mixed group that includes bigger global companies that specialize in semi-finished goods (see Fig. 2.1). For example, Delphi, a harness cable producer for original equipment manufacturers (a.k.a. OEMs—such as FIAT), is a good example to a first tier supplier that uses more sophisticated techniques on the shopfloor.

Among the OEM producers, there exists a hierarchy of products targeted at different consumer groups, which can be classified under four categories: cars for high income group (e.g. luxury brands like BMW, Mercedes, Jaguar; selected SUV brands, and boutique luxury goods such as Ferrari, Lamborghini, Maserati, Porsche), upper-middle income consumers (e.g. Audi, Saab, Volvo), middle income consumers (e.g. family cars produced by a wide range of OEMs such as Toyota Corolla, VW Passat, FIAT Linea; GM Buick; commercial purpose vehicles such as FIAT

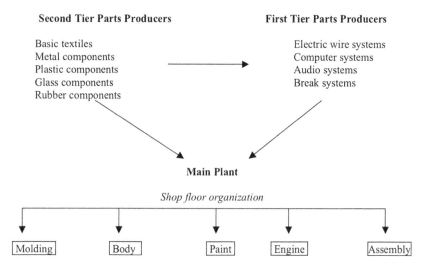

Fig. 2.1 Supplier-chain and producer networks in automobile production

Doblo, VW Caddy, Peugeot Partner) and lower-middle income consumers (e.g. Chinese Chery and Indian Tata/Nano) groups.[14] While the luxury goods and upper-middle class cars that require higher craftsmanship are produced exclusively in advanced industrialized countries in smaller numbers for status seeking customers, the production sites of third and fourth group of cars are based across a wide range of industrializing countries with relatively higher production volumes. For example, in Turkey and Argentina, the automobile MNCs such as FIAT, Renault and Toyota produce a variety of car models that are mostly targeted at middle and lower-middle income groups. Unlike the first and second group of products where the manufacturers maximize profits through selling cars to wealthy customers with relatively high or even exorbitant price tags, companies that produce goods for the middle/lower-middle income group have to keep prices relatively affordable, and need to implement additional techniques on the shopfloor for facilitating surplus extraction and profit maximization. That is why manual and intellectual training of these workers in line with post-Fordist principles on a regular basis becomes a *must* under the new production regime.

In automobile production, surplus labor extraction in second tier parts producers depends less on the control over intellectual labor and more on manual labor. On the other hand, in first tier parts producers (such as

Delphi) and the main plant (such as FIAT), surplus extraction depends heavily on the combination of control over manual *and* intellectual labor. This is where the content of skill formation and worker training programs become important. Ideally, automobile producers would like to recruit well-trained workers with lower mobility prospects (e.g. workers who do not move frequently)[15] and in order to ensure this, they need to cooperate with local officials for creating a pool of skilled workers with attractive opportunities in regions where the production facility is located. Just-in-time, flexible production requires the worker to actively improve surplus extraction. Returns out of this process are maximized when labor turnover rates are minimized and when workers are recruited among those who live in a commutable distance.[16]

In contrast to manual labor, intellectual labor refers to the use of mental skills that enable the worker to make modifications that cut down costs or improve the production process when executing tasks. This requires a more extensive training that focuses on the building of soft-skills. In order to do this, workers must be exposed to behavioral trainings from a very early age—ideally as an apprentice—and use their intellect to exhibit best performance. On the shopfloor, the process simultaneously calls for the transformation of Fordist firm hierarchies into horizontally organized systems that encourage worker participation. Under this new system, production-related information flow is not unidirectional (i.e. from the top to the bottom), rather, the workshops need to be in constant communication and employees are encouraged to work in teams for finding cost-cutting solutions (see Illustration 2.1). To facilitate this, workers need to be willing to acquire new skills such as negotiation, conflict resolution, leadership and ability to work in teams—on and beyond the shopfloor.[17] Early vocational training of the youth is one influential strategy to engender such a commitment and get maximum returns on a worker's input.

Surplus Labor Extraction in Second and First Tier Suppliers

Second tier parts suppliers usually include small and medium sized enterprises that employ between 10 and 100 workers. The production space is smaller and there is no moving band in most of these enterprises: the shopfloor is more like a sizeable workshop. The tasks are relatively simple and could be learned under the supervision of a journeyman or shopfloor leader. Often, these employees have minimum or no vocational training, and workers generally acquire skills on the job.[18] Still, the standardization

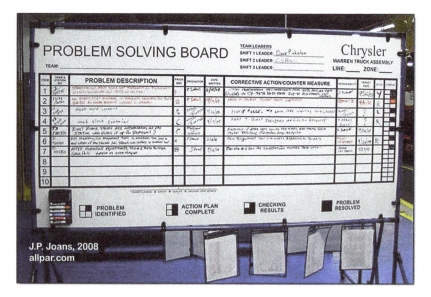

Illustration 2.1 Intellectual participation of workers on a problem solving board at Chrysler

of product quality is of top priority in most of these firms.[19] This is because a small defect in components could completely ruin the overall quality of the final product.[20]

On the other hand, surplus extraction in first tier suppliers is more similar to the techniques used in the main plant. In these enterprises, production space is organized into different workstations, where workers are expected to make small components under heavy time pressure. There is no moving band in most of these factories. The measure of a worker's performance is calculated over how many pieces (i.e. wires, wire components, connectors, brake parts) s/he has completed during a shift. Though the tasks can be repetitive in most of these stations, the management prefers workers who have completed apprenticeship training in a related field, because these employees are much faster and better in detecting and solving problems on the spot. In most of these enterprises, production technology is more sophisticated than the first tier suppliers, which requires employment of workers who can use manual *and* intellectual skills. To that end, the management trains the workers with technical and behavioral modules on a systematic basis.

Surplus Labor Extraction in the Main Plant

Surplus extraction in the OEM is very similar to the process in first tier suppliers, but it is more complicated, scope of the production is bigger and requires careful coordination of tasks with appropriate worker skills. The automobile factories I visited in Bursa and Argentina had at least five production units. These include molding and press, body, paint, engine and assembly. The molding and press division is responsible for building the equipment that will shape large metal parts that eventually constitute the body of an automobile. The workers employed in this department are required to have relevant manual skills for building different molds and operate press machines. In addition, they are expected to make suggestions on how to improve models. Finally, these workers must be flexible, open to frequent changes in model upgrading (every three to four years), work in teams and pay maximum attention to quality improvement.

Once the molding department completes building the initial model, this is used to cut and shape metal sheets in the press department. The pieces are then transferred over to the body-shopworkers, who are responsible for welding pieces using automated, semi-automated and manual techniques. This requires sophisticated knowledge on how to operate welding equipment, and therefore companies generally prefer to hire workers with formal vocational training for this department. Though welding of large auto-parts is done automatically with robots, blue collars undertake majority of detailed work to put together smaller metal components. Just like their fellows in molding and press, body workers are also expected to use their intellectual skills and make regular suggestions on how to improve welding, and participate in team meetings to discuss possible improvements. These suggestions are then re-evaluated by supervisors, and those that are most likely to cut down costs are incorporated into work plans. The worker/team responsible for the improvement generally receives no material compensation, but is symbolically rewarded with some form of recognition for this contribution.

Following the assembly of key metal parts in the body shop, the next station is paint- shop. Workers in this department operate relatively sophisticated tools. In addition to trainings on how these tools are operated, they also need to have some knowledge on chemical composition of the material they work with. Furthermore, because the operation of this equipment is highly sensitive, and even a small mistake could substantially reduce the quality of the coating (e.g. paint could come off after a few months of driving under normal weather conditions), the workers are actively encouraged to look for solutions to reduce the chances of faulty production. Just like the molding, pressure and body divisions, paint-shop workers are expected to make regular suggestions on reducing defects, participate in daily and weekly quality trainings, and work on maximizing their performance as a team to compete for internal awards.

Most multinational automobile companies also have a division on factory premises where they produce and assemble the engines, which are later installed in the automobiles. The workers employed in the engine division need to have higher than average skills. This includes a solid understanding of how a car engine works, and knowledge about general laws of mechanics and physics. This skill-set is absolutely necessary to detect production problems and—ideally—resolve them on the spot because engine is arguably the most sophisticated and expensive component in an automobile. Just like the molding, body-shop and paint-shop divisions, workers in the engine department also work in teams and hold regular meetings for discussing production-related problems and possible solutions. In short, besides manual labor, these workers are also expected to come up with creative ideas to lower production costs. The number of monthly suggestions made by a worker is later taken into account when preparing performance assessment reports.

The assembly-line is the final part in the production process where workers install thousands of small components into a semi-finished car body. Once the body unit is out of the drying oven in paint-shop, all remaining components—including the engine—are assembled on a moving band. Though assembly of parts is not as complex as the previous four tasks, worker proposal system, which is an essential part of quality improvement schemes under post-Fordism, demands blue collars to actively think on what they could do better as they put together various parts. The tasks are repetitive, but in order to maximize the flexibility of the workers, the management regularly rotates workers from one position to another on the same line (e.g. from installing the audio set to mounting bumpers). The band workers are also organized into teams and worker performance is measured based on the number of suggestions.

In order to maximize worker performance, this way of reorganizing production on the shopfloor requires a reliable pool of workers who are willing to accept these principles as the new "normal." An entire group of workers in the main plant need to be stimulated by multiple channels to combine manual and intellectual labor, and voluntarily contribute to surplus extraction under post-Fordism. As we shall see in subsequent chapters, this is not a simple problem that could be solved exclusively by relying on managerial tactics. Especially in developing areas, the cost of repressing/eliminating labor unrest while maximizing commitment is high and private entrepreneurs lack access to resources to establish control over worker preferences. Under these circumstances, preventing the risk of unrest, and avoiding extended protests in a rapidly evolving work environment calls for political intervention in favor of business interests in developing contexts. Needless to say, the type of political intervention is very much influenced by a number of contextual factors, including historical legacies and political institutions.

POLITICS OF SURPLUS LABOR EXTRACTION: *VARIETIES OF CAPITALISM* AND THE MISSING LINK

Some scholars suggest that managing skill formation is a key defining feature of different variants of capitalism. In particular, researchers who seek to map *varieties of capitalism* (VoC) around the globe argue that skill formation and policies that administer these processes explain the origins of liberal and coordinated market economies. The *VoC* (Hall and Soskice 2001) framework provides a series of explanations that highlight the role of the state and its institutions, arguing that these mechanisms shape the behavior of labor and unions in market exchanges.[21] Scholars working in this tradition problematize variation in skill formation systems as an extension of how business associations, labor unions and the state respond to market-induced conflicts (Thelen 2004; Culpepper 2007).[22]

The VoC approach marks a clear distinction between liberal and coordinated market economies (LMEs and CMEs) and highlights the role that national institutions play in resolving collective action problems. These processes led to at least two different routes of capitalist development in advanced industrialized countries. In particular, Hall and Soskice (2001) distinguish between LMEs and CMEs, arguing that firms in the former group strictly adhere to the market mechanisms for resolving coordination problems, while firms in CMEs rely on "non-market" mechanisms—such as organizations and networks at multiple levels—to become competitive players (Hall and Soskice 2001, 8).[23]According to this approach, LMEs (such as the UK and the USA) are characterized by private skill formation systems, while CMEs (such as Germany) accommodate extensive public network of vocational training institutions.

However, there are at least three important points that limit the explanatory capacity of the VoC approach. The first is a lack of attention to the interaction between subnational and central units. Second the model adopts a somewhat problematic conceptualization of non-market institutions. Finally, a third point is related to problems of generalizability of the VoC beyond advanced industrialized countries: this model is limited to account for varying pathways of industrial conflict resolution, vocational training and capital accumulation in countries like Turkey and Argentina.

Almost all of these studies under the rubric of VoC analyze national market institutions to point out diverse impact of the national political context on capital accumulation policies, and do not problematize the role of government structure to map out surplus extraction schemes. With the gradual spread of new management techniques, training policy in CMEs also went through transformation. For example, the vocational education curricula in Germany were restructured with add-on modular courses for specialized tracks (Idriss 2002, 474). Because growing demand for specialized consumption pushed economic zones to focus on their local strength and resources, negotiations on skill formation policies were increasingly carried at the local level. During this process, local dynamics came to the forefront to resolve collective action problems to coordinate and consolidate new skill formation modules. In particular, vocational education and training programs across Germany—a federal system— began to exhibit growing subnational variation (Idriss 2002, 474). In the USA (also a federal system), similar transformations prompted local politicians to prioritize human resource formation. There, the local governments are increasingly getting involved in coordinating vocational training and human resource management together with local business and labor unions, but the content of these schemes vary greatly from one state to next (Brand 1998; Herschbach 1998; Mitchell 1998).

Second, the distinction between "market" and "non-market" institutions for governing the economy is quite misleading, because it conceals how political dynamics played a significant role in resolving coordination problems of the firms not only in CMEs, but also in LMEs. A more detailed look into development of capitalism in advanced industrial countries present further empirical evidence that challenge some of the assumptions of Hall and Soskice, especially on the relative absence of "non-market" institutions in liberal market economies during the processes of human capital formation, surplus extraction and capital accumulation. For example, the initial involvement of the federal state in designing and implementing a national vocational education scheme (with Smith-Hughes Act) at the turn of the twentieth century stands in sharp contrast to the arguments on the USA regarding the absence of coordination between the state, business and labor organizations on the vocational education and training in this "liberal market" setting.[24] Though the US government failed in its later attempts to develop a federal vocational education program, local politicians were initially involved in regional skill formation programs for supplying skilled labor to the enterprises within their district.

Third, the VoC's ideal-typical model exclusively focuses on domestic institutions and overlooks international dynamics (such as international trade, access to export markets...) that had a major influence on the capital accumulation patterns and firm behavior. To be clear, these are substantively different from the experiences of countries like Turkey and Argentina. Development of capitalism in LMEs began much earlier in the nineteenth century in an environment where state support was crucial in exporting goods overseas. For example, while the government intervened relatively less in domestic market exchanges in LMEs, the firms based in England exploited colonial ties of the State to access new markets.[25] Notably, capital accumulation in the UK increasingly relied on profits on exports while the CMEs with no similar access had to rely on national endowments for surplus extraction. A typical example to this is Germany. Late-industrializers (such as Germany) with limited access to overseas markets mobilized surplus extraction through an extensive coordination of skill formation, which led to the emergence of nation-wide network of vocational training institutions.[26]

Re-reading history of capitalist development in this way provides initial clues to identify dynamics that affect the balance between market creation and skills, and sheds additional light on the contrast between advanced industrialized countries (see Figs. 2.2 and 2.3), and semi-peripheral economies. For example, because there was limited access to export markets for capital accumulation during the pre-Fordist era in Germany (i.e. German colonial networks were not strong enough to sustain a steady inflow of capital), governments had another reason to maximize surplus labor extraction through a well-coordinated vocational training system in Germany—after extensive negotiations with employer associations and trade unions. To avoid industrial conflict from disrupting production, the institutional edifice of Germany's *dual system* (where a worker would be trained at school and also at the workplace) under a corporatist arrangement was created (Thelen 2004).

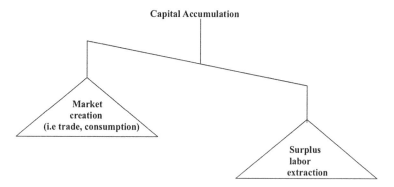

Fig. 2.2   The two legs of capital accumulation in Germany during the early stages of industrial development

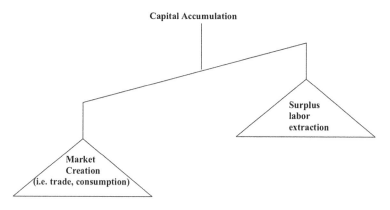

Fig. 2.3   The two legs of capital accumulation in the UK

On the other hand, because private enterprises in England could rely on colonial networks, business groups in England did not share a commitment to standardize surplus extraction through a centralized vocational education and training system—there, profits from international trade were the key to sustain capital accumulation.[27] In England, the state indirectly supported worker trainings by delegating the duty of skill formation to local authorities (Thelen 2004, 141).

In short, by the end of the nineteenth century, emerging policies on skill formation were very much influenced by the capacity of national governments to navigate diverse paths to capital accumulation. Specifically, the early formulation and implementation of skill formation policies in today's advanced capitalist economies were closely related to the ability of rulers to facilitate access to new markets for exporting goods.[28]

By contrast, the politicians in late-industrializing countries like Turkey and Argentina were constrained by a very different context. First, during much of the twentieth century, these economies were ISI-oriented, closed network economies with limited access to overseas markets. This pushed governments to put the emphasis on surplus labor extraction through wage compression—mostly through a mixture of policies that alternated between repressive and populist measures. In both cases, skill formation policies included a publicly (but rather poorly) funded scheme, focusing on the acquisition of technical skills. Second, and more importantly, surplus extraction in the Fordist era often pitted business associations and labor unions against each other, leading to frequent conflicts in the absence of extensive welfare benefits. In many ways, the path to capitalist development in these countries in no way resembles those of advanced industrialized countries.

Training Workers in Turkey and Argentina: A Variety of Capitalism?

Extending the debate on varieties of capitalism to include the experience of Latin American economies, Schneider (2009) has introduced a new term to conceptualize the institutional foundations of capitalist development: hierarchical market economies (HMEs). There are four distinct traits of HMEs that characterize capital accumulation: (1) non-market but diversified business groups, (2) non-market MNCs with hierarchical organization, (3) low-skilled labor, and (4) atomistic labor relations (Schneider 2009, 553). Arguably, these factors together create hierarchical relations—especially in Latin American economies—where firms and business associations neither rely on the market, nor on negotiation with stakeholders when resolving market coordination problems.[29] As a consequence, Schneider argues, these economies are less competitive, and countries characterized by hierarchical capitalism experience frequent market instabilities.

In terms of labor market indicators, hierarchical market economies are characterized by low skills and lower tenure rates (Schneider and Soskice 2009). This is partly because vocational education and training is very inadequate or non-existent since the emphasis is on general skills to enable labor mobility across different sectors. Though Schneider and Soskice recognize that some sectors, such as the automobile industry is an exception to this trend (Schneider and Soskice 2009, 35), they suggest that the cost of these trainings are primarily sponsored by the firm (Schneider and Soskice 2009, 49). In general, business in HMEs has unilateral control over employment decisions, including hiring, firing and benefits packages. Typically, unionization rates are low and labor is not a relevant political actor since majority of the workers are employed in a large informal sector under precarious conditions. Only a fraction of formal sector workers holds quality and stable jobs. These are mostly public employees that are unionized and have access to greater welfare benefits and employment protections (Schneider and Soskice 2009, 34).

At a first glance, Turkey and Argentina both seem to share some of the attributes of a hierarchical market economy as described by Schneider (2013) and Schneider and Soskice (2009). These include diversified business groups and the growing presence of MNCs, especially in the automobile sector. It is true that under ISI-oriented economies, selected business groups including major automobile producers in Turkey and Argentina enjoyed exceptional benefits from incumbent political parties (e.g. selling low-cost cars with a higher price tag in the domestic market in order to facilitate capital accumulation—in contrast to LMEs that exported affordable cars in higher volumes to foreign markets), and later emerged as domestic giants operating across multiple sectors in the market (e.g. Koc Group in Turkey and Macri group in Argentina are typical examples to this). However, it is difficult to classify Argentina or Turkey as a type of HME due to notable differences. First, weak plant-level labor representation is often not the case, especially in most automobile MNCs. In both countries, incoming automobile manufacturers preferred to negotiate with established unions and allowed their workers to enlist as rank-and-file members in formal platforms. While the autonomy of these unions is indeed dubious, MNCs also seek to control potential labor unrest through negotiating with union leaders because this strategy is viewed as more efficient by some managers.

Second, while low skills are indeed a major problem in Turkey and Argentina, both countries have a history of providing middle to high quality vocational training in selected areas through public programs under the ISI regime. The depletion of hard-skills in leading industries, including those in the metalworking and automobile sector, is a recent change that picked up speed after governments in both countries switched to export-led growth while endorsing economic liberalization agendas that called for greater labor flexibility.

In the face of these profound changes, the ability of producers to shape training policies was also influenced by the exchanges between local and national officials in each country. In contexts with a strong centralized government, big conglomerates were much more influential through powerful links to the incumbents. For example, among the HMEs in Latin America, Schneider and Karcher cite Chile—a unitary system—as an exception to government absenteeism in skill formation (Schneider and Karcher 2010), while in countries like Argentina, firms were relatively limited in pushing their plans especially when subnational governments either had a different political agenda or were engaged in a deep conflict with the national government.[30] Though the HME framework is not oblivious to the role of political institutions in skill formation trajectories across Latin America, it exclusively focuses on the electoral system and the negative complementarities generated by a combination of majoritarian and proportional representation systems. Comparative findings from Turkey and Argentina adds further nuance to this focus by revealing how the system of government and the territorial organization of political power play a crucial role in processes of skill formation and labor mobilization.

CONCLUSION

Ever since the birth of the automobile industry, the state has played an important role in the development of this sector through deploying various strategies, such as offering subsidies for research and development projects, networking producers and intervening in processes of surplus extraction at times of stress. However, the extent of state involvement and the tactics deployed in addressing market-induced conflicts varies across time and space. Under Fordism, national officials occupied a key role behind the rise of these companies. After the demise of Fordism in semi-peripheral countries like Turkey and Argentina, local officials emerged as new and relevant actors.

The exchanges between national and local politicians have a notable impact on the industrial performance of these firms as well as on labor mobilization patterns. In that sense, the findings in the subsequent chapters complement Gereffi and Korzeniewicz's (1994) observation, where they classify automobile production as a producer driven sector with entrepreneurs as key actors that drive industrial innovation and capital accumulation. While much of the innovation in automobiles owes to private investment, the implementation of new management techniques involving labor requires tighter state-business linkages.

Unlike the moving band that yields large stocks under mass production, post-Fordism's flexible and lean production lower the costs by eliminating large stocks while increasing the product diversity.[31] In order to address varying demand, the new production system uniquely combines manual and intellectual labor for maximizing flexibility while keeping the profits high. In this way, workers become active agents of surplus extraction, for example through modifying their behavior for making proposals to cut down costs.[32] As intellectual labor becomes an indispensable component of production—complementing manual labor—after Fordism, companies are increasingly compelled to cooperate with public agencies and institutions beyond the shopfloor to communicate their expectations, and ensure hiring workers who already possess the required set of soft-skills.

Across much of the developing world, not all stakeholders welcomed these changes with open arms, and opposition to shopfloor reorganization was common (Atzeni 2009). This variation is even more striking across different production sites of the same corporation. Often, these workers do not necessarily exhibit a similar pace of adaptation: while some endorse new techniques more easily, others have a more difficult time in accepting flexibilization on the shopfloor.

The next two chapters unpack the political dynamics behind these contrasting experiences. During the 1990s, FIAT introduced an ambitious program to produce FIAT 178 platform models across five continents with standardized techniques, demanding all managers to reorganize the shopfloor along the principles of FIAT-branded *integrated production system*—which is a tailored version of just-in-time, flexible production techniques.[33] All of the factories, including FIAT-Bursa and FIAT-Córdoba had to *strictly* follow the same guidelines and principles. While FIAT-Bursa workers initially challenged these tactics, they soon backed off and multiplied company profits with frequent participation in proposal schemes. On the other hand, FIAT-Córdoba workers had a difficult time adapting post-Fordist production techniques and opposed company proposals for a much longer period.[34] A key difference between these two cases is the background of these workers. While Bursa workers were largely recruited out of local vocational schools that modified their curricula to incorporate business expectations and discipline labor (Apaydin 2017), their counterparts in Argentina had no previous exposure as such. Across these contexts, skill formation policies—and labor response to new surplus extraction practices—showed variation, depending on the capacity of local politicians to embed new modules across a network of public schools. The next two chapters unpack these processes in further detail.

NOTES

1. This quote is from http://www.freeliberal.com/archives/003634.html, accessed on 10 January 2010.
2. See "The Auto bailout: how we did it" 21 October 2009, CNN Money, http://money.cnn.com/2009/10/21/autos/auto_bailout_rattner.for-tune/, accessed on 1 March 2010 and "Auto-bailout: French style" *Forbes*, 9 February 2009, http://www.forbes.com/2009/02/09/renault-peugeot-bailout-markets-equity-0209_autos_12.html, and "German government announces auto-industry financial support package," *IHS Global Insight*, 14 January 2009, http://www.ihsglobalinsight.com/SDA/SDADetail15619.htm. Both accessed on 15 January 2010.
3. "Ford Kisa Calisma Odenegine Basvurdu" (Ford Applies to Short-Term Employment Benefits Program) Hurriyet, 18 March 2009. http://www.hurriyet.com.tr/ekonomi/11229130.asp
4. See Chaudhry 1993, Cammett 2006, 2007a, b on how the industrial development histories of late-developers in the semi-periphery are quite different from the experiences of advanced industrialized countries.
5. Recently, scholars from the post-structuralist school suggested that expansion in economic activities beyond the city could best be explained by a focus on *spaces* (Lefebvre 1991; Brenner 2004; Harvey 2006) *city-regions* (Scott 2002), and new *territorialities* (Held 1999). Focusing on alternative conceptualizations of local economies, these approaches argue that globalization reshaped capital accumulation patterns at the subnational level in distinct ways, and the central state played a key role in blurring the political boundaries between subnational units by privileging some regions over others, establishing a hierarchy among economic sectors across different zones (Brenner 2004). Yet, these analyses almost portray public and private agencies at the local level as –almost—complacent actors that tacitly welcome radical changes in economic development policies. In fact, neither in advanced industrialized countries nor in semi-peripheral economies, political actors easily move out of the way, leaving the initiative on industrialization policy to the central government or private actors especially on issues like surplus labor extraction. Relatedly, a focus on *new state spaces* disproportionately aggrandizes the role of central government in

industrial development after Fordism regardless of the territorial organization of the state, because under the newly emerging production regime, local politicians are significantly getting more involved in economic policy-making. For example, Locke (1997) reveals how subnational governments in Italy often struggled with local stakeholders to coordinate contradicting interests when trying to build competitive industrial districts during the post-Fordist transformation in the 1980s. Similarly, Humphrey and Schmitz (1996) find that local and regional governments in Europe played a significant role in European industrial development by assisting firms to build clusters, adopt a customer-oriented approach and build cumulative capacity to produce new technologies in the later stages (Humphrey and Schmitz 1996, 1859).

6. This argument stands in sharp contrast to those who have announced the end of *local politics* as we know it. Some researchers propose that rather than assigning a larger role to local politicians, decentralization in federal systems gradually gave way to the emergence of *local governance* schemes, especially in advanced industrialized countries (Goodwin and Painter 1996; Sellers 2002). Local governance refers to new institutions and organizations that are partially delinked from the representative and bureaucratic institutions of local government, and involves greater societal participation for steering policy implementation with the participation of private and voluntary organizations (Rhodes 1997, 53; Stoker 1998; Lowndes 2001). At one extreme, some researchers have claimed that *governance without government* has become the new norm in political administration (Rosenau and Czempiel 1992), especially at the local level (Rhodes 1997; Wilson 1998; Hajer and Wagenaar 2003). According to these scholars, social networks along with private-public partnerships dominate policy-making and implementation in the post-Fordist era (Bianchi 1992). Under this system, the state allegedly loses power to directly control policy formulation and implementation in regional economic development. Rather, it can only *influence* these processes within certain limits, because government organizations are embedded in a relationship of mutual resource dependency with private actors (Peters and Pierre 1998, 228). According to this perspective, the local government in developing countries would have minimum or no control over setting the course of human capital formation policies after Fordism. Yet, this is an oversimplified version of a highly complex interaction between the local government and societal actors, especially when applied to explain industrial development in the semi-peripheral economies. Local government is far from disappearing from economic policy-making and implementation scene not only in advanced industrialized countries, but also in industrializing economies (Snyder 2001).

7. For an analysis on the role of state in the development of automobile industry in Germany see Tolliday 1995. For a similar analysis on Italy see Fauri 1996. In Japan, the state also played a key role in the development of this critical industry. See Shimokawa 1994. For an analysis on the role of state in British Motor Industry, see Church 1995. The state also played a critical role in the emergence of competitive auto industries in East Asia. See Doner 1991; Abrenica 2002. For the origins and the role of state in automobile sector development in Argentina see Brennan 1992; Catalan 2010.

8. For a comparative analysis on the early forms of control over the production process in the textile industry, see Burawoy 1984.

9. For a collection of essays on Fordism see Beynon and Nichols (eds.) 2006. For a critical discussion on Fordism and Post-Fordism see Jessop 1992.

10. For full credits, see http://www.imdb.com/title/tt0027977/

11. See Tolliday and Zeitlin (1986) for an overview of variations in Fordism in automobile production across Europe and the USA in between the two world wars. Despite some differences, the automobile producers across Europe incorporated the basic production principles of Fordism as ideal and continued to implement them on the shopfloor as long as the national markets allowed them to do so (Tolliday and Zeitlin 1986, 4).

12. This also explains why "personnel management" was the name of today's *human resources* department during the Fordist era, because the supervisors were not yet concerned about the potential contributions the workers could offer using their intellectual ability under this production regime.

13. Others (Veloso and Kumar 2002) classify the suppliers under three to four different tiers, making a further distinction between second tier producers such those that produce semi-components (second tier) and different types of raw materials (third and fourth tiers).

14. For an analysis on the classification of luxury automobiles, see Strach and Everett 2006. It must be noted that some multinational companies manufacture goods targeted at multiple streams of consumers, and accommodate a variety of brands that are produced for high, upper-middle, middle and lower-middle income groups (e.g. VW group makes Lamborghini for luxury consumers, Audi for upper-middle income, Passat for middle income and Bora for lower-middle income groups) (Strach and Everett 2006, 109).

15. Interview #12, 21 November 2007, Bursa, Turkey, and Interview #17, FIAT-Córdoba, 8 July 2008, Córdoba, Argentina.

16. Labor turnover refers to the average period of employment per worker in a given enterprise. Labor turnover rate is calculated by average number of employees lost per year, divided by the average number of total number of

employees during the same period. For a model developed for less developed countries, see Stiglitz 1974.

17. Nearly 50 years after Charlie Chaplin's Modern Times, the transformation in surplus labor extraction techniques was the plot of another Hollywood comedy, *Gung Ho* (1986).This movie tells the story of an uneasy transition from Fordist to post-Fordist surplus extraction techniques at an automobile factory: after a Japanese firm takes over a failed auto plant in the USA, the new managers introduce endless trainings to maximize production quality and pressure the workers to produce more cars in a short time-frame. Following numerous struggles between the managers and the workers, the movie ends with collaboration between the employer and employees on post-Fordist reorganization of the shopfloor, and the factory is "saved" with Japanese management practices: as the end credits roll, we see workers *literally* practicing flexibilization exercises before they start work in the morning. For full credits see: http://www.imdb.com/title/tt0091159

18. While surplus extraction in these enterprises depends on control over manual labor, some of these second tier enterprises recently began to apply carefully picked principles of *Total Quality Management* in order to obtain international quality certificates and seals. Nevertheless, because the rate of unionization at these enterprises is low, workers do not have a strong bargaining power to negotiate the terms of job contract. Therefore, in most cases, the management resorts to punitive tactics in order to ensure worker discipline on the shopfloor: the most common strategies include vacation cuts, payment cuts/delays and increasing the working hours without payment when product quality is low.

19. According to Veloso and Kumar (2002), global OEMs select first and second tier suppliers based on a number of common criteria, which include (1) cost and quality competitiveness, (2) R&D capacity, (3) closeness to the development center, (4) closeness to the location of production (Veloso and Kumar 2002, 11).

20. Perhaps a great example to this is the recent Toyota call-back of Prius model due to a defect in the brake system. Because of a seemingly minor problem, the entire reputation of the company as a leader in quality automobile production has been at stake. See "Prius Adds to Toyota's Woes as Stock Drops in Tokyo" http://www.nytimes.com/2010/02/04/business/global/04toyota.html

21. The theoretical inspiration behind Hall and Soskice's framework is based on the *market vs. hierarchy* ideo-types, first articulated by Williamson (1975). According to this distinction, "transactions that involve uncertainty about their outcome, that recur frequently and require transaction specific investments of money, time or energy that cannot be easily transferred are more likely to take place in hierarchically organized firms.

Exchanges that are straightforward, non-repetitive and require no transaction-specific investments will take place across a market interface" (Williamson quoted in Powell 1990, 296–297). However, this stylized conceptualization of firms versus markets assumes that the organization of the firm is completely independent of the market in which it operates, which is hardly the case. See Powell (1990) and Macneil (1985) for a more extended critique of Williamson.

22. It must be added that the categorization of Germany under CME faces a challenge in the face of new evidence from the 1990s. During this period, some of the collective bargaining and vocational training institutions that characterize coordinated market economies began to disappear, especially after the reorganization of production (Hassel 1999). In a later study, Martin and Thelen also recognize the changing institutions of the CMEs under neoliberal pressures (Martin and Thelen 2007, 2). For a detailed critique of general conceptual problems associated with the VoC literature, see Blyth 2003.

23. Based on the observations of Chandler (1977) and Williamson (1975), Hall and Soskice note a variation in the hierarchical organization of the firms (i.e. corporate structures) across LMEs and CMEs, and argue that firms in liberal market economies (US and UK) are more inclined to rely on these hierarchies (i.e. corporate management systems) in order to resolve market coordination problems while their counterparts in coordinated market economies arguably do much less so, and rely on other organizations and inter-firm networks (Hall and Soskice 2001, 8).

24. For a detailed discussion on the history of vocational education in the USA, see McClure et al. (1985). Especially Chaps. 2 and 3 of this book discusses the federal state involvement in coordinating skill formation programs and documents the push for developing a national skill formation regime during the 1920s and 1930s. Recently, the local government administrations in the USA have become highly involved in coordinating meso-level interactions between business and labor on skill formation. In 2012, the Obama government proposed increasing spending on vocational modules and in 2015, the administration pledged around $200 million to boost vocational education and training (see http://www.reuters.com/article/us-usa-budget-education-idUSTRE81C1Z620120213, and https://blogs.wsj.com/washwire/2015/09/09/obama-administration-to-support-apprenticeships-vocational-school/, both accessed 3 August 2017).

25. For an analysis of protectionist measures of the state in capitalist development of Great Britain and the USA from the nineteenth century until the 1940s, see Shafaeddin (1998); and for an analysis of protectionism in the USA, see Lake (1983). Following the great depression, the US govern-

ment felt increasing pressures from producers to secure export markets, which it did through *bilateral* trade agreements. This facilitated access to foreign markets and sustained capital accumulation at increasing rates. For an analysis of the US trade policy during this period, see Goldstein (1989) and Bailey et al. (1997).

26. For example, Bairoch (1972) finds that prior to the protectionist economic policies in Germany, the free trade era between 1862 and 1879 negatively influenced German economic development during this period. As Wehler (1970) and Brown (1995) show, it was only after a long period of protectionism, investment in domestic infrastructure and an aggressive export policy that Germany emerged as a competitive economic player around 1914. Bismarck's aggressive expansionist policies included colonialist enterprises first for having access to new markets and then to resources for raw material extraction (Kennedy 1972). Yet, because Germany was a latecomer in the scramble for external markets, its efforts to keep up with British colonialism was limited—especially because Germany lacked resources and infrastructure to meet up the high costs of ruling the colonies (Smith 1974, 652). The vocational training programs later addressed this problem by increasing the speed of surplus labor extraction.

27. For a discussion on the diverse preferences of business groups with respect to the role of the central administration in administering skill formation during the late nineteenth and early twentieth centuries, see Thelen 2004, 92–117.

28. Further, this brief overview suggests that the role of the state in creating markets and skills were inversely correlated under Fordism. Because the USA had a clear dominance in the overall market share in automobile production, this sector did not face a stimulus to alter Fordist surplus extraction techniques, which could be sustained without centralization of public vocational education and training system. On the other hand, the UK automobile producers had a significantly lower market share compared with the USA. In order to secure capital accumulation, labor governments supported even the weak and outdated manufacturers at the expense of the more efficient (Dunnett 1980, 35), and encouraged these exports to the commonwealth markets (i.e. New Zealand, Australia, South Africa) (Dunnett 1980, 34). Because *market creation* and support for the motor industry by the British government enabled firms to stay afloat, the producers were indifferent to creating a coordinated skill formation framework. In contrast, the German state had to rely more on surplus labor extraction in the early stages of capitalist development. There, conservative parties in the government played a key role in coordinating human capital formation together with businesses and unions. Despite the lower share of the German motor industry in the automobile markets when compared

with its Western rivals (see Broadberry 1997, 231), controlled and coordinated surplus labor extraction kept the automobile industry relatively more competitive during the early stages.

29. Based on cases from Latin America, Schneider and Soskice (2009) argue that under these circumstances, business organizations strive to impose the logic of *firm hierarchies* on governmental institutions that coordinate economic policies, giving way to *hierarchized market economies*. Under this variety of capitalism, big family conglomerates and powerful business groups take over democratic decision-making processes, compelling politicians to prioritize large conglomerate interests, especially when it comes to administering industrial development policies. Schneider and Soskice further suggest that, firms do this by establishing personal and informal ties with government agencies to prioritize particularized interests (e.g. those of selected firms and businesses) over collective interests (e.g. inclusive decision-making platforms that incorporate labor and pay attention to labor rights). According to Schneider, this process generates a set of negative complementarities that doom these economies to underdevelopment in the long run, interlocking these countries into uncompetitive sectors characterized by unskilled labor and informal markets. Similarly, Teichman (2001) supports these observations in an earlier study on market reform in Latin America, arguing that *policy networks* that operate on personal ties and loyalties (including international and domestic actors) shape the uneven developmental pathways that characterize economic atmosphere in these countries.

30. On the other hand, in Korea and Taiwan, governments followed an ambitious policy to transfer a large segment of the student population to vocational education tracks in order to create skilled a workforce (Bennell and Segerstrom 1998, 274; Bae 1989, 355; 361). Because these economies were primarily concerned with increasing the rate of capital accumulation within a relatively small market, repressive techniques for higher surplus labor extraction were combined with new management methods that required appropriation of worker's intellectual contribution (Amsden 1990, 13–14). Thus, these countries came up with a novel combination of surplus labor extraction techniques through controlling manual *and* intellectual labor, while deploying authoritative means to facilitate collective action. As a result, automobile companies like Kia, Daewoo and Hyundai gradually moved away from assembling parts to manufacturing vehicles using original technology (Green 1992).

31. For a detailed discussion of these new techniques, see Piore and Sabel (1984).

32. In particular, regular interactions between workers are expected to generate cooperation to eliminate problems in order to yield maximum effi-

ciency in production. This requires workers' voluntary participation in brainstorming, data-collection, data analysis, cause and effect analysis and the development of new control techniques (Hutchins 1985, 44). Surveillance, monitoring and the examination of worker participation are necessary but not sufficient for profit maximization. According to the most notable quality gurus such as Crosby (1979) and Peters (1987), quality improvement seeks to develop the principle of self-control.

33. For an analysis of the FIAT 178 world car project, see Camuffo 2002, Volpato and Camuffo 2002a, b, Ozkan 2003, Dunford 2009. As Dunford 2009 shows, the ambitions plan of standardizing the FIAT 178 model did not work in some contexts as the sales of these models went through a sharp decline in fragile markets like Argentina.

34. These techniques have substantial profit-boosting effects. In another study on FIAT-Bursa, Ozkan (2003) finds that in 2002, savings gained through quality circles, *kaizen* and suggestion system reached 42,494,000 Euro by 2002 (Ozkan 2003, 148).

BIBLIOGRAPHY

Abrenica, J. 2002. The Asian Automotive Industry: Assessing the Roles of the State and Market in the Age of Global Competition. *Asian Pacific Economic Literature* 12: 12–26.

Amsden, A. 1990. Third World Industrialization: Global Fordism or New Model? *New Left Review* 182: 5–32.

Apaydin, F. 2017. Uneasy Discipline: Training Workers After Fordism in Turkey and Argentina. *Studies in Political Economy* 98: 151–174.

Atzeni, M. 2009. Searching for Injustice and Finding Solidarity? A Contribution to the Mobilisation Theory Debate. *Industrial Relations Journal* 40: 5–16.

Bae, K. 1989. Labor Strategy for Industrialization in South Korea. *Pacific Affairs* 62: 353–363.

Bailey, M.A., J. Goldstein, and B.R. Weingast. 1997. The Institutional Roots of American Trade Policy: Politics, Coalitions, and International Trade. *World Politics* 49: 309–338.

Bairoch, P. 1972. Free Trade and European Economic Development in the 19th Century. *European Economic Review* 3: 211–245.

Bennell, P., and J. Segerstrom. 1998. Vocational Education and Training in Developing Countries: Has the World Bank Got It Right? *International Journal of Educational Development* 18: 271–287.

Beynon, H., and T. Nichols. 2006. *The Fordism of Ford and Modern Management: Fordism and Post-Fordism (vol.1)*. Northhampton: Edward Elgar.

Bianchi, P. 1992. Levels of Policy and the Nature of Post-Fordist Competition. In *Pathways to Industrialization and Regional Development*, ed. M. Storper and A.J. Scott. London: Routledge.

Blyth, M. 2003. Same as It Never Was: Temporality and Typology in the Varieties of Capitalism. *Comparative European Politics* 1: 215–225.

Brand, B. 1998. The Process of Change in Vocational Education and Training in the United States. In *Changing Vocational Education and Training: An International Comparative Perspective*, ed. Ian Finlay and Stephanie Young. London: Routledge.

Brennan, J. 1992. "El contexto fabril del "sindicalismo de liberacion" en la industria automotriz cordobesa, 1970–75" [The Industrial Context of Liberation Syndicalism in the Automotive Industry in Córdoba]. *Desarrollo Económico* 32: 3–22.

Brenner, N. 2004. *New State Spaces*. New York: Oxford University Press.

Broadberry, S.N. 1997. *The Productivity Race: British Manufacturing in International Perspective*. Cambridge: Cambridge University Press.

Brown, J.C. 1995. Imperfect Competition and Anglo-German Trade Rivalry: Markets for Cotton Textiles Before 1914. *The Journal of Economic History* 55: 494–527.

Burawoy, M. 1984. Karl Marx and the Satanic Mills: Factory Politics Under Early Capitalism in England, the US and Russia. *American Journal of Sociology* 90: 247–282.

Cammett, M. 2006. Development and the Changing Dynamics of Global Production: Global Value Chains and Industrial Clusters in Apparel Manufacturing. *Competition and Change* 10: 23–48.

———. 2007a. *Globalization and Business Politics in Arab North Africa*. New York: Cambridge University Press.

———. 2007b. Business-Government Relations and Industrial Change: The Politics of Upgrading in Morocco and Tunisia. *World Development* 35: 1889–1903.

Camuffo, A. 2002. Rolling Out a "World Car": Globalization, Outsourcing and Modularity. Online Working Paper. Available at: http://dspace.mit.edu/bitstream/handle/1721.1/661/cam-volp1.pdf?sequence=1.

Catalan, J. 2010. Strategic Policy Revisited: The Origins of Mass Production in the Motor Industry of Argentina, Korea and Spain, 1945–87. *Business History* 52: 207–230.

Chandler, A.D. 1977. *The Visible Hand*. Cambridge: Harvard University Press.

Chaudhry, K.A. 1993. The Myths of the Market and the Common History of Late Developers. *Politics and Society* 21 (3): 245–274.

Church, R. 1995. *The Rise and Decline of British Motor Industry*. Cambridge: Cambridge University Press.

Crosby, P. 1979. *Quality Is Free: The Art of Making Quality Certain*. New York: Mentor Books.

Culpepper, P. 2007. Small States and Skill Specificity: Austria, Switzerland, and Interemployer Cleavages in Coordinated Capitalism. *Comparative Political Studies* 40: 611–637.

Doner, R. 1991. *Driving a Bargain: Automobile Industrialization and Japanese Firms in Southeast Asia*. Berkeley: University of California Press.

Dunford, M. 2009. Globalization Failures in a Neo-Liberal World: The Case of FIAT Auto in the 1990s. *Geoforum* 40: 145–157.

Dunnett, P.J.S. 1980. *The Decline of the British Motor Industry: The Effects of Government Policy*. Guilford: Biddles.

Fauri, F. 1996. The Role of FIAT in the Development of the Italian Car Industry in the 1950's. *The Business History Review* 70: 167–206.

Gereffi, G., and M. Korzeniewicz. 1994. *Commodity Chains and Global Capitalism*. Westport: Greenwood Press.

Goldstein, J. 1989. The Impact of Ideas on Trade Policy: The Origins of U.S. Agricultural and Manufacturing Policies. *International Organization* 43: 31–71.

Goodwin, M., and J. Painter. 1996. Local Governance, the Crises of Fordism and the Changing Geographies of Regulation. *Transactions of the Institute of British Geographers* 21: 635–648.

Green, Andrew E. 1992. South Korea's Automobile Industry: Development and Prospects. *Asian Survey* 32: 411–428.

Hajer, M.A., and H. Wagenaar. 2003. *Deliberative Policy Analysis*. Cambridge: Cambridge University Press.

Hall, P.A., and D. Soskice. 2001. *Varieties of Capitalism: The Institutional Foundations of Comparative Advantage*. Oxford: Oxford University Press.

Harvey, D. 2006. *Spaces of Global Capitalism*. London: Verso.

Hassel, A. 1999. The Erosion of the German System of Industrial Relations. *British Journal of Industrial Relations* 37: 483–505.

Held, D. 1999. *Global Transformations*. Stanford: Stanford University Press.

Herschbach, D. 1998. *United States: Local Training Networks*. Geneva: International Labor Organization.

Humphrey, J., and H. Schmitz. 1996. The Triple C Approach to Local Industrial Policy. *World Development* 24: 1859–1877.

Hutchins, D. 1985. *Quality Circles Handbook*. London: Pitman Publishing.

Idriss, C.M. 2002. Challenge and Change in the German Vocational System Since 1990. *Oxford Review of Education* 28: 473–490.

Jessop, B. 1992. Fordism and Post-Fordism; A Critical Formulation. In *Pathways to Industrialization and Regional Development*, ed. M. Storper and A.J. Scott. London: Routledge.

Kay, J.H. 1997. *Asphalt Nation*. Berkeley: University of California Press.

Kennedy, P.M. 1972. German Colonial Expansion: Has the 'Manipulated Social Imperialism' Been Ante-Dated? *Past & Present* 54: 134–141.

Lake, D. 1983. International Economic Structures and American Foreign Economic Policy, 1887–1934. *World Politics* 35: 517–543.

Lefebvre, H. 1991. *The Production of Space*. Oxford: Wiley-Blackwell.

Locke, R. 1997. *Remaking the Italian Economy*. Ithaca: Cornell University Press.

Lowndes, V. 2001. Rescuing Aunt Sally: Taking Institutional Theory Seriously in Urban Politics. *Urban Studies* 38: 1953–1971.

Macneil, I. 1985. Relational Contract: What We Do and Do Not Know. *Wisconsin Law Review* 3: 483–526.

Martin, C.J., and K. Thelen. 2007. The State and Coordinated Capitalism. *World Politics* 60: 1–36.

Marx, K. 1990 [1976]. *Capital, Volume I*. London: Penguin Books.

McClure, A.F., J.R. Chrisman, and P. Mock. 1985. *Education for Work: The Historical Evolution of Vocational and Distributive Education in America*. Rutherford: Fairleigh Dickinson University Press.

Mitchell, A.G. 1998. *Strategic Training Partnerships Between the State and Enterprises*. Geneva: International Labor Organization.

Özkan, S. 2003. More Global Than Ever, as Local as Always: Internationalization and Shop-Floor Transformation at Oyak-Renault and Tofas-FIAT in Turkey. *Actes Gerpisa* 36: 143–160.

Peters, T. 1987. *Thriving on Chaos: Handbook for a Management Revolution*. London: Macmillan.

Peters, B.G., and J. Pierre. 1998. Governance Without Government? Rethinking Public Administration. *Journal of Public Administration Research and Theory* 8 (2): 223–243.

Piore, M., and C. Sabel. 1984. *The Second Industrial Divide*. New York: Basic Books.

Polanyi, K. 2001 [1944]. *The Great Transformation*. Boston: Beacon Press.

Powell, W. 1990. Neither Market Nor Hierarchy. *Research in Organizational Behavior* 12: 295–336.

Rhodes, R.A.W. 1997. *Understanding Governance*. London: Open University Press.

Rosenau, J.N., and E.O. Czempiel. 1992. *Governance Without Government*. Cambridge: Cambridge University Press.

Rothstein, J.S. 2006. Selective Participation: Controlling Workers' Input at General Motors. *Research in the Sociology of Work* 16: 151–175.

Sassen, S. 1994. *Cities in a World Economy*. Thousand Oaks: Pine Forge Press.

———. 2001. *The Global City: New York, London, Tokyo*. Princeton: Princeton University Press.

Schneider, B.R. 2009. Hierarchical Market Economies and Varieties of Capitalism in Latin America. *Journal of Latin American Studies* 41: 553–575.

———. 2013. *Hierarchical Capitalism in Latin America: Business, Labor, and the Challenges of Equitable Development*. New York: Cambridge University Press.

Schneider, B.R., and S. Karcher. 2010. Complementarities and Continuities in the Political Economy of Labor Markets in Latin America. *Socio-Economic Review* 8 (4): 623–651.

Schneider, B.R., and D. Soskice. 2009. Inequality in Developed Countries and Latin America: Coordinated, Liberal and Hierarchical Systems. *Economy and Society* 38: 17–52.

Scott, A.J. 2002. *Global City-Regions: Trends, Theory, Policy*. Oxford: Oxford University Press.

———. 2009. *Social Economy of the Metropolis: Cognitive-cultural Capitalism and the Global Resurgence of Cities*. Oxford: Oxford University Press.

Sellers, J.M. 2002. *Governing from Below: Urban Regions and the Global Economy*. Cambridge, MA: Cambridge University Press.

Shafaeddin, M. 1998. *How Did Developed Countries Industrialize?* UNCTAD Discussion Paper. No.139.

Shimokawa, K. 1994. *The Japanese Automobile Industry*. London: Athlone Press.

Smith, W. 1974. The Ideology of German Colonialism, 1840–1906. *The Journal of Modern History* 46: 641–662.

Snyder, R. 2001. *Politics After Neoliberalism*. New York: Cambridge University Press.

Stiglitz, J. 1974. Theories of Wage Determination and Unemployment in LDC's: The Labor Turnover Model. *The Quarterly Journal of Economics* 88: 194–227.

Stoker, G. 1998. Governance as Theory: Five Propositions. *International Social Science Journal* 50 (155): 17–28.

Strach, P., and A.M. Everett. 2006. Brand Corrosion: Mass Marketing's Threat to Luxury Automobile Brands After Merger and Acquisition. *Journal of Product and Brand Management* 15: 106–120.

Studer-Noguez, I. 2002. *Ford and the Global Strategies of Multinationals*. London: Routledge.

Teichman, J.A. 2001. *The Politics of Freeing Markets in Latin America: Chile, Argentina, and Mexico*. Chapel Hill: The University of North Carolina Press.

Thelen, K. 2004. *How Institutions Evolve: the Political Economy of Skills in Germany, Britain, the United States, and Japan*. Cambridge: Cambridge University Press.

Tolliday, S. 1995. Enterprise and State in the West German Wirtschaftswunder: Volkswagen and the Automobile Industry, 1939–1962. *The Business History Review* 69: 273–350.

Tolliday, S., and J. Zeitlin, eds. 1986. *The Automobile Industry and Its Workers: Between Fordism and flexibility*. Cambridge: Polity.

Veloso, F., and R. Kumar. 2002. *The Automobile Supply Chain: Global Trends and Asian Perspectives*. ERD Working Paper Series No.3. Asian Development Bank.

Volpato, G., and A. Camuffo. 2002a. Global Sourcing in the Automotive Supply Chain: The Case of Fiat Auto "Project 178" World Car. Online Working Paper. Available at http://dspace.mit.edu/bitstream/handle/1721.1/729/cam-volp1.pdf?sequence=1.

————. 2002b. Global Sourcing in the Automotive Supply Chain: The Case of Fiat Auto. Online Working Paper. Available at: http://dspace.mit.edu/bitstream/handle/1721.1/661/cam-volp1.pdf?sequence=1.

Wehler, H.A. 1970. Bismarck's Imperialism, 1862–1890. *Past & Present* 48: 119–155.

Williamson, O. 1975. *Markets and Hierarchies: Analysis and Anti-Trust Implications*. New York: Free Press.

Wilson, D. 1998. From Local Government to Local Governance: Re-casting British Local Democracy. *Democratization* 5: 90–115.

Womack, J., D. Jones, and D. Roos. 2007. *The Machine that Changed the World*. New York: Simon & Schuster.

CHAPTER 3

All Quiet on the Turkish Front: Workers and Skill Formation After Fordism in a Unitary Setting in Bursa

When Ali graduated from a well-known vocational high school in Bursa-Turkey, a prominent multinational auto company based in the same city immediately hired him. During the first two weeks, human resources department assigned him to participate in a company-based training program. As some of the newcomers struggled to digest the principles of quality management, Ali excelled among his peers, demonstrating high leadership skills, willingness to collaborate with his colleagues, and a genuine commitment to problem solving and conflict resolution. "My former exposure to similar exercises helped me a lot" he commented. "I could build on this base...our teachers always told us to produce quality work," he added.[1]

Ali's comments reflect an ideal worker profile demanded by many employers in Bursa. He is hardworking, eager to participate in training programs and interested in learning the most recent techniques. He enjoys teamwork and seeks harmony and discipline in the workplace. Moreover, Ali has flexible skills: he can adapt to rotations across different stations with ease. Unlike his fellow workers employed in the same factory during the 1970s, Ali embodies a new worker profile that came to characterize most workplaces in the city of Bursa today.

This chapter reveals how a political congruence between local and central state officials in a unitary setting helped to mobilize local resources for creating "flexible" workers in Bursa, without a protracted opposition from the workforce. Ali and many of his fellow workers were frequently exposed

© The Author(s) 2018

F. Apaydin, *Technology, Institutions and Labor*, International Political Economy Series, https://doi.org/10.1007/978-3-319-77104-5_3

to trainings inspired by Toyotism as the partnership between public agencies and private actors worked toward embedding these modules beyond the factory. Two major factors facilitated this process. First, economic liberalization, increasing market competition and rising costs of skill formation pushed private actors to seek public support. Second, the absence of a major political conflict between the government in Ankara and the governor in Bursa facilitated the transformation of vocational education schemes through a concerted effort under the auspices of Vocational Education and Training Council.

POST-FORDIST PRESSURES AND THE AUTOMOBILE SECTOR IN TURKEY DURING THE 1990s

Just like Argentina, Turkey switched to an export-led growth model following the economic crisis in 1980 in the hopes that exposure to global competition would facilitate capital accumulation and industrial development. In order to sustain this agenda, the new government under Turgut Ozal took a series of measures to promote high value-added sectors for stimulating growth. As Menem government in Argentina drafted a new policy that officially prioritized the automobile sector as the new locomotive of development, Ozal's ANAP government was busy working on a similar program. Through tax breaks and subsidies, the government in Ankara hoped that the automobile sector would lead the great industrial leap forward, and trigger the diffusion of a new production system inspired by Japan's Toyota Corporation.

Until the late 1980s, automotive sector in Turkey was based on low-tech, assembly-line production organized around Fordist principles. Moreover, under an ISI regime, the production was largely for a non-competitive and small domestic market. Enjoying government protection with guaranteed market share, automobile producers did not feel any pressure to improve quality and diversify their product range. During this period, investment in soft-skills was not yet on the agenda. Thus, Ozal's plan for the automobile industry aimed to prepare the ground by first offering incentives to modernize and upgrade production technology and facilitate a gradual exposure of the sector to foreign competition.

The fifth five-year development program of 1984 set the initial framework to take steps in that direction.[2] The shift of policy toward export-led growth with an emphasis on automobiles required a revision of skill formation policies as well. In that sense, the plan foresaw the preparation of new guidelines to encourage collaboration between the state and private sector to reform vocational and technical education programs.[3] At the same time, the plan stipulated launching of "collective trainings at the workplace" that would induce workers to develop "values that fit the structure of our society, such as mutual love and respect, the consciousness of worker identification with the workplace, the consolidation of their belief in the unity of the state and the nation, and legal principles."[4] The plan also underlined improving worker capacity to adapt to change. For example, Article 517 of the program states that "the content of curricula will be revised in accordance with the goal of increasing students' ability to adapt and improve the quality of education at each stage. The state will collaborate with private sector to realize this goal."[5] In addition, the new plan foresaw the triple collaboration of state, business and unions for creating a mutual fund for financing basic vocational education.[6]

Table 3.1 Automobile production, export and import figures between 1983 and 2001

Year	Total production	Exports	Imports	Production/Export ratio (%)
1983	42,509	3,343	3,219	7.9
1984	54,832	3,888	8,849	7.1
1985	60,353	3,760	12,806	6.2
1986	82,032	4,997	6,975	6.1
1987	107,185	4,987	5,115	4.7
1988	120,796	6,818	4,665	5.6
1989	118,314	8,474	6,854	7.2
1990	167,556	6,122	72,215	3.7
1991	195,574	7,244	33,692	3.7
1992	265,245	8,779	60,134	3.3
1993	348,095	7,177	101,010	2.1
1994	212,651	12,790	28,116	6.0
1995	233,412	32,764	21,651	14.0
1996	207,757	33,404	57,479	16.1
1997	242,780	21,051	150,704	8.7
1998	239,937	32,377	120,967	13.5
1999	222,041	77,459	131,215	34.9
2000	297,476	90,026	258,987	30.3
2001	175,343	142,288	72,259	81

Source: SPO, Automotive Sector Development Perspective Report (2002) p. 27

Before the 1990s, Turkey's automobile exports were largely destined to countries in the Middle East and Central Asian Republics, which had somewhat lower expectations on quality standards. Furthermore, as Table 3.1 puts it, a greater share of the overall car production during this period was for the domestic market. Following the launch of the fifth five-year developmental program, output began to increase and more than doubled between 1984 and 1988, rising from 54,800 to 120,800 units.[7] However, there was no significant increase in the share of automobile exports to foreign markets. Thus, not only the technology employed in car production lagged behind, but also there was no standardized and systematized training policy during this period.

Meanwhile, the Ozal government in Ankara felt growing pressures from international financial agencies (namely, the World Bank and the IMF) to cut back on government expenditure and take necessary measures for maintaining fiscal austerity. Besides financial liberalization, privatization and trade liberalization, these organizations recommended decentralization. This was a major challenge for Ozal, because article 3 of the 1980 constitution describes Turkey as a unitary system. Nevertheless, the government got around this through a series of government decrees and laws that circumvented the constitution.[8] Thus, as Menem took steps toward administrative, fiscal and political decentralization in federal Argentina, Ozal's ANAP bestowed provincial governors with new administrative duties such as the coordination of industrial upgrading.[9] These measures were further justified in the sixth five-year development plan in 1990, which openly designated export-led production in the automobile sector as the new priority.[10] The plan also put renewed emphasis on technological improvement, quality and standardization in production.[11]

While the central government supported automobile producers with subsidies and incentives, the duty of aligning industrial infrastructure to meet producer needs fell on the shoulders of the provincial governors. One of the top items on the agenda was flexibilization. This also introduced further challenges. Not everyone at local industrial zones was happy with the plan. Initially, labor unions were skeptical vis-a-vis flexibilization and associated quality improvement techniques, arguing that this was not their priority unless they enjoyed tangible benefits. Additionally, some vocational school managers seemed uneasy with restructuring curricula under market-induced pressures. Meanwhile, businesses were very keen on introducing new modules as soon as possible. This tension initially posed a significant challenge to governors as they tried to build regional coalitions and revamp existing vocational education and training programs in Bursa.

Reaching Beyond the Shopfloor

As many firms gradually began to modernize their production facilities, FIAT-Bursa also announced that the company would join the trend and upgrade its production systems in order to produce a new model, FIAT Tipo, adopting a semi-mechanized shopfloor plan, installing robotics and laser systems.[12] The efficient use of this technology subsequently called for greater intellectual participation by the blue-collar workers to improve efficiency.[13] This required a major transformation in worker skills and existing training schemes. Now that the provincial government in Bursa was in charge of coordinating vocational education and training activities, FIAT-Bursa management sought logistic support to ensure a well-trained workforce and thereby maximize performance during the transition. As the former human resources manager of the company put it, "FIAT [had to] work with what [was] available [in Bursa]...We had to take care of [this] with people willing to work with us."[14]

Meanwhile, the ratification of the EU Customs Union treaty by the parliament added a new impetus to FIAT to shift its focus on reforming skills. Beginning in 1993, FIAT-Bursa restructured the organization of the factory: the new CEO Jan Nahum in Bursa gradually backed away from vertical integration and introduced a horizontally coordinated management model. The aim was to eliminate efficiency-related problems that arose due to delayed communication between different departments. Likewise, just like their counterparts in Córdoba, the company decided to substantially change its assembly-line-based production system, incorporating the principles of "lean production."[15] Subsequently, FIAT-Bursa introduced flexible techniques on the shopfloor.

Despite these changes, the management realized that company-based trainings were not good enough to create a qualified workforce and ensure their full commitment. Workers were puzzled by these changes. Some were overtly skeptical of the quality improvement modules that focused on their behavior and did not see the connection between changing their attitude toward work and increased productivity. There were also minor tensions between the foremen and the blue-collars as the management now had higher expectations. Despite repeated efforts, the number of worker proposals to cut down costs and improve quality remained very low during the first year after the introduction of these changes.[16] The experience was frustrating for both the workers and the management. The managers were convinced that more seasoned workers were hard to change and sought to replace them with a younger group. Therefore, the company began to look for ways in which they could mobilize and improve local resources for recruiting new workers. As Interview#11 puts it:

> ...FIAT began to contribute quite a lot to vocational schools in Bursa area. For example, we provided them with unused equipment, donated money for setting up training labs. Sometimes the school management would send us off a list of necessary equipment and tools and we would provide them. Our collaboration has been continuous with these schools ever since.[17]

The new workplace environment after Fordism is quite a stressful one for the workers. Sometimes, conflict becomes unavoidable, and the workers find themselves at odds with the management. When that happened at FIAT-Bursa, the resolution of these disputes was relatively fast, however. Even in the case of protests and walkouts involving a larger number of workers—as it happened in 1994 and 1998 respectively—the conflict was effectively contained and workers went back to the line without causing any major delays. According to the management, the frequency of such disputes was further reduced as the share of alumna from vocational high schools increased among FIAT ranks.

The former industrial operations and human resources manager of FIAT-Bursa further underline that collaboration between FIAT and vocational high schools works effectively to (1) recruit workers with basic technical skills and (2) preempt unwanted behavior once these students complete their internship and start working as employees. As the managers communicated their expectations to school managers, changes in the curricula incorporated these requests to develop rudimentary soft-skills.[18] Interviews with the graduates of vocational high schools employed at FIAT-Bursa confirm these remarks: the respondents repeatedly emphasized the perceived value of behavioral trainings at school. While the quality of technical training at school is viewed as "limited," "low" or "not sufficient"—and most workers acknowledge the insufficiency of practical technical knowledge offered by their instructors—they have had prior familiarity with soft-skill training modules such as quality circles, 5S and Kaizen. Overall, workers at FIAT consider their vocational school experience a very valuable asset since they "have a stronger basis compared to others without basic training."[19] Most of the younger vocational school graduates at FIAT highlight the behavioral modules as the greatest value added since it constitutes a crucial base for keeping up with an ever-changing work environment.[20]

THE GREAT TRANSFORMATION IN BURSA: POST-FORDISM AT FIAT

How did FIAT-Bursa manage to transform the labor force from a group of moderately skilled assembly-line operators into a flexible and dedicated group endowed with post-Fordist skills, while minimizing industrial conflict? As of February 2008, around 90% of blue-collar employees at FIAT were graduates of vocational and technical schools. All of the newly hired workers have been systematically exposed to a broad array of behavioral trainings. This figure is well above the national average, where only 61.91% of vocational high school graduates indicate that they received some form of orientation and training in their current position.[21]

The company's current policy of hiring vocational high school graduates sharply contrasts FIAT's earlier policy during the 1980s. During this period, the management saw interns coming from these schools as a burden, rather than potentially valuable future employees. Because they did not feel obliged to hire skilled workers, the managers were not interested in offering a well-rounded training environment on factory premises. But this policy was revised following the exposure to foreign competition—especially after Turkey joined the Customs Union with the EU. In the words of a FIAT manager, "the real change in our company took shape following Turkey's decision to join the Customs Union. When the country goes through a change, we follow[ed] the trend."[22] Thus, beginning in mid-1990s, the company took additional steps to ensure the competitiveness of its brand, and stepped outside the shopfloor to communicate its expectations to bureaucrats and policy makers. This included working with vocational and technical high schools in the area to ensure curricular updates and incorporate modules on soft-skills.

According to the managers, graduates of technical high schools at FIAT-Bursa demonstrate a higher capacity for adaptation following their recruitment. The training manager argues that around 90% of the newly hired workers do not experience major problems when moved to a different workstation.[23] Moreover, the graduates of vocational high schools are arguably much faster in mastering the details of new techniques. During the 1990s, the company regularly exposed these workers to several programs designed to refresh their knowledge, including quality circles, kaizen and zero-defect training.[24]

How effective are curricula updates to build these desired skills? To unpack this, I did semi-standardized interviews with fifty workers at FIAT-Bursa to see whether these workers indeed feel comfortable with these principles.[25] The findings indicate that especially younger workers with a formal vocational degree welcome these values and accept them as the new normal. During these interviews, graduates of vocational high schools repeatedly emphasized: (1) discipline and obedience, (2) self-improvement, (3) hard-work and honesty, (4) dedication to quality work. In addition to having technical skills, workers frequently cited the necessity of being a competitive player, indicated that quality improvement techniques are very useful, highlighted the importance self-discipline, and many noted that they use negotiation and conflict resolution techniques to address problems on the shopfloor (which are reportedly not too many). Moreover, the responses reveal that nearly 90% of the interviewees at FIAT had received early training on, and participated regularly in quality circles.[26]

A former manager of the factory who worked at FIAT until 1998 also confirms these observations: "We worked especially on setting up a [new] culture of questioning among our workers. In order to have continuous improvement, you need to make sure that employees know what they are doing."[27] By "continuous improvement" the respondent refers to a quality improvement technique called Kaizen, which was introduced in 1995. This is a technique geared to maximize efficiency and productivity using very basic steps, such as organizing the workspace, paying attention to order of tools, discarding unnecessary equipment, and keeping the workstation clean. In addition, Kaizen incorporates teamwork into the production process by launching product improvement groups in each department. In the words of a former manager:

Kaizen means setting up a team of 15–20 people where 1/3rd of the group members would be workers, 1/3rd would be technical experts and 1/3rd of the remaining members would be outsiders who have minimum or no information about the technical details of the production process. Of course, you also need to have a knowledgeable moderator…It was Jan Nahum who pushed us into it. As a result, we had high improvement rates, around 40–50% and in some cases, 60%.[28]

After 1995, the company also began to offer *initiation trainings* to the newly hired workers and familiarized them with two additional techniques: *zero-defect training* and *5S technique*. 5S includes five basic principles for improving efficiency and quality: organizing materials and removing unnecessary tools, setting them in order, cleaning the workspace, standardizing production process by identifying normal and unusual conditions, and sustaining quality production by implementing solutions that address the root causes of encountered problems.

When asked about the benefits of these trainings, the interviewed workers rate company-based quality trainings 8 out of a scale of 10 on average. Because Kaizen and 5S are relatively easy to apply, they rank by far as the most popular of all. Overall, the FIAT respondents in Bursa are highly satisfied with these new behavioral trainings on the grounds that it enabled them to be more productive and efficient. My in-depth interviews with other FIAT workers also confirm this. For example, during our conversation with a former FIAT worker (now retired), he frequently mentioned the benefits of vocational education and training seminars, how working at FIAT had been an important reference in finding his next job following retirement (*"in the same sector, that's even better"*). But in return, he acknowledges that the worker has to work more:

> *You get so much education and training that in the end you find yourself overworking, doing the job of two or three people [instead of one]...You end up doing it because you are mentally molded [to do so].*[29]

Could repeated exposure to post-Fordist principles be powerful enough to transform the attitudes of workers in a relatively short amount of time? Intrigued by this, I asked a series of questions to the workers in order to explore the frequency of these trainings and check whether there were any additional sources of behavioral skill training. Among the interviewees, 51% of vocational and technical high school graduates mentioned that they had their first quality training at school. These include basic familiarization with post-Fordist principles. The responses also reveal that workers have been exposed to these modules systematically and through multiple channels: in addition to school-based trainings, most workers participated in trainings on various quality techniques sponsored by the business association of which FIAT was a member during the 1990s. In addition to repeating what students picked up at school and at the factory, additional trainings on similar topics helped participants with no vocational school background to get acquainted with recent modules.

In line with the principle of enhancing flexibility, most graduates of vocational and technical high schools are employed in departments that do not correspond to their technical specialization. At FIAT-Bursa, workers have been frequently rotated and trained for adaptation. Survey results reveal that about 90% of the interviewees are working in a unit that is irrelevant to their primary field of specialization printed on their diploma. Second, within the same group, 58% of the workers have been rotated across different workstations and/or departments at least once. When asked their opinion on this, 66% of the workers expressed that their technical background had nothing to do with their current assignment.[30] Though some workers criticize this practice on the grounds that it depreciates their hard-skills, others express that they are happy to have a breadth of knowledge across different production units, which also enabled some to become team leaders.[31] Those who criticize it also add that they gradually forget technical skills they picked at school.

During the 1990s, there were also workers without any vocational training background employed at the factory, and interviews with these workers reveal that they experience major difficulties in adaptation and adjusting themselves to behavioral trainings, such as quality circles. For example, a former FIAT employee who was laid off during the 1994 crisis thought that his supervisor put him on top of the lay-off list because he did not have any formal vocational training and had difficulties related to performance.

I worked hard, and I really devoted myself to my job, and to this day, I cannot think of any other reason to why I was chosen to be on that list, apart from the fact that I was without [a vocational] diploma.[32]

Even though he participated company-based training sessions, this worker had difficulties on the job. When the manager moved him to a different workstation, he resisted this decision by dragging his feet to perform the assigned tasks on time. When the section leader "lectured him" and other workers on the topic, he saw these training sessions as "passtime and did not think [he] had benefited much."[33] Indeed, this worker's experience as an unskilled worker shows the difficulty of adjustment to post-Fordist expectations without prior exposure at a younger age. It also reveals that unskilled workers do not tacitly accept any change. Did his union representative support him when he resisted following the new orders of the management?

Perhaps not so surprisingly in the Turkish context, the answer is no. What is more surprising, however, is the direct involvement of the union in post-Fordist transformation of worker skills: TURKMETAL (the union organized at FIAT-Bursa) provided similar adjustment trainings at its own headquarters. These trainings—which emphasized quality improvement techniques—were launched during the early 1990s, and workers were encouraged to participate in these sessions together with their families. As the respondent comments in Interview #23: "[our] wives were being trained by female instructors about the activities of the union. [They] wanted to prevent rising opposition from our family members by informing them about our activities and also to train them [on quality] as well."[34] Among the interviewed workers at FIAT, nearly 74% of the workers received behavioral training and/or information from the union on quality improvement. During the 1990s, most of these sessions took place in the local offices of TURKMETAL Bursa. Beginning in 2000, the union headquarters launched a co-sponsored training session in Ankara in collaboration with the Association of Metal-Goods Producers (MESS), of which FIAT-Bursa was a member. In the words of a FIAT manager, "MESS-TURKMETAL training programs are helpful...The communication skills of our workers are enhanced, they become more engaged, the number of innovative [and] improvement related suggestions are increasing."[35]

Besides behavioral modules like *art of negotiation, total quality management* and *conflict resolution*, these three-day seminars also accommodated additional modules including basic economics, globalization, industrial relations and the national ideology-Kemalizm. Overall, these short and brief modules further reminded workers of the rapidly changing market conditions, highlighting intense competition in bold letters. For example, the notes of the training module on total quality management convey this message explicitly:

> *[Q]uality is not the goal, but is a tool that enables competitive power. It would [perhaps] not even be enough to achieve highest levels of quality. The goal is to be one step further from the rivals.*[36]

The module on industrial relations also conveys the need for constant self-improvement and highlights competitive power as the precondition for economic success. This module especially underlines the ultimate goal as "customer satisfaction" and lists necessary tools such as setting up quality circles, employing total quality management, working under time pressure, interactive planning, and in a learning organization, and achieve top performance with a customer driven approach.[37] Furthermore, the new industrial relations training module introduces the concept of *social dialogue* to the participants, arguing that the "most economically advanced countries maintain worker welfare because they implemented social dialogue between the state, business and labor representatives when negotiating over developmental goals."[38]

To some readers, such a dedicated worker profile may sound surprising and others may view it as too good to be true. While there may indeed be selection bias with respect to identifying the respondents, these interviews were conducted in a confidential environment without the presence of managers and under the condition of anonymity. Thus, it is unlikely that workers were trying to please their managers with their enthusiasm. Rather, the overall positive attitude vis-à-vis the new core values of the workplace is a result of concerted public and private efforts to implant business expectations firmly in the minds of workers, first at school, then at the workplace and also at the union. In order to reduce the production costs while maximizing profits, the company managers stepped out of factory campus to create a new worker profile who would align his career objectives with those of FIAT's success. In Bursa, Vocational Education and Training Council played a key role in this process.

THE POLITICS OF POST-FORDIST TRANSITION IN TURKEY

The large-scale transformation in worker profile was possible thanks to a common platform—Bursa Vocational Education and Training Council—that brought together businessmen, local officials and union representatives on a regular basis. This platform served as a key node for networking different stakeholders to enable faster cooperation and upgrade vocational education and facilitate a comprehensive change across institutions of skill formation. The initial seeds of this collaboration were planted when Necati Cetinkaya was appointed as the governor of Bursa in 1992, and continued under Ridvan Yenisen and Orhan Tasanlar, who each paid special attention to accommodating the demands of the producers. Appointed by the right-wing representatives of coalition governments in a unitary setting, these governors played an important role to build durable networks between public and private stakeholders. Unlike their counterparts in Córdoba, the officials in Bursa did not challenge the central government policies and worked through this platform to rapidly address automobile producers' needs. Meanwhile, such close connections to top-level bureaucrats facilitated the broader diffusion of manager demands, especially with respect to content of vocational programs. Through these efforts, the council oversaw the transformation of a future workforce into multi-tasking agents that could combine intellectual and manual labor with ease.

Bursa is one of the oldest industrial provinces, and its economy is largely based on automobiles and textile production.[39] The city has been home to two major multinational auto companies (FIAT and Renault) since 1971. Between 1987 and 2001, manufacturing industry in this city was the fastest growing sector with an average rate of 5.5% per year.[40] Within the manufacturing sector, automotive production has steadily occupied a larger share in the overall economic output and holds the biggest share in exports (see Table 3.2). The rapid growth of this sector subsequently increased employment by creating new job opportunities and demanded skilled and semi-skilled workers, ideally with a vocational training background.

Following the transition to democracy, the modification of vocational education in Turkey took place through decrees and laws that circumvented the constitution beginning in 1986. Since Turkey is a unitary system, education policy is highly centralized and governed by the Ministry of Education. However, the vocational education and training was gradually

Table 3.2 The export shares of Bursa companies, by sector

	2001	2002	2003	2004	2005	2006	% Δ
Food and alcoholic beverages	45.2	34.5	36.9	54.6	60	59.3	−1.2
Textiles	383.7	413.4	586.1	646.6	636.4	639.6	0.5
Yarn	97.1	74.3	87.4	117.5	96.5	93.6	−3.0
Machines and metal goods	151.2	74.3	189.6	300	369	452.2	22.5
Automotives	**755.8**	**1169.9**	**2025.4**	**2544.8**	**2499**	**3873.6**	**55.0**
Leather goods	0.9	0.9	1.2	1.9	1.1	3.6	224.0
Wood	3.3	5.5	12.3	25	21.8	20.3	−7.0
Other	36.9	51.8	33.9	57.5	83.5	75.2	−9.9
Agriculture	94.5	114.9	177.3	224.1	182.7	195.6	7.1
Mining	0.4	0.6	1.1	1.8	2.7	7.3	171.4
Total	1569	2018	3151	3974	3953	5420	37.1

Source: BTSO. Figures are in million $

exempt from this rule due to changing industrial and local needs. As a result, following the passing of Vocational Training Law No. 3308 by the ANAP government in 1986, provincial vocational education and training councils across the country were established.[41] These councils served as a forum where state, business and union representatives would get together regularly to discuss and formulate policies to meet producer demands and incorporate business expectations into the vocational education system.[42] The meeting minutes of this council in Bursa reveal that between 1991 and 2007, unions, business associations and vocational high school principals and training center administrators discussed various issues, including the set-up of new schools, training tracks and specialized modules. In every meeting, at least one representative from these organizations would raise concerns, highlight problems and issue recommendations to address specific demands of leading industrialists.

At the same time, the council lacked economic resources to finance these changes.[43] Moreover, in a unitary setting, the governor had no fiscal authority to raise funds via imposing new taxes on local residents. In the face of this challenge, local businesses were encouraged to accommodate a greater number of interns on production premises. This measure aimed to expose vocational students to these new techniques without additional costs of investment in teacher training, teaching materials and curricular readjustments as they would gain first-hand experience. The process was initiated under governor Erol Cakir's tenure but also continued under his successor M. Necati Cetinkaya—who was also appointed by DYP controlled Ministry of Interior—in 1992 (Table 3.3).

Besides the coordination of business demands, the council was also responsible for the launching of new vocational schools and programs. The responsibility for overseeing this process together with bureaucrats from the Ministry of Education's local office now rested on the shoulders of the new governor. Planning the location, size and specialization of these schools calls for expert knowledge involving education professionals and business representatives. However, since Necati Cetinkaya did not have any expertise on the details of this process, the council members contacted the local business association BTSO—which was known for its close ties to the government—and encouraged them to help vocational high school and training center managers.[44]

Table 3.3 Percentage of total funds that are allocated to the use of vocational education council (nation-wide)

Year	Income funds for vocational education council	Funds transferred to the general budget	
		Amount	Percentage
1987	17,645	–	–
1988	44,672	12,533	28
1989	118,218	35,370	30
1990	228,650	83,860	37
1991	388,061	188,551	49
1992	447,772	326,452	73
1993	1,055,610	753,010	71
1994	1,699,557	1,373,321	81
1995	3,046,405	2,513,720	83
1996	5,929,909	5,032,424	85
1997	11,371,744	9,376,812	82

Source: Eighth Five-Year Development Program, Secondary Education, General Education, Vocational Education, Technical Education, Private Advisory Committee Report 2001. (The figures are in TL)

Bursa Governors and Mobilization of Local Networks

Working with businessmen from BTSO, it was under Cetinkaya's term as the governor when the bare foundations of a public-private partnership to reform the vocational school curricula were laid on the ground. During this period, the council committed itself to build new training centers within the close proximity of industrial zones and facilitate internship agreements between factories and technical schools in Bursa.

Vocational education in Turkey is neither a favorite subject nor occupies the center of popular debates. Though the issue rarely makes it to national headlines, there is an ongoing interest among politicians and bureaucrats to capitalize on skill formation for various reasons, including for political returns. Students who end up on the vocational track often have a rural or working class background and are not expected to exhibit top-level academic performance. While those who come from middle-class families compete for college education, graduates of vocational schools are trained to become employed as blue-collar workers or as middle-men with technical skills. In that sense, vocational education in Turkey stands a mechanism of social control, limits inter-class mobility opportunities and reproduces class-based hierarchies by interlocking generations into similar positions. Given these attributes, governments in Turkey always seek to reform the vocational education framework in a way to serve their own political ends, and mobilize the bureaucracy—including the governors—under their control to carry out proposed changes.

While appointed governors in Turkey arguably have no partisan affiliation, some cannot hide their greater political ambitions. The experience of Governor Cetinkaya is a case in point. Cetinkaya's later political career as an MP from DYP following the 1995 general elections reveals that the governor was indeed motivated by other goals. In order to be elected, however Cetinkaya first had to prove himself to the party leadership cadres as a capable networker—as this is an implicit expectation from any candidate—so that he would be nominated from the DYP list. Bursa governorship was therefore a great opportunity for Cetinkaya to demonstrate his skills. Working under time pressure to impress the party headquarters, the governor—among other things—oversaw the initial formation of collaborative vocational training schemes with the participation of businesses and education bureaucrats.[45]

In 1993, Cetinkaya was replaced with another DYP-appointed governor, Ridvan Yenisen.[46] A lawyer by training, Yenisen also worked as a teacher before embarking on his career as a bureaucrat, and showed concern for vocational education and training reform. More importantly, the new governor had some understanding of administering education reforms.[47] As the automobile producers were undergoing profound restructuring, the governor saw the need to retrain the labor force, upgrade their skill-set and avoid industrial conflict. Arguably, Bursa's success would be Yenisen's success and maybe carry him to the national parliament with a prestigious position as an MP, or perhaps as a minister.

In 1995, Yenisen was promoted to the governorship of Istanbul and Orhan Tasanlar—a former police officer, known to be very close to Prime Minister Tansu Ciller from DYP—was appointed as his successor.[48] Tasanlar had a very tumultuous career, and during the first days in office, he was involved in a scandal on torture in his former capacity as the Chief of Istanbul Police Department. In order to cast away the accusations, Tasanlar tried to deflect attention by focusing on regional development policies.

As a former police officer, the new governor was relatively inexperienced in industrial policy management but was dedicated to keep any industrial unrest under control. Tasanlar's reputation was not a very positive one: he was accused of pushing the legal limits, especially when dealing with leftist groups. Openly antagonistic toward labor, Tasanlar was highly responsive to accommodate the demands of business—including those as specific as quality improvement—and frequently participated in the award ceremonies of the factories that received ISO quality certificates.[49] Moreover, he paid close attention to the infrastructural development of the Demirtas industrial district that accommodated FIAT, and mobilized public and private actors to raise the necessary funds for facilitating the implementation of further development of this area.[50]

As a result of continuous efforts between 1991 and 2000, the number of area-specific modules offered at vocational high schools increased substantially, with a special emphasis on automobile production. Unlike Córdoba, this is largely due to the absence of polarization and conflict among central and local state actors on the key tenets of economic development policy and market reform (e.g. privatization, decentralization and flexibilization of labor force). Location of schools and content of modules were collectively decided in semi-annual meetings with the participation of governors, Ministry of Education officials, business organizations and union representatives. An overview of council decisions reveals that between 1994 and 2005, 39 out of 40 new tracks were directly addressed to meet the needs of main automobile and parts producers located in the region.[51]

For appointed governors and bureaucrats, FIAT-Bursa was an important enterprise whose input mattered because the local partner of FIAT, Koc Family, had strong ties to the government.[52] Thanks to this privileged status, the managers could communicate their demands rapidly and effectively. For example, on 12 July 1994, FIAT sent a letter to the council recommending a change in high school curricula—from credit-based system where students would be evaluated on individual course work to a semester-based system with a final examination—arguing that the latter would improve disciplinary behavior among the young apprentices. This was a period when the factory management particularly focused on consolidating work discipline among the apprentices. As one manager recalls, during the early 1990s these students were having a hard time understanding the basic principles of work and discipline in the factory.[53]Some of these students would be "loitering around, seeing the apprenticeship as a pass-time," a requirement that had to be dealt with.[54] Once the management discovered that the unwilling students were causing delays and lowering the productivity of their colleagues, company managers warned their vocational school partners to take necessary measures to ensure a stronger consolidation of values such as paying attention to workplace safety and health, participating in teamwork, making proposals and focusing on improving quality.

Until 1990, there were twelve vocational high schools in Bursa. Between 1990 and 2007, this figure more than doubled, reaching thirty schools in total. The sharp increase in the number of vocational schools that are financially supported by local businessmen is an important sign of a strong and consistent collaboration between local officials—including governors and ministry of education—and the businessmen. Between 1990 and 2006, not only FIAT but also prominent companies such as Ozdilek, Sonmez Holding, Coskunoz Holding, Dortcelik, as well as businessmen like Sarik Tara and Necati Yilmaz and Bursa Chamber of Trade and Commerce (BTSO) sponsored the construction of and supplied the necessary equipment for eight out of a total of thirteen newly built vocational schools. During this period, personal connections of these businessmen to the government facilitated the mobilization of resources to upgrade training schemes. These producers—organized under BTSO—gave a blank check to the government in Ankara on the flexibilization of labor relations.

The Role of Education Bureaucrats

In addition to close contact with governors, businesses had direct interactions with school managers who were in charge of training the next generation of workers. As the vocational council meeting records reveal, at least one principal from a vocational high school was present during the meetings, often serving as the secretary of the council. Among those principals, Hakki Bayrakci deserves a special attention. Between 1990 and 1998, Bayrakci was the principal of Demirtaspasa Industrial Vocational High School and participated in council meetings in his capacity to voice the needs and problems experienced by all schools in the province. Working with DYP-appointed governors from 1991 onwards (i.e. Erol Cakir, Necati Cetinkaya and Orhan Tasanlar), Hakki Bayrakci played an important part in restructuring the school administration and curriculum.[55] Importantly, the principal was now responsible to the governor to implement curricular changes.

As an education professional in the public sector, Bayrakci had to be quick, efficient and practical, otherwise he would face the risk of losing his position as a principal. To facilitate student exposure to new production technologies, Bayrakci turned to BTSO representatives he met at the council and convinced some of them to accommodate students as interns in these factories. In return for apprenticeship training, students worked in these factories on a minimum wage. This collaboration did not go unnoticed, and was also backed up and approved by the governors and Ministry of Education officials. A few years later, Bayrakci's school was promoted to a higher division among the vocational schools, and Demirtaspasa acquired Anatolian Technical High School status, where the language of instruction would be in English.[56]

Following Bayrakci, Ugur Nikbay took over his position as the secretary of the council in 1999. Though he is a newcomer, Nikbay was aware of the impact of ongoing budget cuts on vocational schools. Thus, he relied on his predecessor's network and mobilized the students and technical teachers to generate additional income by setting up deals with local producers, including FIAT.[57] According to this agreement, the students would be subcontracted by local firms to participate in production. The precondition required students to be employed in a field that is related to their specialization at school. While the students would acquire practical and behavioral training, they would also supply goods at a much lower price than the market value to the producer.[58] As a result of this, and a number of other collaborative income generating engagements, Demirtaspasa High School could cover the basic costs of curricula upgrading without additional funds from the central government.

At the same time, Nikbay continued to regularly participate in the vocational education council meetings and used his contacts at BTSO to set up similar deals.[59] He also took an active lead in initiating a school-based training program for effective student participation in teamwork in 2001. Additionally, together with other school principals, he co-authored a handbook on total quality management to be used in vocational and technical education.[60] The book specifically highlights customer demands as the driving force of the new economy and underlines the indispensability of competition for constant improvement in quality, arguing that this could be primarily achieved through a collaborative teamwork among workers. The book also describes additional techniques for enabling smoother communication and cooperation first at school and then in workplace.

Besides Demirtaspasa High School, Tophane Industrial and Technical High School principal Orhan Savaseri also helped subsequent governors to mobilize schools and businessmen. Between 1971 and 2001, Savaseri served as this school's principal until his retirement. Beginning as early as 1978 with the OSANOR project, Savaseri used established networks as an opportunity to strengthen the cooperation between Tophane and local business by placing students as trainees in Bursa factories. In 1986, with Savaseri's initiative, a foundation was established to strengthen local business and school cooperation in technical education. Today, this foundation continues under a different name (Foundation for Strengthening Bursa Tophane Technical and Vocational High School) and serves as an important institution for mobilizing resources through an extensive network of school's alumni. Additionally, under Savaseri's management, Tophane signed a cooperation and "brotherhood" agreement with Hans Wildorf Schule in Germany as early as 1985. As a result of this collaboration, Tophane students were exposed to quality trainings as early as the second half of 1980s. In 1987, an electronics training track and an Anatolian Technical High School was added to the Tophane group. The opening of engine and computer science tracks followed this in the 1990s.

As a result of these efforts, Tophane Vocational High School began to produce CNC equipment in the school workshop to generate extra income for training students with most up-to-date curricula and equipment.[61] The students were directly involved in the production of these machines and gained practical experience on the spot. The melding laboratory used for this purpose was built in collaboration with funds from BTSO and the curriculum was structured taking business demands into account. By 2006, Tophane schools also began to supply the Ministry of Education with computer equipment (around nearly 4000 machines) and programming support.[62] These activities enabled students to gain extensive hands-on experience before graduation.

The alumni statistics as of March 2008 show that over two hundred former graduates of Tophane vocational high school went on to set up their own businesses in Bursa. Perhaps not so surprisingly, majority of these small or medium enterprises operate in the metalworking and auto-production industry.[63] Most of these factories produce metal goods, car parts, textiles and wood-works, destined to many export markets. Exceptionally, five of these Tophane graduates are among the founders of biggest domestic holding groups in the province. Some of these former graduates regularly visit Tophane to lecture students on entrepreneurship values and the importance of familiarizing oneself with ever-changing market conditions.[64]

Through these direct exchanges between school principals and entrepreneurs, post-Fordist expectations found their way into the classroom smoothly. These efforts gradually changed the hiring practices of many companies. According to school's principal Rahmi Ozyigit, "the founders of these companies [were] well aware of the significance and necessity of technical education for [high quality in] production so they are very eager to recruit our graduates...last year [2007] we had seven hundred fifty graduates and none were left unemployed."[65] FIAT-Bursa managers exclusively prefer graduates of Tophane, Hurriyet, and Demirtaspasa Vocational Schools when hiring and speak very highly of their talent and training.[66]

In sum, led by appointed governors and Ministry of Education officials eager to please their superiors in Ankara, exposure to behavioral modules and on-the-job training for many students became increasingly common in Bursa. The businessmen operating in the automobile sector not only showed interest in what was being taught at schools, but also many of these enterprises collaborated with the school management in the placement of the recent graduates. Through these channels, the businessmen had immediate access to school principals to communicate their demands. In particular, FIAT directors were very exacting about the attitudinal and technical skills of the interns, and conveyed their expectations directly to the Tophane and Hurriyet Vocational and Technical High School principals. Though the factory managers did not make detailed proposals about the curriculum of vocational skill training programs, they informed school managers and teachers about the most recent changes in production techniques.[67] In return, the Undersecretary of Ministry of Education responsible for the curricula prepared syllabi for metalworking and car production tracks, and then sent those to the representatives of the industry asking for feedback.[68]

Besides FIAT, other BTSO affiliated companies have set up similar deals for vocational training of young students and workers. Recently, Bosch, which produces brake-systems for many multinational auto companies including FIAT and Renault, established a vocational center on factory premises for training young students in 1999. The center operates in collaboration with Bursa Ataturk Vocational Training Center, BTSO, and the company itself. Besides technical instruction, the students are also exposed to behavioral trainings focusing on teamwork, problem solving and strategies of total quality management. Upon successful completion of the program, Bosch employs most of these students as workers.[69]

In addition to companies, business organizations in Bursa also set up a foundation and collaborated with the state officials for improving vocational education in the city. For example, BTSO sponsored the launching of a foundation for the improvement of education (BEGEV) in Bursa in 1999. The foundation completed 82 vocational training and vocational improvement courses since 2001, including programs on molding, textile and apparel production, CNC, automation and quality control (Aydagul 2006, 37). Besides the contributions of local businessmen, BEGEV also cooperated with the National Employment Office in Bursa (ISKUR) and also received financial benefits for the participation in SVET/MEGEP program between 2003 and 2007.[70]

Another business foundation that works toward strengthening vocational education in Bursa is Coskunoz Education Foundation. Founded by late Kemal Coskunoz, who was a former graduate of Tophane Vocational Industrial school and the founder of Coskunoz Holding—also a member of BTSO—that supplies car parts to multinational companies based in Bursa, the foundation offers employment guaranteed training programs to regular high school graduates without any vocational skills. The training program lasts for 18 months. Upon successful completion, participants are offered positions to work at related positions within the company. In addition, the foundation financially supports working students to obtain a vocational diploma by attending evening courses at high schools in Bursa. The foundation also works hand in hand with vocational high schools closely, offers financial and technical support to school management, provides scholarships to graduates of these schools who want to study further to specialize in the field of their vocation (Aydagul 2006, 37–38).

After Fordism: Faster Surplus Labor Extraction and Declining Interest in the Union

Between 1990 and 1999, the union also encouraged participation of their members in "leadership seminars" which ran parallel to the modules operated by the Bursa branch. These trainings equipped rank-and-file members on technological and economic change, the impact of globalization, negotiation and conflict resolution techniques, quality improvement as well as propaganda and member recruitment techniques.[71] Interviews with FIAT managers reveal that they were very supportive of union-based behavioral training modules. The human resources manager of FIAT particularly noted the difference between those workers who attend the seminars and those who did not. According to this observation, those who come back to the factory after this brief exposure are more interested in the technical details, ask more questions, are eager to participate in factory-based training schemes, and there is a modest increase in the number of cost-cutting proposals they make. Other managers also note that there is some improvement in the communicative abilities of the workers after having participated in union seminars on behavioral training.[72] During the economic crisis of 2000, instead of sending workers out for unpaid vacations when market demand fell sharply, the managers launched an intense training program to keep workers active.[73] Simultaneously, TURKMETAL leadership in Bursa launched a new training program on quality improvement techniques.[74] Among the respondents, 39% are familiar with union sponsored quality and productivity improvement trainings and about 28% participated in union-led quality improvement modules. According to one shopfloor representative, budget limitations only allow a portion of workers to attend these trainings. Still, some workers identify the selection process as unfair and add that only those who are close to their shopfloor representatives are able to go to these sessions. Those who participated in such trainings do not remember having learned something radically new, however. Rather, these sessions include refreshment modules on topics that they are already familiar with. In the words of one respondent:

We took classes from 9 am till 5 pm in the evening. There [were courses on] quality, workplace safety, team work, defect identifying systems, pokayoke... (Worker THL)

Interviews with these workers also confirm how a regular exposure to these trainings from a very young age facilitates a smoother surplus labor extraction without frequent business-labor conflict. In the words of one worker:

We always want something. We work for extended hours, and we always want something [in return]. But what else are you doing for this factory other than production? Have you ever said 'let me do six instead of five'? Some people are done early [and] they don't do anything. Does he ever say 'let me work on improvement'? But you always ask for more. (Worker BTC)

What is even more surprising is the spillover of these techniques into the everyday lives of the workers. In one case, a worker recounted how he adopted the proposal system at home:

We follow the proposal system outside [as well]. They told us that we should adopt the proposal system even at home. I did this. It is a habit I picked up here. My kids do the same, they put proposal notes on the fridge. (Worker HFB)

While FIAT-Bursa workers give consent to the implementation of these modules, they also recognize that worker proposals, if accepted and implemented, primarily boosts company profits and not their salaries:

> *Proposal system is a part of our lives. We made a proposal...which was recognized as the proposal of the year [by the management]...But we did not get any [extra] pay...We made them save 126 billion TLs.* (Worker RRL)

As workers gradually accepted Toyotism-inspired modules as the new normal, the union managers at FIAT-Bursa systematically encouraged workers to also participate in schemes that reaffirm the need for such rearrangements. By supporting this, TURKMETAL's Bursa leaders who served in office during the 1990s hoped to secure a guaranteed due-paying rank and file base since the company management expected all workers to enlist under TURKMETAL, albeit informally.[75] The policy was in perfect harmony with the officials and businessmen in Bursa who pushed for creating a competitive workforce to facilitate surplus extraction without a major worker opposition.[76] Perhaps not so surprisingly, the union's uncritical approach generated strong feelings of apathy and resentment toward the union, and gradually led to a decline in worker commitment to pursuing collective action.[77] There is a growing indifference toward the union management, strongly mixed with resentment. In the words of these workers:

> *...the union management just takes my money, and does not do anything else.*[78]

> *...the union leadership...does not come and talk to us, they don't ask our opinion on anything.*[79]

These findings concur with an earlier study on the same factory by Nichols and Sugur (2004). While the decline in the overall unionization rates in Turkey was led by increasing repression of labor movements under center-right governments, the new production principles of the post-Fordist regime further contributed to growing feelings of worker apathy vis-à-vis collective action. The emphasis on adopting new habits for higher productivity and efficiency has created a new generation of workers who constantly worry about their individual performance and keeping their job above everything else.

CONCLUSION

The experience of FIAT workers in the face of new skill formation policies in Bursa shows that a unitary administrative system enabled a comprehensive embedding of new production principles through a concerted training scheme that emphasized soft-skills. There, appointed governors mobilized local resources for undertaking industrial reforms demanded by the central government. Potential career rewards were the key motivation behind the commitment of public officials to this agenda. In that sense, the story of Bursa suggests how political institutions and the absence of a major political conflict between local and central officials shape worker responses to industrial upgrading in unitary systems.

The pro-business orientation of governors and weak bargaining power of labor unions in Bursa allowed local state officials to make long-term investments to manufacture labor consent first at vocational schools, then at the workplace and finally through the union. Over time, this generated a decline in worker mobilization rates and allowed businesses to snatch further concessions from the union leaders. Partly as a reward for their role in keeping industrial unrest under control, Bursa governors were either promoted as civil servants or recruited to run as MP candidates from the DYP following the end of their tenure. For example, Erol Cakir was reappointed twice as a local governor to Izmir and later Istanbul—provinces that are known to be higher among the Ministry of Interior appointment hierarchy because of their economic and political importance. Similarly, Ridvan Yenisen was subsequently appointed as the governor of Istanbul in 1996. The other two governors later ran for office as MP candidates from DYP: while Necati Cetinkaya was elected, Orhan Tasanlar lost the competition but worked for the party until its practical dissolution in 2002 (Apaydin 2012).

However, prioritizing economic development at the expense of labor autonomy and unions comes at a price. While the rising profits and growing exports after a major overhaul of vocational curricula in Bursa strengthened the corporatist ties that held the business community and the government together, it simultaneously led to a major decline of trust in the union among the rank-and-file. The workers at FIAT are officially enlisted as members of TURKMETAL and their dues are automatically deducted from their monthly paycheck. However, majority of the respondents exhibit very little confidence in their shopfloor leaders on the grounds that union bureaucracy is pursuing their own material interest and is largely corrupt.

Declining interest in the union and apathy in TURKMETAL reached its zenith in 1998 when workers collectively resigned from the union after the leadership accepted a wage increase way below the rank-and-file expectations. Upon receiving the news, FIAT workers walked off the factory and blocked a major highway, protesting the union for letting them down once again. Next, FIAT workers collectively handed-in their resignation to TURKMETAL headquarters in Bursa, and prepared to enlist under the rival BIRLESIK-METAL, a more progressive union with a history of left-wing militancy. When the company management blocked this move, workers refused to enlist under any union. In this case, even though the decline in worker wages was part of a broader scheme initiated by the arrival of post-Fordist production technologies, the workers did not protest the company management but the union and chose to resign from TURKMETAL as a solution.

The lack of trust in the labor union for representing workers' interests is just another manifestation of a general decline of labor as a relevant political actor in Turkey. The gradual absence of unions from the political negotiations over the last two decades had lasting implications on the process of de-democratization (Blind 2009). As progressive unions lost their steam and were increasingly marginalized, neo-conservative political movements gained further strength. In that sense, Turkey's recent drift toward a competitive authoritarian regime under the AKP rule (Esen and Gumuscu 2016) could be partially explained by an ever growing decline of labor unions as relevant actors in the political scene. This stands in stark contrast to the Argentine experience where labor unions continue to be indispensable actors in negotiations over economic policy and reforms.

NOTES

1. Interview with undisclosed FIAT worker, 28 January 2008, Bursa, Turkey.
2. As stated in this report, "the automotive sector including car and parts producers will have a structure that is open to foreign competition, performing based on principles of economies of scale, using modern technology, and producing in line with international standards" *Fifth Five-Year Development Plan*, p. 68.
3. As stated in this report, "in order to improve efficiency and fluidity of labor, on-the-job trainings and vocational education will be given particular attention. Necessary regulations will be undertaken in order to ensure the participation of private sector, in addition to state support, keeping in

mind that vocational and technical education at every level will meet the demands of this country" Article 495 of fifth five-year development plan, SPO (1985) p.134.

4. *Fifth five-year development plan*, Article 496.
5. Ibid., Article 517.
6. Ibid., Article 551.
7. *Sixth Five-Year Development Plan*, p.339.
8. For a discussion of Ozal government's approach to decentralization, see Ozal 1987.
9. The new law (#3360, article 14) granted the provincial government to plan and implement regional development programs. In addition to law that regulated the rights and duties of provincial governments, the central government issued decrees to provide legal status to regional organized industrial zones. For example, Demirtas Organized Industrial Zone in Bursa—which accommodates FIAT was granted a special status with Government Decree on 16 October 1989 (#20314).
10. As stated in the report, "a yearly increase of 13% in production in this sector is planned in accordance with improvements in demand and exports." *Sixth Five-Year Development Plan*, p. 243.
11. The report also states that "quality in production and issues in standardization will be prioritized...In order to ensure the life-security of the public and improve export opportunities, the documentation of product standardization will be done in accordance to the rules and regulations determined by international and regional institutions." *Sixth Five-Year Development Plan*, p. 243.
12. "Oto Dunyasinda Hareket Var" (Action in the auto world) *Cumhuriyet*, 10 August 1990.
13. "Japonlara karsi FIAT'ta devrim" (Revolution at FIAT against the Japanese), *Cumhuriyet*, 5 June 1990.
14. Interview #11, Former FIAT Manager, 29 November 2007, Istanbul, Turkey.
15. Before this system, FIAT used to work with large stocks and the costs would increase tremendously when stocks were not eliminated in due time. Also, this created serious problems when there were production defects. Under the new system, once the target was reached, the management altered the production line and eliminated stations that produced specific parts so that new stations for updated and upgraded models could be installed. As Interview#11 reveals "when you are work with large stocks, it becomes very costly to re-install the former station and produce old parts to replace those with production errors." Interview #11, Former FIAT Industrial Operations Manager, 29 November 2007, Istanbul, Turkey.

16. Interview #12, FIAT Manager, 21 November 2007 and 15 January 2008, Bursa, Turkey.
17. Interview #11, Former FIAT Manager, 29 November 2007, Istanbul, Turkey.
18. Interview #11, Former FIAT Manager, 29 November 2007, Istanbul, Turkey.
19. Interview#3, FIAT Manager, 30 January 2008, Bursa, Turkey.
20. This finding is also consistent with the national survey across vocational and technical high school graduates. When asked to evaluate the contribution of vocational attitudes (*mesleki tutum*) and work-habitualization (*is aliskanligi*) acquired at school, around 68% of the respondents found these trainings "highly useful" or "useful" in relation to their current position at work. Report on the Follow-up project of Vocational and Technical School Graduates (Mesleki ve Teknik Egitim Kurumlari mezunlarinin izlenmesi projesi raporu) June 2007, Ministry of Education (Milli Egitim Bakanligi) Ankara, p. 44.
21. Report on the Follow-up project of Vocational and Technical School Graduates (Mesleki ve Teknik Egitim Kurumlari mezunlarinin izlenmesi projesi raporu) June 2007, Ministry of National Education (Milli Egitim Bakanligi) Ankara, p. 39.
22. Interview #12, FIAT Manager, 21 November 2007, Bursa, Turkey.
23. Interview #6, FIAT Manager, 21 November 2007 and 26 December 2007, Bursa. This rate is consistent with an earlier finding of another survey conducted by the employee association MESS among their members: according to a 1994 research, 87% of vocational training center and vocational school graduates were evaluated as either "very quick" or "highly quick" in adapting to their new work environment during the first basic orientation program. See MESS Bulletin (Bulten), December 1994, p. 15. These findings also resonate with the results of the 2006 Ministry of Education national survey conducted among employers. For example, when asked about why they prefer vocational high school graduates, 29.89% of the respondents rank the ability of these graduates to adapt changing technology and work environment more smoothly as the primary reason; 29.57% of the employers highlight the overlap between the curriculum at school and production operations at the workplace; and finally, 21.14% of the respondents underline the higher ability of these graduates to communicate effectively and participate in teamwork. See Report on the Follow-up project of Vocational and Technical School Graduates (Mesleki ve Teknik Egitim Kurumlari mezunlarinin izlenmesi projesi raporu) June 2007, Ministry of National Education (Milli Egitim Bakanligi) Ankara, p. 75.

24. Interview #6, FIAT Manager, 21 November 2007 and 26 December 2007, Bursa, Turkey.
25. These workers were selected based on block sampling criteria I submitted to the management. The sample consists of 50 workers (all male), in four different age brackets. Half of the sample included workers who have been working in the factory for more than 20 years. The other half included workers with less than 20 years of work experience.
26. In addition, workers also participated in CEDAC schemes. CEDAC stands for *Cause and Effect Diagram with the Addition of Cards*. It is visual, team-oriented problem solving methodology developed by Dr. Ryuji Fukuda. (See Fukuda 1996). According to Interview #11, "this was a lighter tool that was much easier for the workers to accept without much difficulty. In this way, the workers could identify and propose solutions to efficiency and productivity problems on the spot." Interview #11, Former FIAT Manager, 29 November 2007, Istanbul, Turkey.
27. Interview #11, Former FIAT Manager, 29 November 2007, Istanbul, Turkey.
28. Interview #11, Former FIAT Manager, 29 November 2007, Istanbul. Jan Nahum served as FIAT CEO between 1993 and 2002.
29. Interview #23, Former FIAT worker, 3 November 2007, Bursa, Turkey.
30. In a way, this finding is also consistent with the findings of the Ministry of Education 2007 survey: among the graduates of vocational high schools, around 42.27% of the respondents are employed in a position that is *somewhat related* to their school training, while 19.68% of the graduates have jobs that are totally unrelated to their technical specialization at school. When combined, 62% of the total interviewees are employed in positions that do not directly correspond to their specialization. Report on the Follow-up project of Vocational and Technical School Graduates (Mesleki ve Teknik Egitim Kurumlari mezunlarinin izlenmesi projesi raporu) June 2007, Ministry of Education (Milli Egitim Bakanligi) Ankara.
31. It must be noted though, that at FIAT, transfer from blue-collar to white-collar status is extremely hard and competitive.
32. Interview #20, Former FIAT worker, 1 November 2007, Bursa, Turkey.
33. Interview #20, Former FIAT worker, 1 November 2007, Bursa, Turkey.
34. Interview #23, Former FIAT worker, 3 November 2007, Bursa, Turkey.
35. Interview #12, FIAT Manager, 21 November 2007, Bursa, Turkey.
36. Turkmetal training module notes (no date) (Turkmetal egitim ders notlari), p. 30.
37. Ibid., p. 37.
38. Ibid., p. 38.
39. For a history of industrial development in Bursa see Kaygalak 2008. For studies that examine contemporary industrial development dynamics in

Bursa, see Eraydin and Aymatli-Koroglu 2005; Taymaz and Kilicaslan 2005; Sugur and Sugur 2005.

40. Prominent Industrial Sectors in the Cities (Illerde One Cikan Sanayi Sektorleri), Basbakanlik DPT Publications, August 2006, p. 131.

41. ANAP was founded by Turgut Ozal in 1983, following the transition to democracy. DYP was founded a few years later, and Suleyman Demirel, the arch-rival of Ozal, was elected as the party leader in 1988. ANAP was a right-liberal political party with an open admiration for Reagan and Thatcher style reforms. The business community that supported ANAP included some industrialists, but it overwhelmingly mobilized services and financial sector behind Turgut Ozal's economic liberalization agenda. On the other hand, Suleyman Demirel's DYP followed the line of AP, and endorsed a more statist approach to industrial development.

42. The Council was also a platform to facilitate local interaction and transfer of information with respect to changing human capital needs of the city. Besides vocational education council, the participants also got together to debate employment related problems and concerns in two additional platforms: the Employment Council for the City of Bursa (*Il Istihdam Kurulu*) and Local Council for Employment Consultation (*Mahalli Danisma Kurulu*). Both of these institutions brought business and union representatives under the coordination of the local representative of National Ministry of Labor to discuss, evaluate and resolve employment related problems.

43. The funds allocated for the use of the council were transferred to the general budget, instead of the budget of the local department of National Ministry of Education. The report also notes: "it is unacceptable of the state to raise resources for the use of improving the vocational education system and then not using the funds for this purpose. It will not be possible to convince people, organizations and institutions to donate to education as long as incorrect [policy] implementations like this are allowed" *Eighth Five-Year Development Program, Secondary Education, General Education, Vocational Education, Technical Education, Private Advisory Committee Report*, 2001 (Sekizinci Bes Yillik Kalkinma Plani, Ortaogretim, Genel Egitim, Meslek Egitimi, Teknik Egitim, Ozel Istisare Kurulu Raporu), p.78.

44. During the 1990s, BTSO had close connections to DYP, and prominent members of this organization from textile and automotive sectors ran for an MP position (e.g. A. Osman Sonmez and Cavit Caglar). Some ended up in DYP government as ministers. See "Bursa Ithal Aday Cenneti" (Bursa is a Heaven of Import Candidates) *Milliyet*, 7 December 1995.

45. In fact, Cetinkaya continued to voice his concern over reforming the apprentice training centers and vocational high schools once he was elected

as an MP from DYP, in the national parliament. In 1997, Cetinkaya accused the ruling coalition-parties, including ANAP, of paying abysmal attention to human capital formation in a changing world of production. See http://www.tbmm.gov.tr/develop/owa/Tutanak_B_SD.birlesim_baslangic?P4=472&P5=B&PAGE1=65&PAGE2=67.

46. Ridvan Yenisen was a close figure to DYP leader Tansu Ciller and campaigned in support for her during the 1995 elections. See Musa Agacik, Interview with Tansu Ciller and Ridvan Yenisen, 12 September 1995, *Milliyet*, p.17. He was also a frequent participant in party's social gathering activities. See "DYP'nin Mangal Partisi" (DYP's Barbecue Party), *Milliyet*, 3 January 1995, p.14.

47. Yenisen was actively involved in the launching and administration of short-term skill training modules in Istanbul during his tenure as a Vice-Governor in Istanbul in 1987. During his period, Yenisen administered 151 courses in 42 vocational fields. See "Beceri kurslari issizligi onluyor" (Training Courses remedy unemployment) *Milliyet*, 23 June 1987, p.3.

48. Orhan Tasanlar later ran for MP from DYP in 2002. See "Adaylarin sagi solu yok" (There's no left or right in candidates) *Milliyet*, 9 August 2002, p.20.

49. See "Yesim Tekstil'de kalite bayrami" (Quality Fest at Yesim Tekstil) *Hurriyet*, 28 July 1998.

50. Tasanlar set up an association for building a waste disposal and water cleaning system in the district and raised funds for installing the equipment necessary for this project. See interview with Erdem Saker, http://www.yenibursa.com/Artik&Adaylik&Dusunmuyorum&12.html.

51. Source: Bursa Vocational Education and Training Council Meeting Minutes, 1991–2004. Compiled by the author.

52. In 1997, Rahmi Koc (the CEO of FIAT's partner Koc) was awarded with Supreme Service Medal for his services to the Turkish Republic by Suleyman Demirel, the president and the founder of DYP. The founder of Koc Holding, Vehbi Koc, was a close figure to the DYP line and had warm relations with Suleyman Demirel dating from the 1970s. (See for example, Demirel Koc'la gorustu (Demirel met Koc), *Milliyet*, 30 March 1993; "Demirel: Koc'un Reklamini Yapiyorum" (Demirel: I promote Koc) *Milliyet*, 4 December 1993; Yilmaz Cetiner: Koc'un Mutlulugu (Yilmaz Cetiner: Koc's Happiness), *Milliyet*, 29 June 1995). It must be noted that though Demirel left the party leadership position in 1993 following his election to the presidency of Turkish republic, he had informal control over DYP cadres throughout the 1990s.

53. Interview #6, FIAT Manager, 21 November 2007 and 26 December 2007, Bursa, Turkey.

54. Interview #12, FIAT Industrial Operations Manager, 21 November 2007 and 15 January 2008, Bursa, Turkey.
55. For example, during the early period in his leadership, a new department for *auto-engine studies* was opened in 1985. This was followed by the launching of *computer, electronics* and *press* departments in 1988. See http://www.demirtaspasa.k12.tr/.
56. Right before his retirement, Bayrakci also worked toward launching of a leveling department, and opened up Anatolian technical high school of for engine studies as a part Demirtaspasa Vocational High Schools.
57. According to Nikbay, in contrast to FIAT, other prominent firms, such as Renault (also in Bursa) had always declined to accommodate interns until 2012. See http://www.hurriyet.com.tr/oib-de-otomotiv-egitimi-alan-ogrenciye-universitede-ogretecek-bir-sey-kalir-mi-21482689, accessed on 1 June 2017.
58. This practice was becoming more common across other vocational schools in Turkey. For example, in 2004 Samsun Atakum Vocational industrial high school also took a similar lead to produce sound systems and energy systems for computers and created an additional source of income for the school management. For news coverage, see *Sabah*, 6 April 2004.
59. In 2010, Nikbay was appointed as the first principal of a new vocational high school (Otomotiv Endüstrisi İhracatçıları Birliği Teknik ve Endüstri Meslek Lisesi) which exclusively focused on training future workers to be employed in automobile firms. See http://www.hurriyet.com.tr/oib-de-otomotiv-egitimi-alan-ogrenciye-universitede-ogretecek-bir-sey-kalir-mi-21482689, accessed on 1 June 2017
60. National Ministry of Education, Total Quality System in Technical Education 2001 (MEB Teknik Egitimde Toplam Kalite Yonetimi) MEB: Ankara.
61. CNC is a computed based parts producing device. Upon entering the necessary commands, the equipment controls machine cutters to produce the material with desired shape. This is a very widely used tool across a broader array of industries, including automobile production.
62. http://www.egitimportali.com/haber.php?hid=1691; accessed on 12 April 2010.
63. Some of these graduates and their companies are: Fahrettin Gülener, Ermetal; Atilla Öztelcan, Kuzuflex; Mehmet Ülker, Meka Teknik; Serkan Köristan, Gera Makina; Ali Olağaner, Mutlusan; Necmettin Pınar, Pınar Metal; Ali Altınipek, Omega Otomotiv; Hulusi Burkay, Burkay Tekstil; Abdullah Bayrak, Elsisan; Nurettin Akbal, Ceyantek; Burak Selamet, Ünimak; Zeki Tunaoğlu, Tunaoğlu AŞ; Yusuf Meriç-Kadir Gümüş, Yuneka; Ali Tosun, Mutfakçılar AŞ; Sabri Evci, Revsan; Cengiz Malkoç, Karmod; Emin Işıkverenler, Başarır Kalıp; Yusuf Keser, ŞRK AŞ; Vehbi

Varlık, İnoksan; Harun Keser, Kema Makine; İhsan Gürsu, Türkkar Otobüs; Erhan Kara, Hidro Tek; Fahri Tuğral, Tuğra Makina; Veli Kaynar, Hidrosel; Turgay Şenel, Modsan; Fevzi Uçar, Mimsa; Hüseyin Şahinkul, Şahunkul AŞ.

64. Interview with Rahmi Ozyigit, *Bursa Ekonomi Dergisi* (Bursa Economy Journal), December 2007.
65. Interview with Rahmi Ozyigit, *Bursa Ekonomi Dergisi* (Bursa Economy Journal), December 2007.
66. Interview #6, FIAT Manager, 21 November 2007 and 26 December 2007, Bursa, Turkey.
67. Interview #11, Former FIAT Manager, 29 November 2007, Istanbul, Turkey.
68. Interview #12, FIAT Manager, 21 November 2007 and 15 January 2008, Bursa, Turkey.
69. The curriculum is modeled after the dual system in Germany, where the students receive theoretical training in the training center and have practical training in the factory. At Bosch Training Center, Bursa Ataturk Vocational Training Center management, which operates under the Ministry of Education office in Bursa, is responsible for the theoretical training, while the company is responsible for the practical training of young apprentices. BTSO is responsible for carrying the examination and accreditation of skills. http://www.boschtr.com/press/bulliten/bulliten_detail.asp?bid=66
70. More recently, besides collaborating with the local politicians, BEGEV managers also applied to the EU and World Bank funds to finance the trainings.
71. Interview #38, Former Turkmetal Bursa Branch Leader, 2 November 2007, Bursa; and Interview #25, Turk-Is Confederation Regional Representative, Bursa, 10 January 2009. As Interview #38 puts it "...the union also needs to offer support services to secure [the loyalty of] members...these [workers] are paying their dues..[they] want to see something in return...that the union is doing service with their money." Though the union leaders encouraged worker participation in leadership and quality seminars, some workers initially criticized the rules of participation and expressed their discontent with the selection process and criteria. In response, the union management excluded these older workers who were known to openly criticize union politics and leaders. Rather, the management selected younger and newly recruited workers to participate in the seminars on a non-random basis. The shopfloor leaders usually prepared a list of candidates among those who were relatively recently recruited to the union.
72. Interview #12, FIAT Manager, 21 November 2007 and 15 January 2008, Bursa, Turkey. Interview #6, FIAT Manager, 21 November 2007 and 26

December 2007, Bursa, Turkey. The behavioral trainings that FIAT workers participate under Turkmetal since 1999 are also partially supported by FIAT's contribution to MESS. According to the management, the behavioral trainings offered by the union do not radically alter the behavior of a worker from one day to next, but they have an incremental effect to refresh and reaffirm what the workers have already been exposed to.

73. Interview #12, FIAT Manager, Bursa, 21 November 2007.
74. Interview #38, Former Turkmetal branch leader, Bursa, 2 November 2007.
75. The willingness to transform the human capital profile of the rank-and-file in line with changing market demands was also reflected in the words of these former leaders. According to Interview #38, Turkmetal chose to negotiate and collaborate with the employers because "[they] did not want to have [rank-and-file] members laid off so [they] agreed to work without payment and have unpaid vacations when production would go low. Most of the workers received trainings in large enterprises like FIAT and Renault during times of crisis...It is the legal right of the employer to protect himself [by postponing production]. We are in favor of those enterprises [and people] that invest in this country and create new jobs. FIAT and Renault do this." Interview #38, Former Turkmetal Bursa Branch Leader, 2 November 2007, Bursa, Turkey.
76. In addition to the Bursa representatives of Turkmetal, the general leader of the union in Ankara, Mustafa Ozbek, was known to be an avid champion of DYP during the 1990s, and explicitly supported Demirel and Ciller government policy on decentralization, flexibilization and privatization. See "Susurluk'tan Turkiyem Topluluguna" 20 June 2006, http://www.etikhaber.com/content/view/19212/40/, accessed on 15 February 2010.
77. The overlapping political orientation of the union leaders and company management also contributed to the development of further cooperation in behavioral training. Some researchers classify the relationship between the union, the company and the state as corporatist (Interview #37, Eskisehir, Turkey September 2007 and see also Nichols and Sugur 2004). Moreover, due to lack of democratic election mechanisms, Nichols and Sugur classify the union as autarchic. Other accounts reveal that the collaboration between Turkmetal and the company had non-democratic characteristics as well. For example, during the 1998 collective bargaining process many workers affiliated with Turkmetal withdrew their membership from the union to protest union leaders' lack of dedication for higher wage increase rates. In response, the company managers are said to join Turkmetal leaders and are accused of pressuring and threatening the workers with lay-offs if they refuse to join back Turkmetal (see Nichols

et al. 2002). My interviews with the factory management show that the managers classify the relationship as one that is based on maintaining "industrial peace and harmony." The union representatives use a similar expression to define the relationship: "collaboration for mutual benefits."
78. Interview with worker RSD, Bursa, January 2008.
79. Interview with worker NTK, Bursa, January 2008.

BIBLIOGRAPHY

Apaydin, F. 2012. Partisan Preferences and Skill Formation Policies: New Evidence from Turkey and Argentina. *World Development* 40 (8): 1522–1533.

Aydagul, B. 2006. *Beceriler, yeterlilikler ve meslek eğitimi: politika analizi ve oneriler* [Skills, Abilities and Vocational Education: A Policy Analysis with Recommendations]. Istanbul: Sabanci University.

Blind, P. 2009. *Democratic Institutions of Undemocratic Individuals*. New York: Palgrave.

Eraydin, A., and B. Armatli-Köroğlu. 2005. Innovation, Networking and the New Industrial Clusters: The Characteristics of Networks and Local Innovation Capabilities in the Turkish Industrial Clusters. *Entrepreneurship & Regional Development* 17: 237–266.

Esen, B., and S. Gumuscu. 2016. Rising Competitive Authoritarianism in Turkey. *Third World Quarterly* 37 (9): 1581–1606.

Fukuda, R. 1996. *CEDAC: A Tool for Continuous Systemic Improvement*. Portland: Productivity Press.

Kaygalak, S. 2008. *Kapitalizmin tasrasi* [The Rural of Capitalism]. Istanbul: Iletisim.

Nichols, T., and N. Sugur. 2004. *Global Management, Local Labor: Turkish Workers and Modern Industry*. Basingstoke: Palgrave Macmillan.

Nichols, T., N. Sugur, and E. Demir. 2002. Beyond Cheap Labor: Trade Unions and Development in the Turkish Metal Industry. *Sociological Review* 50: 23–47.

Ozal, T. 1987. Turkey's Path to Freedom and Prosperity. *The Washington Quarterly* 10 (4): 161–165.

Sugur, N., and S. Sugur. 2005. Gender and Work in Turkey: Case Study on Women Workers in the Textile Industry in Bursa. *Middle Eastern Studies* 41: 269–279.

Taymaz, E., and Y. Kiliçaslan. 2005. Determinants of Subcontracting and Regional Development: An Empirical Study on Turkish Textile and Engineering Industries. *Regional Studies* 39: 633–645.

CHAPTER 4

A Persistent Refusal: Córdoba's Contentious Workers in Federal Argentina

In 1989, the election of Carlos Menem to the presidency of Argentina from PJ against Eduardo Angeloz from UCR was a critical turning point that intensified existing political rivalries in Córdoba for nearly an entire decade during the 1990s.[1] First, a deepening political conflict between the provincial and federal capital pushed Angeloz government into isolation, turning Córdoba into a political and economic "island." By the end of 1995, the province was on the brink of bankruptcy and societal groups in the city of Córdoba directly experienced pains of a severe financial crisis. Second, the tension between two powerful figures from these rival parties aggravated existing socio-political rifts in Córdoba.

When PJ and UCR took opposing sides on a number of critical economic issues, daily protests by public and private sector unions frequently disrupted production as business organizations fought among themselves and with the local government. Most notable of these cases was the experience of FIAT. Unlike their counterparts in Bursa, FIAT-Córdoba workers were caught up in a political storm, and in the shadow of a rivalry between UCR and PJ politicians, these workers persistently opposed a post-Fordist restructuring of production and training techniques. As FIAT-Bursa factory went through profound changes to increase its competitive edge, Córdoba workers launched protests, factory occupations and walkouts—which lasted much longer than similar outbreaks in Bursa—in the face of pressures to create a more flexible labor force. How should we account for

© The Author(s) 2018   109
F. Apaydin, *Technology, Institutions and Labor*, International Political
Economy Series, https://doi.org/10.1007/978-3-319-77104-5_4

the divergence in FIAT workers' response as both factories were going through a similar process of post-Fordist reorganization on the shopfloor? This chapter shows how federal institutions are more conducive to harboring political conflicts between the central and provincial officials, creating opportunities for organized labor groups to stay in opposition at times of industrial conflict. Consequently, strategies adopted by the same multinational company took a different path in Córdoba. As we shall see, the changes in the production regime are subject to political intervention, which pushed managers to re-negotiate components of new skill formation schemes with local stakeholders. Further, the comparison built around two FIAT factories in Bursa and Córdoba reveals that surplus labor extraction processes are shaped by factors *beyond* the company, most notably, the degree to which new technologies are embedded in wider societal and political networks.[2] Drawing on comparisons with Bursa, this chapter reveals that governors in Córdoba—including Eduardo Angeloz and his successor Ramón Mestre—were unwilling to comply with the economic reform policies of the federal government under the control of a rival party, PJ. Thus, unlike Bursa, producers in Córdoba, including FIAT, had to rely on firm-based solutions to train workers along post-Fordist technologies, which resulted in uncoordinated and decentralized schemes. Consequently, isolated efforts to consolidate post-Fordist skills did not initiate a comprehensive transformation as in Bursa. The deskilling of workers during this process further contributed to industrial troubles during the second half of the 1990s, creating an additional excuse for the relocation of most manufacturing firms (i.e. parts producers) to Brazil, especially after the 2001 crisis.[3] Though FIAT partially remained in the province of Córdoba, the worker profile in this factory was very different than their counterparts in Bursa.[4]

In order to illustrate how federalism created institutional barriers to the broader consolidation of post-Fordist training schemes, the first part of this chapter maps out the trajectory of skill formation schemes in Córdoba during the 1990s. This section raises a few important questions: how did this limited change from Fordist to post-Fordist production unfold in Córdoba? Why did select-few companies implement on-site vocational training programs independently? To explain this in comparative perspective, I begin by highlighting the partisan preferences of organized interest groups and their origins. The second part of this chapter shows how these political rivalries intensified under a growing political tension between unions and business organizations at the local level.

These divisions blocked communication between politicians, businessmen and labor unions, which imposed limitations on policy options available to local politicians. Because the successive UCR governments in this province were engaged in a protracted political conflict with the federal government, the latter sidestepped the local government and took the initiative to finance boutique-style training programs in multinational car companies.[5] However, rather than facilitating a broader embedding of new production principles, federal politicians handpicked companies to implement shopfloor-based modules only. Between 1990 and 1999—or during the post-Fordist transition—company-based training prevailed as the dominant arrangement in Córdoba.

THE ARRIVAL OF POST-FORDISM IN CÓRDOBA

In 1991, FIAT-Córdoba began to reorganize the shopfloor along the principles of just-in-time production.[6] Similar to FIAT-Bursa, the management introduced quality circles to facilitate team-building among the blue-collars. However, few workers showed genuine commitment and shopfloor leaders had little trust in the promoted merits of these meetings.[7] Meanwhile, encouraged by the federal government and intrigued by attractive regional market opportunities, FIAT decided to expand its production and make a 600-million-dollar investment in its Córdoba factory to produce the new *Siena* model in 1996.[8] After FIAT signed a new investment deal, the company began to look for local support to upgrade production. In addition to negotiations with the local government on infrastructural support, (i.e. subsidies on energy and water costs), the managers wanted to transform the labor profile, replacing the existing one with flexible labor contracts in addition to reorganization of production on the shopfloor. In order to facilitate the transformation, the company arranged a deal with the pro-PJ *Sindicato de Mecánicos y Afines de Transporte Automotor* (SMATA), welcoming the union to organize workers on the premises, under the condition that the new collective agreement recognize new production principles and accept flexible shopfloor reorganization.[9]

The new scheme offered symbolic rewards for individual performance for all workers regardless of experience.[10] This decision was taken after negotiations with SMATA leaders who were promised a guaranteed quota of rank-and-file members. However, once the workers found out about the new terms, they launched a violent protest on September 20th 1996, occupying the factory for several weeks, blaming wage-readjustments on

just-in-time production and staunchly opposing shopfloor rearrangements.[11] This conflict quickly escalated, some of the workers attacked the
machinery and the management again began to lay off workers.[12] Once
the initial anger subsided, workers continued with their protests—which
lasted with interruptions over into a year. During this process, some workers refused to join SMATA, first formed an independent union and then
joined a new branch under SMATA's rival *Unión Obrera Metalúrgica*
(UOM).[13] Meanwhile, other workers at FIAT's suppliers also joined the
protests mobilized under UOM.

The company management deliberately handpicked (SMATA)—known
to support Menem's faction in the PJ—to organize workers at FIAT
because SMATA leadership accepted the proposed changes.[14] Subsequently,
the management began to hire new workers and informed seasoned
employees to expect drastic changes, assigning some of the older workers
to new workstations. Simultaneously, the management began to lay off
older workers that had adaptation difficulties, hiring new ones with no
relevant training or former work experience.[15] This sparked major tensions
between the workers and the management (Anner 2011).

In face of ongoing protests and lack of political support from the local
government, FIAT eventually signed a bilateral training agreement with
the Menem government.[16] According to this deal, the federal government
would cover the training costs of newly recruited workers under *Programa
Emprender*, while FIAT's own instructors would train old and new workers on factory premises.[17] All of these programs emphasized behavioral
skills over technical trainings to facilitate worker rotations.[18]

Just like FIAT-Bursa, the new production plan in FIAT-Córdoba
required the workforce to be endowed with manual and *intellectual* skills
to maximize the participation of the workers in production. To that end, in
1995, the new training program ran by ISVOR (a side company of FIAT),
focused on endowing workers with values such as (1) identification with
FIAT, (2) individual and group responsibility, (3) team spirit, (4) attention
to internal and external clients, (5) interdepartmental integration, (6) vertical and horizontal communication and (7) flexibilization.[19] In the words of
Andrea Franco, the organizational director of FIAT, the most important
component of these modules is the prioritization of general, soft-skills over
highly specialized technical trainings (Illustration 4.1).[20]

Why did FIAT prioritize the acquisition of general over specific skills? A
former FIAT director suggests that this is closely related to containing undis-
ciplined worker action.[21] The new economic era required uninterrupted

Illustration 4.1 Brochure that summarizes the principles of World Class Manufacturing system

production with better product quality, and the older workers of the company were unable to adapt to these new conditions.[22] That is why the company chose to replace the old logic of ISI (an era where keeping up with international competition was not a priority) with a new one that would ensure worker self-identification with the company. The respondent also added that whenever necessary, they had to lay off older workers who had adaptation problems and replace them with young and inexperienced workers. These workers also got some technical training, but unlike their counterparts in Bursa, most of these workers got their first training on the job.

However, unlike FIAT-Bursa, the management in Córdoba did not require a formal vocational degree when hiring a new set of blue-collar workers, on the grounds that the production was increasingly based on computerized systems. In fact, a top-level manager noted that quality of education in technical schools has been quite low and therefore he did not believe in their merit. According to the management, the best training for a worker is on the job, and the key figure in this process should be the supervisor.[23] Another manager of FIAT-Córdoba also shared a similar opinion, arguing that the company does not have a high opinion of vocational schools in this province.[24] For the management, maintenance of factory discipline and worker dedication are ultimate priorities in recruiting.[25] This stands in sharp contrast to Bursa, where the managers were deeply involved in restructuring the curricula of schools that supplied a large share of their employees.

LEGACIES OF POLITICAL CONFLICT IN A FEDERAL SETTING

These differences in the perspectives of FIAT's Bursa and Córdoba managers regarding the merits of vocational training are largely influenced by the broader political context in which they operate. The struggles on post-Fordist transformation of worker skills in Córdoba during the 1990s were intensified in a federal setting that pitted politicians, businesses and unions camped under two major political parties: UCR and PJ. Córdoba is often referred to as a bastion of the Radicalist movement (UCR)—the key opposition to Peronist PJ. During the pre-ISI period, immigrant middle classes, together with agricultural producers and big landowners of Córdoba, constituted the majority of this party's base (Snow 1963; Moran 1970).[26] Even though the city and the province temporarily turned to Peronism between 1943 and 1955, Córdoba reoriented itself toward UCR after 1955.[27] As opposed to Peronist populism, general inclination of the *radicals* was to advocate liberal values and oppose the state's role in economic development.[28]In Córdoba, most UCR members had close links to the agricultural sector, maintaining a distance to Peronism during the twentieth century. However, during the 1960s the newly forming industrial working classes (organized under unions such as SMATA and UOM) leaned toward the pro-industrial PJ. Thus, the clashes between businessmen and labor unions during the 1960s and 1970s in Córdoba left indelible marks on the industrial scene, characterized by mutual suspicion, distrust and antagonism.[29]

Argentine industrialization under ISI required a large base of labor force to be employed in the manufacturing sector during the second half of the twentieth century. Aware of this, Juan Perón and his PJ took measures to create a skilled labor force with strong ties to the party and centralized the fragmented vocational training system by simultaneously expanding technical school network across the industrializing zones.[30] In Córdoba, this process led to the creation of a number of factory-schools (*escuelas fabricas*) during the 1940s and establishment of a worker university

Table 4.1 Historical legacies: partisan preferences of socio-economic groups in Córdoba

UCR	PJ
Immigrant middle classes	Industrial working classes
Agricultural producers, agro-industrialists and big landowners	Heavy industrialists; metalworking sector and automobile producers

campus (*Universidad Obrero Nacional-Córdoba*) during the 1950s.[31] Moreover, technical-vocational high schools were brought under the jurisdiction of the federal government. These institutions were among primary channels that consolidated partisan allegiance of manufacturing sector workers to PJ under a Fordist ISI-oriented regime, because they served as important centers for the dissemination of Peronist ideology and recruitment of new advocates (Table 4.1).

The partisan allegiances of these organized interest groups survived following the transition to a democratic regime after 1983. As Córdoba accommodated growing number of automobile firms, subnational politics in this federal setting was dominated by a struggle between two major business clusters: agro-industrialists who leaned toward the UCR and the metalworking sector that leaned toward the PJ.[32]

Competition Among Local Unions in a Federal Setting

The labor unions in Argentina are the products of a state corporatism, gaining further prominence under the early rule of Juan Perón through the umbrella confederation CGT. However, the political orientation of these unions has gone through a major transformation during the second half of the twentieth century, with major break-ups from the mainstream Peronist line especially after the 1990s. A major factor that facilitated this change is political competition under a federal system. First, some of the public sector workers disengaged themselves from the PJ because they were excluded from the pro-liberal economic reform coalition formed under Menem. These groups suffered due to Menem's ambitious privatization agenda.[33] In Córdoba, public workers opposed these reforms extensively, and launched a series of disruptive protests.

Second, political factions within unions organized in the private sector also gained further prominence during this period. In Córdoba, local branches of the metalworking unions (i.e. UOM and SMATA) rejected proposals on the deregulation of the labor market. In search of enlarging his circle of political allies, governor Eduardo Angeloz first refused and then delayed the implementation of the law on labor market flexibilization. However, this proved ineffective in the face of a counter-move by Menem. The President managed to lure UOM's rival, SMATA, into the reform coalition and got their support for the new labor law in return for promising to increase their rank-and-file base.

Though both UOM and SMATA have close connections to the PJ, their response to the Peronist party's economic reform agenda could not have been more different. The official leadership of these unions had links to rival political factions under the PJ, which intensified the competition between UOM and SMATA.[34] UOM was mostly organized in small and medium size enterprises, while SMATA controlled workers in larger domestic enterprises and multinationals. Unlike SMATA's member base, the workers organized under UOM were the least protected under the new automobile regime.[35] Given the configuration of interests as such, factional divisions within the Peronist party encouraged UOM to oppose whatever SMATA defended (see Table 4.2).

In this divided political environment, when the PJ-controlled federal government under Menem announced the new industrial development initiative and prioritized the automobile industry, many UCR politicians in Córdoba were skeptical about this. None of these officials had close connections with auto producers or the unions.[36] During this period, the UCR government in Córdoba lacked the political will and economic capacity to mobilize resources for coordinating vocational training in line with post-Fordist schemes. Consequently, Córdoba's experience with post-Fordist skill formation sharply differed from Bursa, where no such political fault-lines existed in a unitary setting.

Table 4.2 Preferences and factional alliances of Córdoba unions during the 1990s

SMATA-Córdoba	*UOM-Córdoba*
Pro-Menemist line (PJ); supports economic liberalization only with selective industrial protections for the automobile producers	Pro-De la Sota line (PJ); prefers limited economic liberalization with increased protections, especially for the parts producers

BUENOS AIRES VERSUS CÓRDOBA: EARLY STAGES OF A POLITICAL STRIFE

The arrival of economic liberalization and exposure of local producers to increased competition posed new challenges to governors Eduardo Angeloz and his successor Ramón Mestre during the 1990s. In particular, local officials faced increasing demands for infrastructural support from the manufacturing industry, especially with respect to training the labor force. Yet, both governors were unable to mobilize resources for sustaining this transformation in workplace arrangements, production systems and adaptation to new technologies. While workers in select companies were exposed to behavioral modules of just-in-time and lean production, others who were excluded from these programs were gradually sidelined and experienced deskilling in a rapidly changing production landscape. Most prominently, the political conflict between central and local government in a federal setting provided an additional impetus to the unraveling of the vocational education system in Córdoba.

Following the transition to democracy in 1983, Eduardo Angeloz was elected as the governor of Córdoba from the UCR. Angeloz was a lawyer by training and he had joined the UCR during the 1950s as a young student at the *Universidad Nacional de Córdoba*. His political views on economic development were formed amid fierce debates between the two major opposition groups within the UCR during the early 1950s. Eventually, Angeloz sided with politicians who promoted private entrepreneurship and called for reduced state involvement in the economic domain. This stood in sharp contrast to the early statist line of PJ.

During his tenure as the governor of Córdoba, Angeloz emerged as a political figure with close relations to the agro-industrial groups, advocating policies that prioritized agro-industrial exports.[37] In addition to subsidies and infrastructural support, Angeloz government launched publicly sponsored vocational training programs to meet human capital needs of this sector.[38] Additionally, Angeloz government financed new centers to retrain unemployed individuals for labor market reintegration, with a special focus on agro-industry related modules.[39] Further, the government supported research and development programs with the purpose of maximizing the competitiveness of agro-industry in export markets.[40] In addition to infrastructural support, he also offered attractive credit options to agro-producers in this province. Indeed, state-owned *Banco de Córdoba* was the primary means through which Angeloz channeled resources to the agro-industry: the bank gave nearly 20% of its available total investment credit to agro-businesses as of August 1991.[41] In 1991, Angeloz proudly noted that agro-business grew 2.8 times faster than other sectors, producing 42% of brute product in Córdoba, and outlined his policy for supporting agriculture on a product-by-product basis.

Angeloz's close relationship with agro-business in Córdoba is also evident in his composition of cabinet members. Agro-industrialists such as José Porta (Minister of Industry and Commerce, owner of drinks company Porta S.A.), Luis Fernando Farias (Minister of Agriculture, owner of the granary Luis Fernando Farias e Hijos S.R.L.), Jorge Caminotti (Minister of Economy, and one of the first executive directors of the confectionary company Arcor) and Oscar Juan Carreras (Ministry of Agriculture, former president of A.M. Sancor) occupied key positions in the local government. Even though automobile producers made significant contributions to the economy in Córdoba, no minister with close links to automobile production was in the cabinet (see Table 4.3).[42]

Under governor Angeloz, vocational training schemes in Córdoba lacked a well-coordinated and updated framework. Schools that performed above the bar primarily addressed the needs of an industry with close ties to the local government. As decentralization and post-Fordist pressures called for

Table 4.3   The industrial mosaic of Córdoba in 1993

Sector	Number of factories	Percentage %	Number of employees	Percentage %
Processed food and drinks	**2,343**	**43.62**	**25,727**	**32.29**
Textiles	371	6.91	6,252	7.85
Industrial wood products	434	8.08	2,226	2.79
Paper and print	218	4.06	2,274	2.85
Chemical products	327	6.09	6,454	8.10
Mineral products	285	5.31	5,268	6.61
Basic metal Products	75	1.40	1,658	2.08
Machinery and equipment	**1,258**	**23.42**	**29,561**	**37.11**
Other	61	1.14	248	0.31
Total	5,372	100	79,668	100

Source: Córdoba in figures, Governorship of Córdoba, 1994

reskilling workers, Angeloz government faced a significant challenge to connect schools, private enterprises and workers. Facing a mounting public debt and lacking resources, the governor could only arrange short-term training agreements with business organizations that were known to be closer to UCR line, focusing on the needs of agro-industry, construction and services.[43] Though the governor acknowledged the significance of automobile sector in Córdoba, he was skeptical of Menem's prioritization of automobile industry at the expense of his traditional business allies. Thus, Angeloz's discursive support did not materialize into a comprehensive support. A former minister who served under Eduardo Angeloz notes that skill formation during this period was very limited and economic problems faced by the local government pushed them to identify sectors that needed less costly training programs, such as construction and tourism.[44]

Aware of the diminishing resources for publicly funded vocational training opportunities in the province, some multinational car companies based in the industrial belt around Córdoba launched their own training programs beginning in the early 1990s. In this way, old and new workers were exposed to general and specialized modules on factory premises. Meanwhile, small and medium sized suppliers of automobile manufacturers—which were already experiencing financial difficulties due to shortages in credit—were not in a position to undertake a similar training program, and therefore continued to hire unskilled workers to be trained on the job and focused on the acquisition of technical skills for newly hired workers as best as they could. However, volatilities in export markets put these firms in a difficult position as they had to lay off trained workforce especially after the 1994 economic crisis. Thus, unlike the multinational producers, parts suppliers faced a faster depletion of skilled workforce during the first half of the 1990s.

Why did Angeloz seem less enthusiastic about supporting the automobile industry—a sector with the second largest source of income for Córdoba's economy? Angeloz's position on human capital formation was very much influenced by the political stance of UCR vis-à-vis business groups in Córdoba. Because UCR did not have organic ties to the pro-PJ business organizations, neither Eduardo Angeloz, nor his successor Ramón Mestre had any political interest in catering to their costly training needs.

The producer associations based in the Córdoba were historically organized around sectoral interests and had divergent political connections. The agro-industrialists gathered around *Union Industrial Córdoba* (UIC), while the metalworking sector was organized under CIM, headed by Roberto

Avalle, known to be closer to the PJ.[45] In particular, businessmen organized under the latter supported Menem's economic liberalization program.[46] At the same time, these businesses expected preferential treatments to benefit small and medium sized enterprises, mostly organized under CIM. On the other hand, UIC members stood closer to the UCR because of historical ties between the party and the agro-industrial sector (see Table 4.4).

As Menem announced the details of preferential treatment program for the auto-industry, the multinational companies welcomed these incentives to expand direct investment in Córdoba. Aware of the sector's growing potential for job creation, the UCR politicians initially tried to establish closer ties with the producers in the region. With this goal, Angeloz set up a local council, bringing representatives of different industrial sectors together and mobilize resources for worker training programs toward a liberalizing economy.[47]

However, the conflict with the Menem government on a number of policy areas including decentralization of education system, labor flexibility and privatization sharpened the existing partisan rivalries between organized interest groups, polarizing businesses and unions along political lines in Córdoba. During these exchanges, CIM realized that protections announced by Menem only benefited big multinational automobile producers, and excluded small and medium sized enterprises. In response, CIM gravitated toward Menemists' rival, allying themselves with de la Sota line. Meanwhile, UIC sided with Angeloz in order to continue enjoying benefits from the UCR government. This polarization among the metalworking and automobile industry in Córdoba along rival political factions further debilitated the political capacity of Angeloz to address changing needs of automobile producers. These rivalries eventually marked the end of UCR era by the end of 1990s.

Table 4.4   The partisan links of producer group organizations in Córdoba during the second half of the twentieth century

Pro-UCR	Pro-PJ
Union Industrial Córdoba (UIC); dominated by mostly big agro-industrial groups and construction companies	Camara de Industriales Metalurgicos Córdoba (CIM); includes small and medium sized metal goods and auto parts producers

THREE EARTHQUAKES THAT SHOOK THE GROUND: AREAS OF CONFLICT BETWEEN CÓRDOBA AND THE FEDERAL GOVERNMENT

Between 1990 and 1999, Menem's PJ imposed three major public policy changes: decentralization of education, deregulation of the labor market and privatization. As the public debate on each issue intensified, organized interest groups readjusted their position vis-à-vis proposed changes based on their partisan preferences. As a result of rising tension between Córdoba's UCR government and PJ-controlled federal government, mobilizing local resources for a post-Fordist transformation became more and more difficult to achieve first for Angeloz, and later his successor Mestre.

The Decentralization of Education

Since the early days in office, a major component of President Menem's political agenda was decentralization of key public services, including education. In this way, the federal government was planning to cut back on expenses that constituted a sizeable portion of the state budget. Yet, once the central government announced transferring educational services to the jurisdiction of provinces, Angeloz government fiercely opposed this proposal. The transfer required the local government to bear the costs of mandatory education. Because Córdoba was already in dire straits, governor Angeloz was unwilling to accept decentralization of education without supporting funds and infrastructural backup from the center.[48] This tension between local and central government also marked the beginnings of a long-term crisis between businesses and unions that belonged to rival partisan factions in Córdoba.

The new education policy created an additional burden on the provincial budget, and introduced a new set of problems in terms of maintenance and education quality.[49] In particular, vocational schools and teachers persistently opposed the proposal, fearing that economic rationalization of public costs would eventually result in the elimination of the public vocational education.[50] The provincial ministry repeatedly opposed the Menem government and argued against transferring teacher-training centers under Córdoba's jurisdiction.[51] Meanwhile, teachers unions in Córdoba began a series of strikes and protests against the decentralization of education, and asking for salary increases.[52]

As the debate intensified between Angeloz and the Federal Economics Minister Domingo Cavallo, businesses began to take opposing sides. Some sided with Cavallo, backing up his arguments in favor of a lesser state involvement in public good provision. During this period, a survey by a private research company found that among the local businessmen in Córdoba, 98% of the industrialists backed up Cavallo and his economic agenda including decentralization.[53] Meanwhile, UIC appeared more hesitant to pressure local government in favor of a total abandonment of public vocational education.[54]

Initially, the UCR government in Córdoba was not opposed to the idea of decentralization and privatization of public services. For example, Angeloz's Minister of Economy, Jorge Caminotti strongly argued in favor handing education and health provision over to the responsibility of local municipalities.[55] The local governor's precondition for this support included federal funds. Yet, federal government renounced this request, arguing that the provincial government should raise necessary funds by itself.[56] Under increasing pressure from Menem, an agreement on school transfers was signed in 1994. In response, teacher unions continued with a series of strikes and protests. For the business organizations that demanded social stability, the rising tension had a negative impact on the credibility of UCR government in crisis management.

Meanwhile, the metalworking unions had mixed response to this debate. Because UOM workers were excluded from the benefits of a preferential treatment for automobile producers, they were critical of Menem's proposals. According to UOM leaders, decentralization of education would significantly reduce resources channeled to vocational and technical schools, and thereby initiate a deskilling process. Therefore, UOM leaders and workers opposed the federal plan.[57] On the other hand, SMATA kept a low profile and gave passive support in favor of Menem.[58] By the end of 1999, the first signs of a decentralized education system on vocational training was more visible. As resources channeled to public schools were significantly reduced, vocational schools faced decreasing enrollment rates and an erosion of their reputation in Córdoba toward the end of the decade.

Deepening of Political Crisis: Deregulation of the Labor Market and Flexibilization

In addition to decentralization of education, Menem's proposal on deregulating labor market relations intensified a decade-long struggle between business organizations that supported this plan and labor unions that opposed it. During the late 1980s in Córdoba, the automobile sector also experienced a crisis due to sharp fall in demand. As a result of worsening economic conditions, the automobile workers began a series of protests including walkouts and strikes. In order to control these incidents, Menem government issued a decree, proposing to limit union rights to strike. In response, Angeloz opposed this and announced that Córdoba province will not put Menem's decree in effect, on the grounds that banning strikes is unconstitutional.[59] Eventually, the decree was not put into effect, but this time Menem pulled out the flexibilization card to reduce chances of labor unrest.[60] In justifying his move, Menem argued that flexibilization would be a great stimulus for job creation. If the decentralization of education sharpened already existing political divisions, the crisis on labor market deregulation further polarized the federal and local government.

Menem government used the 1990–1991 crisis in the automobile sector to convince the industry to maximize its competitiveness in regional markets.[61] On the policy end, this move required flexibilization of production and labor market deregulation—two measures that Menem government was willing to implement without further due. However, provincial ministers in the Angeloz cabinet did not share the same opinion with the federal government. Jorge Sappia, Córdoba's Minister of Labor, did not see any merit in the flexibilization of labor law without protections for workers: according to Sappia, this would not resolve problems incurred by the ongoing economic crisis.[62] UCR leaders were also skeptical vis-à-vis the proposed changes. In Buenos Aires, Senator Luis Brasesco from the UCR also argued against flexibilization, on the grounds that this would not create more jobs.[63] Thus, the UCR block in the senate voted against the provisional law on the introduction of new forms of labor contract agreements such as subcontracting of work, in addition to the creation of temporary and part-time contracts.[64] Meanwhile, despite UCR opposition, the new principle was slowly making its way into the new contracts signed by multinational companies who were planning to invest in Córdoba, including General Motors, Renault and FIAT.[65]

In response to the federal government's move, Córdoba launched a stimulus plan to encourage industrial investment by offering provincial tax reductions of up to 33% for selected companies.[66] However, Angeloz government's list of companies to benefit from tax deductions excluded a large segment of auto-part suppliers in the metalworking sector (see Fig. 4.1).[67] Because Córdoba refrained from joining a fiscal pact with

Excluded companies (grouped by sector)	
Light Metalworking	77
Chrome and chrome containers	5
Cutting, folding y lustration	28
Industrial assembly	10
Automobiles, auto parts y motors	165
Motorcycles and motor parts	25
Others	42
Total	*352*
Included Companies	
Basic metal-mechanics	3
Equipment machinery	21
Railway equipment	1
Aircraft equipment	1
Total	*26*

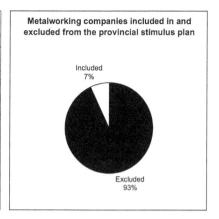

Fig. 4.1 Companies excluded from the stimulus program (Source: *La Voz del Interior*, 27 January 1994, 7A)

Menem, it was unable to extend the stimulus plan so as to cover all producers in the province. That's why Angeloz and his government had to prioritize companies, which ended up pitting CIM against UIC and Angeloz government.

Angeloz's list triggered instant reaction from the CIM on the grounds that the governor was discriminating against these producers, because the government offered favorable investment opportunities to a select-few companies.[68] Faced with a fierce opposition from excluded businessmen in CIM, Jorge Caminotti, Córdoba's Minister of Economy, put the blame on the federal government, arguing that it was Domingo Cavallo who pressured Angeloz to do so.[69] In response, CIM approached Domingo Cavallo and COPIC (Federal Council for Production, Investment and Growth) to pressure Angeloz to enlist their companies in the stimulus program.[70] On the other hand, UIC was unwilling to pursue the same route, in order to avoid any deterioration of relations with Angeloz.[71] These contrasting partisan allegiances of producer groups in Córdoba shaped their responses in the face of new economic policies, repeating a historical pattern. While the automobile producers approached PJ for help, agro-industrialists turned to the UCR.[72]

Meanwhile, as the rival provinces got federal support and Córdoba was denied funds, the phrase "Córdoba is an island" was frequently uttered in political circles.[73] Gradually, excluded businesses blamed Angeloz and his mismanagement. In response to criticisms, Jorge Sappia staunchly defended the UCR line against the PJ. Indeed, the policies followed by the Córdoba government were far from creating new jobs. As Córdoba refrained from supporting Menem and entered a recession, the rate of job creation also fell behind the national average.

An important component of Menem's decree on flexibilization included the decentralization of collective bargaining. According to the new law, companies could sign the new agreements on a firm-by-firm basis. Furthermore, the decree required each document to include a clause for respecting the guidelines of Cavallo's economic liberalization plan.[74] Even though UCR politicians were willing to enter negotiations between the workers and companies behind the scenes, the Ministry of Labor Jorge Sappia persistently opposed the new law proposed by PJ on the grounds that this package did not include additional modifications proposed by UCR, and did not protect the workers.[75]

In the face of conflicts generated by the debate on flexibilization, metalworking unions in Córdoba were also divided. While SMATA was supportive of labor deregulation measures, UOM's local leaders fiercely opposed this. In fact, UOM was frequently on the streets of Córdoba to protest Menem, along with other unions who opposed this proposal. Meanwhile, SMATA was supportive of this policy because it recently signed off a privileged deal with FIAT management on the condition that it would accept flexible labor contracts and reorganization of production. In response, UOM leaders were furious and argued that acceptance of this new contract would deteriorate workers' organizational power in the long run.[76] As UOM took it to the streets, SMATA took a pro-Menemist position. Meanwhile business organizations began pressuring Angeloz to accept the proposal. By mid-1990s, Córdoba's political landscape was sharply divided by fault-lines of an ever-deepening conflict between the local and federal government.

The Last Straw that Broke Angeloz's Back: Privatization

Menem represented the neoliberal wing of the PJ, sending out mixed messages to the electorate on his development policy during his electoral campaign, combining economic liberalization with classical Peronist ideas on industrial development. In fact, it was initially his rival Eduardo Angeloz who called for the deepening of the economic reforms that Alfonsin launched, highlighting trade liberalization, good standing with international financial institutions and privatization of state-owned enterprises as the main components of his electoral campaign (Stokes 1998: 353). However, he had to radically revise his discourse following the financial troubles faced by Córdoba during the 1990s.

After Angeloz lost the presidential campaign, he returned to his post as the governor. The 1989 economic crisis left Córdoba in dire straits and the rising inflation worsened the balance of payments problem. In order to pay the public employees, Angeloz passed legislation in the local parliament allowing him to pay public employees in government bonds. However, this triggered a serious of protests by employees who demanded their wages, and opposed receiving back payments and pensions in the form of an asset that they did not know what to do with. Faced with a deepening social crisis with growing protests in the streets, Angeloz turned to the federal government, demanding cash injection.

Menem was quick to take advantage of this position, and made a conditional offer to his former rival: Angeloz could retrieve funds as long as Córdoba government agreed to a number of federal government reforms, including the privatization of public enterprises such as the Bank of Córdoba (Bancor) and the Córdoba Energy Company (EPEC). In particular, the Economy Minister Domingo Cavallo pressured Angeloz to agree to a complete privatization of the very profitable EPEC, which had more than US$1 billion in assets and employed around 4000 workers. Local business organizations, including UIC, were all pressuring the governor to take the privatization route as soon as possible.[77] Once a promoter of privatization, Angeloz initially resisted this proposal but nevertheless managed to pass another legislation that authorized the local government for the partial privatization of this lucrative enterprise. Still, Menem government refused to release funds on the grounds that his preconditions were not met.[78] The federal government was exploiting every political opportunity to pressure Angeloz for an unconditional acceptance of the economic reform agenda on their own terms.

The public employees demanded their wages with protests on the streets, but the unions they were affiliated were not supportive of privatization as a solution. The metalworking unions were also divided over the issue. UOM—which still had a notable rank and file membership base in the public sector enterprises—fiercely opposed Menem and Cavallo plan, rejecting privatizations. On the other hand, SMATA managers gave passive support to Menem, since SMATA's stronghold remained in private sector enterprises, and especially in automobile producers. In fact, SMATA's Córdoba leader José Campellone repeated the need to adapt to changing work conditions in a new economic era, and this included support for lesser state involvement in production if necessary. As privatization put these unions into opposing camps, and business organizations in Córdoba criticized Angeloz for his intransigence vis-à-vis the Menem-Cavallo plan, the governor felt increasingly isolated.

Faced with severe balance of payments problem, Angeloz then turned to private financial institutions in the USA for credit, and began a series of negotiations with the Dillon Read Bank. However, determined to pressure Angeloz, and carry on with privatizing public enterprises, Menem government intervened in the negotiations, declaring that the federal government will not be the guarantor of a loan should Córdoba fail to pay it back.[79] Alarmed by the high risks induced by political uncertainty, Dillon Read Bank declined Angeloz, and the deal fell through. According to the former governor, it was Menem and Cavallo who sabotaged the negotiations.[80] In counter-attack, Angeloz government published full-page ads, arguing that the central government has abandoned Córdoba way before the crisis.[81]

Despite attempts to save his reputation, the reception of Angeloz's failure in Córdoba was disastrous. As protesters attacked the UCR building in Córdoba, Angeloz found himself in a political quagmire.[82] Faced with no other option, the governor of Córdoba resigned out of office on 6 July 1995, nearly six months before the end of his term would be due. "I am resigning because I am not willing to get down on my knees to any messianic technocrat" were his last words before facing a series of trials on corruption and mismanagement after his 11-year term as the governor.

THE FEDERAL-PROVINCIAL RIVALRY UNDER RAMON MESTRE

As Angeloz was desperately trying to pull the budget together during the final months of his term in the office, Menem was signing one agreement after another with multinational automobile producers that would invest in Córdoba.[83] The negotiations behind closed doors over the conditions of investment enabled Menem government to quickly respond to alleviate concerns of multinational companies, such as FIAT, to ensure an uninterrupted flow of investment capital by foreign investors.

However, for the multinational firms, contacts with the provincial government were also important. Thus, the leading figures of the European and the US automobile firms also paid a visit to Angeloz, meeting up with the cabinet members to ensure favorable investment and production conditions.[84] However, because Angeloz was facing a serious legitimacy crisis and was unable to mobilize societal partners to satisfy the expectations of incoming FDIs, the task awaited his replacement. Meanwhile the investors toyed around with the idea of relocating production to Brazil. In the face of this subtle threat, Menem government was determined to take necessary measures to sustain Córdoba as an attractive site of investment for automobile producers.

After Angeloz's resignation, Ramón Mestre—the former mayor of Córdoba City from the UCR—took up the position as the governor. As soon as he arrived in the office, he convened all business and union representatives in search of a solution to the ongoing economic crisis. His pragmatic approach to problems and initial reconciliatory approach toward the PJ government in Buenos Aires were immediately noticeable. Meanwhile, Mestre made important replacements in the local government.[85] To some, these changes came as no surprise, because he had long been heading the internal opposition group that fiercely criticized the former governor.

The arrival of Mestre as the new governor raised the spirits of businesses and unions who longed for local political support. The business organizations in Córdoba (i.e. both UIC and CIM) initially welcomed Mestre's choices and publicly endorsed the new government.[86] However, Mestre—though he enjoyed support from broad segments of society during these early days—was unable to meet the expectations of small and medium sized producers and worker unions. At the same time, the resurgence of political conflict between the federal and local government put Mestre's career on the line toward the end of his tenure. As a result, the governor's capacity and willingness to invest in vocational training schemes was very limited.

As soon as Mestre arrived in office as the new governor, he cut a deal with Menem in order to get Córdoba out of political and economic isolation. This temporary reconciliation between Mestre and Menem promised a new opportunities.[87] On the vocational policy front, Mestre welcomed short-term training programs formulated by the provincial and federal government in order to make up for rapid depletion in skilled labor force.[88] Because decentralization of education required the local government to channel additional funds to keep schools afloat, the new education minister under Mestre, Jorge Perez, was strongly against the idea of investing funds in technical education.[89] Instead, the education minister worried about declining quality of general education in public schools.[90] Gradually, Mestre government faced severe criticism for neglecting technical schools, and abandoning common platforms set up by his predecessor in Córdoba.[91]

Mestre saw short-term training programs as a remedy in response to rising unemployment in the province.[92] However, these modules were far from meeting the specific demands of the automobile industry.[93] At the very least, the curricula of trainings did not include an emphasis on the development of soft-skills as demanded by the new production regime.[94] Furthermore, unlike Bursa, most of these trainees did not have a vocational school background. The participants of these short-term training programs included recent graduates of secondary and/or high schools without any work experience or skill training. Without a solid foundation, short-term trainings did not have the intended impact on a large group of inexperienced participants.[95]

Most small and medium sized businesses were interested in hiring these workers, but rather than seeing them as valuable assets, managers treated them as cheap labor for jobs that did not require sophisticated technical knowledge.[96] However, this approach increased the labor turnover rate, and discontented workers quit their jobs after a short time.[97] Thus, small and medium sized enterprises were unable to keep a committed group of employees. Consequently, most of these businesses failed to obtain international quality certificates. By 1997, only one auto parts producer registered with CIM qualified for an ISO 9001 certificate.[98] At the end of 1998, when the crisis in Brazil hit the shores of Córdoba, the producers were ringing alarm bells for declining competitiveness and called on Mestre to look for measures to rejuvenate the sector.[99]

Awakened by the growing importance on quality and training, CIM decided to set up a training center in order to catch up with an ever-intensifying competition.[100] However, unlike their counterparts in Bursa, CIM was unwilling make yet another appeal to Mestre who repeatedly ignored the demands of auto parts producers for incentives. As a result, CIM mobilized its resources for establishing a training center. However, the priority was given to updating managers on the latest production and management techniques, and blue-collar trainings were neglected.[101]

Meanwhile, UOM—the union organized in FIAT-Córdoba until 1996—refused to accommodate soft-skills into its own training program because the union managers did not want to lose control over the rank-and-file. In the words of a former shopfloor representative affiliated with UOM, "these trainings [were] intended to brainwash the workers," and did not have anything to do with developing skills.[102] These views are shared by the current leader of Córdoba UOM, Augusto Varas, who was a close witness of the changes in shopfloor organization during the mid-1990s. Thus, feeling neglected by the federal and the local government, UOM-Córdoba took the initiative and set up a training center in 1997. The goal was to secure rank-and-file allegiance to the union and avoid unemployment due to lack of qualification.[103] However, unlike trainings offered by companies, the content of union-sponsored programs was oriented toward enhancing technical skills of workers rather than an emphasis on soft-skills and behavioral adjustments.[104] On the other hand, José Campellone—then acting as the leader of SMATA-Córdoba—supported post-Fordist behavioral training programs as part of union training schemes as well.[105]

Meanwhile, the honeymoon between the new government and societal actors did not last for long.[106] During the first year of Mestre's term in office, labor strikes and protests continued in Córdoba's public and private sector unions. In particular, metalworking and the automobile sector workers launched militant protests against job cuts and rising unemployment after the national government passed the decree on the flexibilization of labor relations.[107] At the same time, Mestre was also struggling to accommodate local business demands for creating more favorable investment infrastructure.[108] However, he lacked financial resources to meet the demands of these producers.

In order to channel credit to the investors, Mestre first had to obtain funds from the central government. This meant he had to sign onto Cavallo's plan, accept the terms of fiscal pact and start privatizing Banco de Córdoba and EPEC.[109] To pull the economy together, Mestre had to decide soon on his next political move, because as the crisis deepened, the industrial production in the province was further going downhill.[110] To get Córdoba out of economic and political quagmire, Mestre took a reconciliatory step, and avoided confrontation with Domingo Cavallo. However, this tactic created severe divisions within the UCR in Córdoba due to within party fragmentations.[111]

By 1996, Mestre had made up his mind and decided on a temporary alliance with the Menem government on a number of critical issues, including decentralization of education, flexibilization of labor code and fiscal discipline.[112] Having seen Angeloz's political decline, the new governor was taking cautious steps in order to avoid Córdoba's financial isolation by the federal government.[113] By 1997, Mestre and Menem were making joint statements on the case of constitutional reform in Córdoba and continuation of restructuring education policies in the province.[114] In the field of economic development, Mestre took a proactive position to accommodate the incoming multinational automobile producers.[115] However, his exclusionary approach vis-à-vis the domestic parts producers raised severe criticisms from unprotected small and medium sized business owners organized under CIM, as well as protests from the worker union (UOM) organized in these workplaces.[116] By excluding the parts producers from the game, Mestre followed the footsteps of his predecessor. Further, by approaching Menem to justify this position, Mestre took a controversial political stance. This move not only alienated the traditional agro-industrial base of UCR Córdoba, but also aroused a significant opposition from the pro-PJ unions that supported de la Sota faction.

Further, in order to increase his weight in local politics, Mestre proposed important changes to be made in the Provincial Constitution, which pitted Angeloz supporters against pro-Mestre groups.[117] This division aggravated political divisions in Córdoba. In particular, Mestre's welcoming approach to privatization triggered a series of union protests in the streets.[118] Furthermore, Mestre's neglect for the agricultural sector also angered these groups, and triggered new protest mobilizations against the governor toward the end of his term.[119] Eventually, just like his predecessor Eduardo Angeloz, Mestre failed to build a coalition for labor force transformation: new trainings were only implemented in handpicked companies with financial support from the federal government.[120]

Menem government realized that Mestre was bounded by the growing social unrest, which prevented him to focus on working closely with the federal government to accommodate the multinational company demands in the long run.[121] Therefore, in order to facilitate the skill formation and secure MNC investment deals, Menem government sidestepped the local governor, who demonstrated a weak ability to exercise political control, and backed up a special deal with FIAT, and launched *Programa Emprender*, exclusively designed to sponsor training of workers at FIAT-Córdoba factory. The small and medium sized producers were excluded from this plan.

With programs like *Programa Emprender*, most MNCs—including FIAT—enjoyed benefits of a contained investment in worker skills on factory premises, supported by federal government programs.[122] Interviews with current FIAT-Córdoba workers who have been employed since 1996 present a highly motivated group who benefited from general skill trainings (with an emphasis on behavioral modules such as attitudinal modifications for quality improvement), and on-the-job technical trainings.[123] Some of these workers were selected to attend advanced programs that build soft-skills (i.e. leadership training for team leaders) in Brazil and Italy for longer periods.[124] The content of these trainings reveal that the same quality improvement techniques (such as Kaizen, TQM, 5S), and FIAT company principles (such as teamwork, zero-defect production, continuous improvement and flexible production) constitute the core modules of factory-based trainings.[125] Most workers acknowledge the drastic changes that took place since the mid-1990s and cite long working hours (around 50 hours or more per week). For example:

> *The mindset of the workers has changed. In 1995, the management... reduced the salaries and had problems with laid-off workers. Those who stayed, like us, tried...we chose the company to save ourselves.*[126]

> *Methodology, structure [has changed]. There was a time when the factory shut down. There have been many changes. At first, I did not adapt well...*[127]

Interviews with managers also reveal a heavy emphasis on behavioral training modules rather than an emphasis on technical trainings.[128] However, despite this emphasis, FIAT-Córdoba has been unable to rise among the corporation's internal rankings, and remained way below FIAT-Bursa, which, as of 2009, occupied the top position in terms of competitiveness and product quality, surpassing its top rivals in Italy.

Moreover, the seemingly positive response of the workers to new behavioral training modules do not always reduce conflict on the shop-floor. In the words of one worker:

> *[A common problem is] disagreement on the form of work—we are not always in agreement on how to do [things]*[129]

Indeed, when conflict becomes unavoidable, it takes a much longer time to resolve it. The FIAT worker protests of 1996–1997 discussed at the beginning of this chapter reveal this more clearly. While the arrival of new technologies on the shopfloor also sparked resentment among workers in Bursa, their counterparts in Córdoba opposed these adjustments and carried their protests on-and-off for almost a year. As the local governor was embroiled in a lasting political conflict, the militant workers took advantage of this local-federal fight and found an opportunity to voice their demands in bolder terms.

As of 2008, SMATA branch leader, Omar Dragun expressed his support for these programs. According to Dragun, quality trainings are crucial components of a modern production system. At the same time, Dragun argues that it is not the primary duty of the union to provide this training to the rank-and-file and that the companies should take measures to update worker skills whenever necessary.[130] Unlike in Bursa, the dominant view by union representatives on skill formation favors shopfloor as the primary location of such trainings and the company is expected to take greater responsibility.

It must be added that the experience of workers in small and medium sized auto parts producers has been worse than those employed in big multinational car producers. A research done in Córdoba on the training patterns in among SMEs in 1999 reveals that approximately 56.7% of these businesses did not adapt any of the internationally recognized quality control norms (Parisi 1999: 86). About half of the companies in the sample do not provide any type of training, while those who sometimes offer some type of training is around 22% (Parisi 1999: 97).[131] Unlike MNCs that promote behavioral modules, a large segment (64.3%) of the small and medium sized producers see training as a necessity primarily for incorporating new technology (Parisi 1999: 103). To put it differently, behavioral training modules are not implemented by first and second tier suppliers even though the managers would like to use them.[132]

In fact, after citing financial concerns, respondents in the Parisi sample have pointed the lack of resources for worker training and poor human capital quality among the list of explanations when accounting for capital flight after 1998 economic crisis (Parisi 1999: 134). Indeed, during this period, these producers got neither financial nor infrastructural support from the provincial government and were unable to compete in export markets.[133] Thus, workers employed in small and medium sized companies that produce parts were not exposed to a similar training that their fellow workers have received at major MNCs like FIAT. During 1990s, businesses organized under CIM were unable to influence decision-making processes due to conflicts intensified by political rivalries. By the end of 1990s, only a handful of these enterprises had international quality certificates as indicators of competitiveness in export markets.

CONCLUSION

PJ politicians in Buenos Aires who intervened in post-Fordist skill formation processes in a top-down fashion were unable to initiate a comprehensive transformation in Córdoba. While *Bursa Vocational Education and
Training Council* served as a key platform for information exchange on
new skill requirements and contain potential labor unrest due to
technological disruptions, *Consejo Economico y Social* (Economic and
Social Council), the common platform of exchange founded by Angeloz
in 1987, failed to survive under his successor Mestre, due to political
regroupings and competitions.[134] In the automobile sector, the federal
politicians took an exclusionary route, financing training expenses of
SMATA-affiliated workers only.

Because UOM-affiliated workers were left out of the protective
schemes, and in the absence of mechanisms to restrain labor mobilization
as in Turkey—rank-and-file launched a series of strikes and protests. In
some cases, both the national and local government resorted to obligatory
conciliation to intervene and control the situation because labor unrest
lasted exceptionally long.[135] While the national government used obligatory conciliation to pressure unions that walked off the Menemist line, the
local government used it to secure control over labor unions that were of
critical importance to the UCR's business base. In Córdoba, the national
government exercised this power particularly to intervene in protests initiated by UOM.[136] Similarly, Menem's ministry of labor, Jorge Triaca also
used personal influence to intervene directly in the ongoing protests
between UOM and the employers.[137] On the other hand, the local labor
minister Jorge Sappia exercised this power to intervene in strikes launched
in sectors that are of critical importance to the UCR base.[138] When UOM
initiated protests, Sappia avoided intervention.[139]

In the backdrop of these politically charged labor unrest, politicians in
Córdoba were not interested in public programs to train workers along
post-Fordist schemes. Given this bi-partisan competition in a federal setting, uncoordinated diffusion of new modules across selected multinational companies did not have the desired impact during the 1990s.
Additionally, these findings show that partisan allegiances of organized
interest groups are critical factors that could enhance or debilitate the
capacity of local politicians to build coalitions for faster surplus extraction
in federal settings.[140]

While these challenges delay a smooth adaptation to technological upgrading, a federal system also provides opportunities for the survival of the democratic regime at times of crisis by means of accommodating labor demands. In that sense, Argentina's democratization process stands in stark contrast to that in Turkey. By the end of 1990s, both countries experienced a major economic crisis that replaced the incumbents with new leaders. In Argentina, Eduardo Duhalde government resigned in December 2001 and chaos ensued until the election of Nestor Kirchner into the Presidency in 2002. In Turkey, the coalition government members suffered a major decline in their vote share and lost the elections to AKP in 2002. As Argentina survived major challenges to democracy in the immediate post-crisis period, the Kirchner government also displayed a firm commitment to upholding democratic institutions (Levitsky and Murillo 2005: Ranis 2004). In doing so, the President relied on support from formal labor unions in addition to accommodating demands of other societal groups, including unemployed worker associations and community-based movements (Etchemendy and Garay 2011: 283). During this period, unionization rates were on the rise and labor unions in Argentina experienced a promising revival in contrast to their counterparts across other liberalizing economies (Cató et al. 2011).

On the other hand, the AKP in Turkey took a different route: the new government repeatedly challenged separation of powers, systematically violated core values of liberal democracy, and eventually made historic amendments to the constitution by concentrating substantial power in the hand of the President in 2017. During this 15-year period between 2002 and 2017, labor unions were conspicuously absent in the political arena. Unlike their counterparts in Argentina, none of the labor unions or big confederations appeared indispensable to the AKP rule. Meanwhile, unions in opposition were systematically harassed and/or repressed. As unionization rates plunged, the opposition parties got increasingly weaker without a powerful labor-based movement to challenge the government and curb its rising authoritarian tendencies. In that sense, the Turkish experience raises additional questions on the democratic resilience of unitary systems with an authoritarian past in the absence of organized labor as a critical mass: without this important societal force, democratic accountability mechanisms are very much likely to falter.

NOTES

1. Eduardo Angeloz was then the governor of Córdoba from UCR. The poor economic performance under the UCR-led federal government between 1983 and 1989 put this party in a disadvantageous position for the 1989 elections. Further, under president Raul Alfonsin, developmental policies failed short of reviving the manufacturing sector, triggering a negative outlook on the credibility of the UCR politicians. Overall, the economic problems under Alfonsin put Carlos Menem in a favorable position against his rival Eduardo Angeloz (Remmer 1993, 398).

2. As I discussed in Chap. 2, OEM factories are embedded in a network of suppliers, which need to be equally competitive because the parts provided by the second and first tier suppliers need to satisfy a minimum threshold of quality. As much as this depends on the fixed-cost investments by the management, maximizing sector-wide quality could be best ensured through a systematic coordination of vocational training programs.

3. See for example "En Argentina no existe politica industrial" *La Voz del Interior*, 27 February 1997, 11A; "Automotrices amenazan con irse a Brazil" *La Voz del Interior*, 26 July 1998, 11A.

4. In 2010, FIAT-Bursa received the Silver prize in World Class Manufacturing, surpassing all other FIAT production centers across the globe. See "Tofas FIAT Uretimde Dunyanin En Iyisi Oldu" accessible at http://www.tofas.com.tr/Haber.aspx?id=414. Moreover, FIAT-Bursa occupies the second place after Italy in Research and Development. Córdoba is not yet included in the rankings. "FIAT'in 2. Buyuk Ar-Ge Ussu Olduk," *Gazete Vatan*, 8 February 2010. One indicator of competitiveness is the quality certificates, such as ISO 9000 and 9001, obtained by the companies. In Córdoba only five companies possessed this as of March 1996. Most parts producers in the city lacked resources to obtain an internationally recognized quality certificate. See "Las Pyme en busqueda de calidad" *La Voz del Interior*, 31 March 1996.

5. This is different than the previous vocational training system under the ISI period where federal government played a greater role in human capital formation. Before the 1990s, formation of vocational skills was primarily administered from the center with minimum local involvement because technical schools were under the jurisdiction of Federal Ministry of Education. The skill formation framework in Bursa during the ISI regime has resemblances with the one in Córdoba during the same period.

6. Interview #2, FIAT Manager, Córdoba, 5 May 2008.

7. Interview #18, Former FIAT worker and shopfloor leader, 8 August 2008, Córdoba, Argentina.
8. "Una fabrica integrada" *La Voz del Interior* 20 December 1997.
9. Interview #30, Expert, Federal Ministry of Labor, Department of Training, 6 June 2008, Buenos Aires, Argentina.
10. "Política de recursos humanos en la integración" *La Voz del Interior*, 8 June 1997.
11. See "Los operarios de FIAT Auto mantenian ocupada la planta" *La Voz del Interior*, 23 January 1997, Frontpage; and "Movilizacion a la casa del gobierno por los despidos en FIAT," *La Voz del Interior*, February 1997; "Marchas contra las cambios laborales" *La Voz del Interior*, 22 February 1997. The conflict continued for months and the insurgent workers pushed for a better deal. See "El paro profundizo el conflicto en FIAT," *La Voz del Interior*, 25 April 1997, 11A. When the leader of the protests was laid off by the company, the workers mobilized against FIAT management and asked for Mestre's help—but in vain. See "Obreros de FIAT reclamaran a Mestre" *La Voz del Interior*, 26 May 1997, 9A.
12. "Fiat Auto ratifico los 41 despidos" *La Voz del Interior*, 31 January 1997.
13. "UOM Nacional ratifico la decisión de constituir la seccional Ferreyra" *La Voz del Interior*, February 1997.
14. Though both UOM and SMATA support the PJ, they belong to opposing camps within the party. These divisions date back to 1980s where the Peronist union leadership split into four main factions: the 62 Organizaciones (the "62"), the Grupo de 25, the Ubaldinistas, and the Grupo de 15 (McGuire 1992: 37). While SMATA joined the Grupo de 15, supporting Menem's campaign, UOM was in the 62 Organizaciones in opposition (McGuire 1992: 72).
15. Interview with former HR Manager of Fiat-Córdoba, 17 June 2008, Córdoba Argentina.
16. *La Voz del Interior*, 27 September 1995; 1 November 1995 and 10 February 1996.
17. Isvor Fiat S.A. Proyecto Argentina Presentation Brochure 1997.
18. "Política de recursos humanos en la integración" *La Voz del Interior*, 8 June 1997 and "Con la mira en la capacitación" *La Voz del Interior*, 20 December 1997.
19. Even though the legal framework of *Programa Emprender* indicated that it was destined to meet the demands of new companies or companies who expanded their investment, in practice, the training program was exclusively designed for FIAT. Interview #7, 17 June 2008 and Interview #57, 24 June 2008. Programa Emprender was launched with resolution no 90/96 of the Federal Ministry of Labor and Social Security. The training

bulletin of ISVOR reveals that the workers are especially trained to acquire the new values of the company listed above. Source: ISVOR FIAT S.A. Proyecto Argentina Presentation Brochure 1997. The intensified training period for the blue-collar workers ranged from 55 days to 280 days, depending on the position and experience of the worker.

20. "Politica de recursos humanos en la integracion" *La Voz del Interior*, 8 June 1997. Also the Worldwide CEO of the FIAT company Cesare Romiti repeated the importance of investment in human capital as a company policy during a visit to Córdoba in 1997. See "Córdoba colmo nuestras expectativas" *La Voz del Interior*, 4 July 1997, 10A. Similarly, FIAT's rival company, Renault, also had a private training facility on its premises in operation under the *Centro de Formacion Renault* and the workers and young students had a focused skill training targeted to respond to the changing production organization at the factory. Also see "Formamos a los profesionales del siglo 21" *La Voz del Interior*, 20 April 1998, Supplement, p.2.

21. Interview #7, Former FIAT-Córdoba Manager, 17 June 2008, Córdoba, Argentina.

22. Interview #36, also confirms this and argues that technological change in production does not always call for intense technical training because the operation of the machines is relatively easy and does not require detailed knowledge to make it work. Rather, she views these training programs as tools for disciplining the workers in order to create a new profile during the 1990s, rather than a genuine investment. Interview #36, 11 August 2008, Buenos Aires, Argentina.

23. Interview #2, 5 May 2008, Córdoba, Argentina. The respondent noted that many of the technical schools were closed, and as of 2008, approximately 20%–30% of all factory workers were graduates of such schools. The percentage of vocational-technical high school graduates in the FIAT-Bursa factory is over 90%.

24. Interview #17, FIAT-Córdoba Manager, 8 July 2008, Córdoba, Argentina.

25. As of August 2008, general skills, and especially behavioral training modules, continued to dominate the agenda. Furthermore, the human resources manager of the Córdoba factory has noted that prior to hiring, candidates are subject to a psychological test and an interview. Interview #17, Manager, FIAT-Córdoba, 8 July 2008, Córdoba, Argentina.

26. These groups were further split into different cleavages on the direction and content of economic development program. For the first half of the twentieth century, within-party political competition revealed the contradicting views on economic policy, ranging from the proponents of nationalizing the entire economy to groups who called for the elimination of the

capitalist system to economic liberals who envisioned a system based on private entrepreneurship. The party was far from having an ideological unity during this period (Snow 1963). At the same time, though some groups within the party advocated industrial development, the UCR did not pursue a well-thought-out industrial policy once it was at power and the old rural elite continued to influence the party's economic development policy (Moran 1970, 77–8; 87). At the beginning of the twentieth century, the newly rising agro-industry business had a strong influence under the leadership of UCR's Marcelo Alvear. These producer groups are powerful in Union Industrial Argentina (Moran 1970, 83), whose founder base is largely composed of agricultural industrialists.

27. For a detailed analysis of the UCR politics in Córdoba during this period, see Tcach 2006(1991).

28. These principles were endorsed after the 1960 party congress. The convention eliminated nationalist and statist understanding of economic development with a new doctrine that (1) respects private property, (2) foresees cooperation between state and private education and (3) accepts foreign capital for the development of natural resources (Snow 1963: 523–4). For a comparison of UCR and PJ and their relationship with populism, see Saettone 2006; Sabatini 1996.

29. Perhaps the most significant incident in the collective memory of the entrepreneurs and the workers is the Córdobazo protests of 1969.

30. During this period, coordination of technical education was centralized under Comision Nacional de Aprendizaje y Orientacion Profesional-CNAOP. It should be noted that Peronist regime did not create a technical education system from scratch. PJ's primary role in this process was centralization of a patched system that characterized the 1930s. Technical education during the pre-Peronist era was provided through multiple social factors including the church, unions and businesses. For a detailed discussion on the evolution of technical education under Juan Perón, see Dussel and Pineau 1995. For an analysis of the foundation of Workers University under Perón, see Sanchez-Roman 2007. Levitsky (2001) suggests that such links constituted informal ties that link broader segments of the population to the Peronist Party.

31. Among the factory-schools, the Córdoba Aviation Factory served as a vocational school for most workers in the region. The worker university was founded under Juan Perón and was converted into a Technical University in 1963. The institution still serves a large body of students who have mostly working class backgrounds and offers degrees in engineering.

32. PJ's agricultural policies have often generated uproar from the agro-industrial groups, resulting with massive protests. In 1993, Menem was the target of criticisms as a result of his economic liberalization program and faced a major protest from these groups. See "El campo protesta y el gobierno prepara medidas" ("The agricultural producers protest and the government prepares measures [to respond]" *La Voz del Interior*, 27 July 1993.

33. For example, teacher unions are among those who broke off from CGT and join a new confederation CTA protesting the Menemist line. For a detailed analysis of teacher union protests and the political dynamics behind it see Murillo 1999. For an analysis of reform coalitions under Menem government in Argentina, see Etchemendy 2001.

34. The division within the Peronist party was marked by two major factions: Juan Manuel de la Sota and his Movimiento de Unidad Peronista and Julio Cesar Araoz's Frente de la Victoria. Originally from Córdoba, Juan Manuel de la Sota was the leader of the movement within the Peronist party that opposed the economic policies of Menem and Cavallo. UOM was among the group of unions that supported him, taking a more critical position against the federal government. See "Los Gremios se alinean para la interna del Justicialismo" *La Voz del Interior*, 8 December 1992. To suppress opposition from Córdoba, the Peronist headquarters intervened in the local party management, and renouncing De la Sota's provincial authority. See "La Intervencion al PJ seria de 90 dias" *La Voz del Interior*, 30 December 1992; and "El PJ Nacional desconoce la autoridad de De la Sota" *La Voz del Interior*, 30 March 1993. Two years later, De la Sota set up a local alliance with Juan Schiaretti to take the lead in the provincial headquarters of the PJ and was back on the political scene. See "De la Sota y Schiaretti: esta vez juntos" *La Voz del Interior*, 28 July 1995, 3A. The division among the Peronist party also affected SMATA. According to the former manager of training at SMATA-Córdoba, the center in Buenos Aires and Córdoba Branch had a rough relationship by the end of 1990s. While the central management supported Menem, SMATA-Córdoba moved toward the de la Sota line. Interview #5, 28 June 2008 and 3 July 2008, Córdoba, Argentina.

35. See "Las Pyme estan siendo expulsadas del modelo economico" *La Voz del Interior*, 24 August 1992. When the central government finally announced a support plan for SMEs, the metalworking sector was again excluded. See "Se ampliaron a comercio, agro, y servicios, creditos para Pyme" *La Voz del Interior*, 23 December 1992.

36. For example, criticizing the new industrial regime pursued by Menem, Eduardo Angeloz argued that this was an adventure. See "Pagaron haberes y desocuparon la fabrica Materfer" *La Voz del Interior*, 25 May 1991.

37. Angeloz's cabinet mostly included owners or managers of powerful agro-industrial groups in Córdoba. For more on this see below.
38. Confirmed by Interview #27, former government official under Eduardo Angeloz, 8 August 2008, Córdoba, Argentina. These programs are Emeta (Expansion y Mejoramiento de la ensenanza technica agropecuaria) and Emer (Expansion y Mejoramiento de Educacion Rural). Both projects foresaw new investments to be made in schools, machinery and tools, development of education programs beyond the school, curricular modification and retraining teachers. "La Interaccion entre educacion y trabajo" *La Voz del Interior*, 22 February 1991, p.3.
39. "*Siempre es tiempo de aprender*" *La Voz del Interior* 22 February 1991, p.4. Throughout the province, the capital—Córdoba City—had the highest number of adult training centers (168) offering programs in the field of agricultural technology and automobile technology. The participants are granted a certificate after completing the program that lasts for two years.
40. "Invertiran 600.000 dolares en area de ciencia y tecnica" ([Córdoba] will invest 600.000 in the area of science and technology) *La Voz del Interior*, 28 February 1992.
41. "Angeloz detallo su politica para el sector rural" *La Voz Del Interior*, 7 August 1991, 5A.
42. Yet, even though UCR politicians did not play a great role in the development of this sector, Angeloz saw a political opportunity in the growing importance of automobiles (i.e. in terms of job creation). To signal interest, Angeloz went to the grand openings of a few multinational factories in the greater metropolitan area of Córdoba and met with automobile producers to deliberate on resolving the problems they faced in a globalizing economy. See "Angeloz encabezara la presentacion de Cormec" *La Voz del Interior*. 25 November 1991. 7A. However, the tension between Angeloz and the central government authorities during the inauguration of the new factory was quite visible.
43. Interview #32 30 June 2008, Córdoba, Argentina and Interview #1, 24 July 2008, Córdoba, Argentina.
44. Interview #32, 30 June 2008, Córdoba, Argentina.
45. In 2008, Avalle was the Ministry of Industry and Commerce under the Peronist Juan Schiaretti government in Córdoba. As of 2017, he continues to serve in the same position.
46. "Industriales Reclaman una Apertura Total de la Economia" (Industrialists demand a total opening of the economy) *La Voz del Interior*, 15 June 1990. 9A.
47. "Crean el consejo provincial permanente de capacitacion" (A Permanent Council for Training is created) *La Voz del Interior*, 16 December 1990.

48. "Angeloz cuestiono traspaso de servicios educativos" *La Voz del Interior*, 12 September 1991.
49. For example, Córdoba did not have any infrastructure for training teachers and this was an important infrastructural problem. "Por ahora es imposible formar a formadores" *La Voz del Interior*, 13 September 1991.
50. "Protestas en la ensenanza tecnica" *La Voz del Interior*, 22 June 1992.
51. "Córdoba no recibira los centros nacionales de formacion docente" *La Voz del Interior*, 27 November 1992, 12A.
52. "Posicion de la provincia ante el reclamo docente" (Position of the Province against teacher demands) *La Voz del Interior*, 8 March 1993, 7A. and "La UEPC ratifico el paro y la marcha de manana" (UEPC approves the strike and the march tomorrow) *La Voz del Interior*, 31 March 1993. In particular the teachers unions opposed the delegation of educational services to the local municipalities. See "Docentes rechazan el traspaso de escuelas a los municipios" *La Voz del Interior*, 24 August 1993.
53. "Posicion empresaria ante el costo social del plan" *La Voz del Interior*, 27 October 1991.
54. Interview #35, 7 July 2008, Córdoba, Argentina.
55. "El 93 sera el ano de la descentralization de los recursos" (1993 will be the year of decentralizing resources) *La Voz del Interior*, 27 December 1992. E1.
56. Córdoba was the last of all provinces to accept the decentralization of education. "Educacion nego fondos a Córdoba" *La Voz del Interior*, 11 August 1994.
57. Interview #54, Córdoba-UOM, 15 July 2008, Córdoba, Argentina.
58. In a research done four years later, a respondent from SMATA quoted in Parisi (1999) notes that the technical schools in Córdoba was of low quality, and argues that decentralization of education should have taken gradually, and with modernization of the curricula. (A SMATA respondent quoted in Parisi 1999: 177.) Even though SMATA initially gave passive support, the union management was not happy with the outcome.
59. "Córdoba no aplicara el decreto sobre huelgas" *La Voz del Interior*, 19 October 1990. 1A.
60. Menem's proposal on flexibilization of labor included introducing contracts for part-time and work-on-demand positions. This would significantly reduce the power of organized labor because flexible labor force is much more difficult to unionize. Second, as a result of decline in unionization rates, the unions would lose a good portion of their stable income.
61. Interview #36, Federal Ministry of Labor and Social Security, 11 August 2008, Buenos Aires, Argentina.

62. "La ley de empleo no solucionara nada" *La Voz del Interior* 10 March 1991. In another report, Sappia likens the proposed changes to "a Dracula movie" labeling the proposal as terrorizing. "Sappia: La reforma es terrorrifica" *La Voz del Interior*, 22 October 1992. 7A.
63. "Luis Brasesco: no servira para nada" *La Voz del Interior*, 21 July 1991.
64. "Aprobaron flexibilizar los regimenes laborales" *La Voz del Interior*, 14 November 1991.
65. "Firman convenio con flexibilidad laboral para obreros del Smata" *La Voz del Interior*, 9 December 1993.
66. "Metalmecanica y alimentacion tendran beneficios impositivos" *La Voz del Interior*, 21 November 1993.
67. Córdoba was not the only province that launched a tax-deductible investment stimulus plan. The autonomous city of Buenos Aires and the province of Santa Fe also had similar plans. On the other hand, Santa Fe, which participated in the fiscal pact, was quick to receive the resources from Buenos Aires to extend the stimulus plan. "Habra rebaja generalizada de aportes en Santa Fe" *La Voz del Interior*, 23 February 1994, 7A.
68. "Los industrias insisten en desgravaciones" *La Voz del Interior*, 8 January 1994. The producers in the metalworking particularly opposed Angeloz's stimulus plan on the grounds that the metalworking sector was excluded from this preferential treatment plan: the head of the CIM argued that they were exposed to external competition in the absence of protections. Of all metalworking industry in Córdoba, only 26 companies were included while 352 were excluded. The "winners" of the stimulus program mostly included producers in the agro-industrial sector (milk and milk products, fruit and fruit-based products). The selected companies in the metalworking sector are machinery suppliers to agro-industrialists such as tractor producers and other agro-industrial equipment assemblers. "Los mayores beneficios senalan hacia este" *La Voz del Interior*, 9 January 1994.
69. "Caminotti: la nacion nos obliga a discriminar" *La Voz del Interior*, 11 January 1994.
70. "Industriales metalurgicos aguardan a Copic" *La Voz del Interior*.
71. In an interview the head of UIC ruled out this option, arguing that it is the UIA (the umbrella organization in Buenos Aires) that needs to negotiate with the central government and Domingo Cavallo and UIC would only talk to local government. "Leonida Panaioti (UIC): El actual esquema es mas distortivo que otra cosa" and "Hugo Paladini (CIM): Ahora tenemos la competencia en las provincias vecinas" *La Voz del Interior*, 23 January 1994.

72. In response to Angeloz's stimulus plan, UIC also called on the government to expand the number of companies to be included in the program. In fact, UIC sided with Menem government on the flexibilization of labor market, but this organization was careful to tone down its critique against Angeloz because many UIC companies were included in the local stimulus plan.

73. "La Plaza Córdoba es tampoco una Isla" *La Voz del Interior*, 6 January 1995, 7A.

74. "Se establecio el nueva sistema de negociacion salarial y laboral" *La Voz del Interior*, 20 March 1993.

75. "Queremos descentralizar las negociaciones colectivas" *La Voz del Interior*, 23 February 1994.

76. Because flexible work would generate fluctuations in the worker wages, the union management was highly likely to be deprived of a stable financial income when the rank-and-file is unable to pay their dues regularly.

77. "La UIC insiste por la reforma provincial" *La Voz del Interior*, 10 February 1995.

78. "No habra avales del creditos" *La Voz del Interior*, 24 June 1995.

79. Interview #1, 24 July 2008, Córdoba, Argentina.

80. Interview #1, 24 July 2008, Córdoba Argentina.

81. "La Nacion abandono a Córdoba antes que comenzara la crisis" *La Voz del Interior*, 28 June 1995.

82. "Asalto y incendio de la casa Radical" *La Voz del Interior*, 24 June 1995 and "Temores y consequencias del paquetazo" *La Voz del Interior*, 24 June 1995.

83. "Chrysler confirmo la inversion de US$80 millones en Córdoba" *La Voz del Interior*, 22 March 1995, 11A; and "FIAT se decidio por Córdoba" *La Voz del Interior*, 11 April 1995.

84. "Llega FIAT para hacer conocer su proyecto industrial" *La Voz del Interior*, 22 March 1995, 11A.

85. Jose Porta was the only minister who survived from the Angeloz administration and he retained his position as the Minister of Industry and Commerce under the Mestre government.

86. "Preocupacion por los conflictos laborales" *La Voz del Interior*, 27 July 1995.

87. According to a former Consultant to the Minister of Labor, because Mestre was under pressure to pull the economy together by reducing public expenditure, his temporary alliance with Menem helped him to facilitate targeted labor training through using federal funds for training programs. Interview #55, 21 July 2008, Córdoba, Argentina.

88. Some of these programs include PRONAPAS (1994–1995), Programas de Apoyo a la Reconversión Productiva (Jovenes) (1994–2000),

Capacitacion Ocupacional (1995–1996), Programa Aprender (1995–1997), Capacitacion para empleo (1996) and Projecto Joven (1997–2002). Source: Maria Estela Lanari, "Las Politicas del Empleo en los Paises del Mercosur," Working paper. Also these training programs got notable public attention. See "Capacitacion laboral para 20 mil personas" (Labor training for 20,000 people) *La Voz del Interior*, 8 October 1997, 10A. Furthermore, the federal government promoted these programs and asked the producers to sponsor them in return for tax reductions. See "Las empresas podrian desgravar los gastos para capacitar personal" (Companies can eliminate tax on the expenses to train personnel) *La Voz del Interior*, 18 October 1997. In addition, some of these programs were partially sponsored by the Interamerican Development Bank. "Capacitacion para Pyme en la provincia" (Training for SMEs in the province) *La Voz del Interior*, September 1998.

89. Even though Perez had to soften his words in the face of rising protests from the parents of students who had their children enrolled in these schools, the minister continued with his dismissive attitude vis-à-vis public vocational education in Córdoba. See "Perez flexibiliza su postura sobre la educacion tecnica" *La Voz del Interior*, 13 March 1997, 13A. In an interview, a former government member also noted the lack of funds for undertaking a large-scale investment program in these schools. Interview #31, 7 August 2008, Córdoba, Argentina. Moreover, Perez's predecessor, Juan Carlos Bocco severely criticized Perez on neglecting technical schools. Interview #8, Former Minister of Education, 1 August 2008, Córdoba, Argentina.

90. "El nivel educativo en Córdoba no es bueno admitio Perez" *La Voz del Interior*, 8 June 1997.

91. "Demoran inicio de clases en el Cassafousth" *La Voz del Interior*, 27 February 1997; and "El Gobierno analiza restablecer talleres en el Cassafousth" *La Voz del Interior*, 12 March 1997. Indeed, a former government member under Angeloz, argues that the price for neglecting technical schools in Córdoba has been quite high especially during the later stages of industrial development. Interview #32, 30 June 2008, Córdoba, Argentina.

92. Rising unemployment was a major problem that Mestre was unable to resolve during his term in the office. The 1997 figures indicated that Córdoba city suffered from an increasing rate of unemployment (18.8%) which was above the national mean. See "¿Córdoba: entre las ciudades con mas empleo?" *La Voz del Interior*, 8 January 1997, 8A. In order to minimize risks associated with unemployment, Mestre government launched short-term training programs for the youth and also signed a short-term training program deal with the Renault Foundation as a part

of *Programa Crecer*. See "Capacitacion" *La Voz del Interior*, July 1998; and "1700 chicos en riesgo reciben capacitacion para el trabajo" *La Voz del Interior*, 1 December 1998. In fact, the federal government used the same technique after the 2001 crisis. Interview #36, Ministry of Labor and Social Security, Director of Institutional Capacity, 11 August 2008, Buenos Aires, Argentina.

93. A news report on skill formation programs notes that Córdoba is unable to meet the growing demand of qualified labor force in multiple sectors, including automobiles. See "Por Ahora 'la docta' se va a marzo" *La Voz del Interior*, 23 March 1997, 2E. In fact, Mestre's minister of production and work, Jose Porta, notes that the growth in automobile sector in Córdoba is unlikely to address the problem of unemployment. See "Este renacer industrial no solucionara el desempleo" *La Voz del Interior*, 9 May 1997, p.9. A program that was launched by the federal government also proved ineffective and soon became the target of accusations and critiques for discrimination and ineffectiveness. See "Plan Trabajar: cruce de acusaciones" *La Voz del Interior*, 19 November 1998, 9A; and "Programa trabajar: ¿quien discrimina a quien?" *La Voz del Interior*, 6 December 1998, 14A. It should be noted that *Plan Trabajar* was intended to employ the poor in public works projects but vocational training was not an integral part of the program.

94. Indeed, this transformation of the labor force constitutes the backbone of new training programs during the 1990s. Interview #36, 11 August 2008, Buenos Aires, Argentina.

95. Interview #24, CIM, 17 July 2008, Córdoba, Argentina.

96. Interview #19, 19 July 2008, Córdoba, Argentina and Interview #28, 30 July 2008.

97. Labor turnover rate is the rate of employee replacement in a given time period. This is an indicator of stability of the workforce.

98. "Sin certificacion, ni cotizariamos" *La Voz del Interior*, 9 May 1997, Supplement, p.9.

99. "Córdoba debe mejorar su competividad" *La Voz del Interior*, 28 December 1997, p.3E.

100. "Capacitacion y calidad: ejes del desarollo" *La Voz del Interior*, 9 May 1998, p.2.

101. Interview #24, CIM, 17 July 2008, Córdoba, Argentina.

102. Interview #18, 31 July 2008, Córdoba, Argentina. The same finding resonates in an earlier study by Parisi (1999), where an interviewee, when asked about labor training programs, responds by arguing that the proposed changes have a harming effect on the work relations because [flexibilization] is exclusionary (Parisi 1999: 181,184).

103. "La capacitacion como herramienta esencial" *La Voz del Interior*, 6 September 1997. UOM was not the only union, in fact, unions in a similar position and organized in other sectors also took up the challenge of offering training to their workers. See "La capacitacion laboral es el pilar de la tarea gremial" *La Voz del Interior*, 18 March 1998, 13A.

104. Interview #54. 15 July 2008, Córdoba, Argentina.

105. Until 1999, SMATA managers were more supportive of new training programs for labor training, including behavioral trainings. In the words of a SMATA manager "it is coming, through other countries, that the labor instability is not the same as before, the companies—with technological advancement—need less labor force each time…because of that we have the responsibility to train our members so that they can face a new situation if they end up losing their job" Interview by Parisi 1999, 186a.

106. "Primera pulseada entre Mestre y los gremios" *La Voz del Interior*, 31 July 1995.

107. "SMATA marcha contra las suspenciones" *La Voz del Interior*, 31 July 1995; "Se logro acuerdo para una huelga provincial" *La Voz del Interior*, 3 August 1995.

108. "La UIC solicito a Mestre bajar las tarifas electricas" *La Voz del Interior*, 10 August 1995.

109. "Mestre insistio en la gravedad de las finanzas" *La Voz del Interior*, 19 August 1995, 6A.

110. "Descendio el 8.1% la produccion en Córdoba" La Voz del Interior, 26 September 1995. Among the sectors, transport materials had a decline rate of 40.9%, while the volume of production in auto-motors and auto-parts went down by 23.9%.

111. "Angelocistas se resisten aceptar a un mestrista al frente del congreso" *La Voz del Interior*, 6 March 1996; and "Una pelea que puede durar hasta 1999" *La Voz del Interior*, 23 February 1997, 8A.

112. During the initial time of Mestre in office, the local Peronists gave open support to him. In fact, contrary to the critics who accused Mestre of deploying authoritarian means to govern, the ultraperonists like Leonor Alarcia, argued that the governor was doing whatever he could to pull Córdoba together. See "Leonor Alarcia: Mestre esta haciendo lo que puede" *La Voz del Interior*, 19 January 1997. Also see "En el PJ crece el fantasma del pacto Menem-Mestre" *La Voz del Interior*, 23 February 1997, 9A and "Confirman que Menem avala el proyecto de Mestre" *La Voz del Interior*, 28 February 1997, 8A.

113. "El Menemismo acepto los plazos que quiere Mestre" *La Voz del Interior*, 25 February 1997, 5A.

114. "Menem y Mestre se profundizan coincidencias" *La Voz del Interior*, 4 March 1997.

115. Under Mestre big multinational companies such as Chrysler, Iveco, FIAT, Renault and Volkswagen made new investments in Córdoba (all are located around the city of Córdoba). This wave of MNC investment initially triggered a rise in the overall automobile production figures in 1997. (See "Córdoba sera el gran centro automotor" *La Voz del Interior*, 2 September 1997, p.7.) However, Mestre's policies excluded any detailed plan of support for the small and medium sized enterprises supplying parts to the multinational car companies, which left SMEs in a disadvantageous position. "¿Quien financia la reconversion de las Pyme?" *La Voz del Interior*, 12 May 1997, 12A. Toward the end of 1997, the automobile sector was experiencing difficulties due to an ongoing crisis in global markets. The automobile producers began to slow down production beginning from November 1997 onwards. See "El sector automotor desacelara la produccion" *La Voz del Interior*, 14 November 1997, 12A.

116. "Cesantias y suspensiones en las autopartistas" *La Voz del Interior*, 6 February 1998.

117. The proposal included reducing the number of provincial deputies in the local parliament. In a way, Mestre wanted to maximize his political power by reducing possible opposition against his policy line. See for example "¿Por que y para que reformar la constitucion de Córdoba?" *La Voz del Interior*, 22 April 1997, 13A. Supporters of Angeloz continued with their critiques against Mestrist plan, especially concerning the proposal on constitutional reform that aimed to centralize the power of the provincial governor. See "El Angelocismo se opone al proyecto de Mestre" *La Voz del Interior*, 2 May 1997, 6A.

118. See "Bazan suplica y exige el apoyo de todos los gremios" *La Voz del Interior*, 10 March 1997.

119. "El Campo anuncio movilizacion contra Mestre" *La Voz del Interior*, 22 July 1998, p.11A.

120. As tension between the federal government and Mestre intensified, the governor lost the elections to the Peronist José Manuel de la Sota in December 1998. "De la Sota Gobernador" *La Voz del Interior*, 21 December 1998, Frontpage.

121. Meanwhile, Mestre government accused rival groups from the PJ of supporting protesters and their militant means to bring down the government of Córdoba. "Intentan quebrar al gobierno de Córdoba" *La Voz del Interior*, 24 May 1998, 13A; "Marcha pacifica, con fuertes criticas a Mestre" *La Voz del Interior*, 30 May 1998, 10A; "Córdoba bajo el signo de la protesta" *La Voz del Interior*, 31 May 1998.

122. An expert in the Federal Ministry of Labor, Training Department notes that during the 1990s, most MNCs specified the content of these trainings according to their production needs. Interview #30, 6 June 2008, Buenos Aires, Argentina.

123. It must be noted that the selection of these workers was primarily done by the human resources department, and despite my appeals, the management did not follow the block sampling guidelines I submitted. In contrast to their counterparts in Bursa, these directors were extremely cautious when administering the survey. In fact, the manager edited the questionnaire line by line and took out sections and questions that he considered sensitive. Interviews took place in the HR management room in the presence of other HR department employees. This is in stark contrast to my experience in Bursa where the management did not intervene in any of the questions. Therefore, positive worker responses to questions on Toyotist training modules in Córdoba may not accurately reflect a broader trend.

124. Interview #46, 29 April 2008, Córdoba Argentina.

125. Source: Trabajo en Equipo, FIAT Argentina (Scarpatti y Asociados, Consultores en gestion Organizacional), and FIAT Internal Training Documents, 2007. As stated by a FIAT worker, the company provides trainings around these themes every month. Interview #46, 29 April 2008, Córdoba Argentina. My interviews with multiple FIAT workers also confirm this observation. In a personal interview, a FIAT worker cited company-based quality and leadership trainings as the most influential components in his training. Interview #47, 14 June 2008, Córdoba, Argentina.

126. Interview #46, 29 April 2008, Córdoba Argentina.

127. Interview #48, 18 June 2008, Córdoba Argentina.

128. According to a FIAT manager, 5S technique is the most influential tool to maximize worker efficiency in production, Interview #17, 8 July 2008, Córdoba, Argentina.

129. Interview #47, 14 June 2008, Córdoba, Argentina.

130. Interview #15, SMATA-Córdoba, 27 June 2008, Córdoba, Argentina.

131. Parisi (1999) interviewed 157 small and medium sized enterprises in Córdoba. The lack of training rate is particularly high in small sized companies, above 50% (Parisi 1999: 98).

132. For example, when the managers of these enterprises are asked about basic attributes that would have enhanced education for work, they list the ability to work as a team and a dedication for constant improvement as their top choices (Parisi 1999: 109). Most of these businesses prefer that these values and the initial base for training should be provided by the education system, rather than the company itself (Parisi 1999: 110).

133. As Mestre's alliance with Menem began to deteriorate during the second half of his term in the office, the governor initially saw a political opportunity in providing infrastructural support to the small and medium sized enterprises who had been calling for help. "Córdoba tramita que la nacion

promueva un regimen especial para las autopartistas" (Córdoba makes a new arrangement so that the central government promotes a special regime for the auto parts producers) *La Voz del Interior*, 8 October 1997, 10A. However, he soon abandoned his discursive support. For example, despite repeated demands from the small and medium sized business for cheaper electricity rates from Epec (the public electricity provider) the local government was unwilling to give privileged treatment to these business owners.

134. Interview #1, 30 June 2008, Córdoba, Argentina.
135. The exercise of obligatory conciliation was mostly motivated by political concerns of the ruling politicians. In this way, the strike would be suspended by the intervention of the government (local or provincial) until the parties would reach an agreement. The negotiations would restart, going back to the pre-strike conditions.
136. For example, see "Intervendra el Ministerio de Trabajo en el conflicto de la UOM" *La Voz del Interior*, 25 May 1990, 5A; "Conciliacion obligatoria para el conflicto en Perkins" *La Voz del Interior*, 20 July 1990, 5A; "Nueva mediacion en el conflicto metalurgico" *La Voz del Interior*, 10 December 1990; "La UOM suspendio las medidas de fuerza al acatar el arbitraje" *La Voz del Interior*, 6 April 1991.
137. "La UOM suspendio los paros por mediacion de Triaca" *La Voz del Interior*, 1 December 1990, 5A.
138. "Traen a Córdoba el conflicto del Arcor" *La Voz del Interior*, 11 April 1992. On 22 April 1992, Jorge Sappia intervened in the strike in Banco de Córdoba using obligatory conciliation.
139. "Amplio apoyo tuvo el paro de UOM" *La Voz del Interior*, May 1992.
140. It must be added that in Córdoba, political divisions that polarized businesses and unions were somewhat reconciled following the 2001 economic meltdown. Indeed, 2001 crisis reset the terms of political divisions among local actors, and from this date onwards, partisan preferences of business groups and unions were gradually de-polarized under Juan Manuel De la Sota's leadership.

Bibliography

Anner, M. 2011. *Solidarity Transformed: Labor Responses to Globalization and Crisis in Latin America*. Ithaca: ILR Press, an imprint of Cornell University Press.

Cató, J., P. Ventrici, and R. Bresnahan. 2011. Labor Union Renewal in Argentina: Democratic Revitalization from the Base. *Latin American Perspectives* 38 (6): 38–51.

Dussel, I., and P. Pineau. 1995. De cuando la clase obrera entro al paraiso: la educacion tecnica estatal en el primer Peronismo [Since the Working Class Entered the Paradise: State Sponsored Technical Education During the First Peronism]. In *Discursos Pedagogicos E Imaginario Social En El Peronismo: 1945–1955*, ed. S. Carli, vol. VI. Buenos Aires: Editorial Galerna.

Etchemendy, S. 2001. Constructing Reform Coalitions: The Politics of Compensations in the Argentine Path to Economic Liberalization. *Latin American Politics and Society* 43: 1–35.

Etchemendy, S., and C. Garay. 2011. Argentina: Left Populism in Comparative Perspective (2003–2009). In *The Resurgence of Latin American Left*, ed. S. Levitsky and K. Roberts. Baltimore: Johns Hopkins University Press.

Levitsky, S. 2001. An Organized Disorganization: Informal Organization and the Persistence of Local Party Structures in Argentine Peronism. *Journal of Latin American Studies*. 33: 29–65.

Levitsky, S., and M.V. Murillo, eds. 2005. *Argentine Democracy: The Politics of Institutional Weakness*. University Park: The Pennsylvania State University Press.

McGuire, J.W. 1992. "Union Political Tactics and Democratic Consolidation in Alfonsín's Argentina." 1983–1989. *Latin American Research Review* 27 (1): 37–74.

Moran, T. 1970. The 'Development' of Argentina and Australia: The Radical Party of Argentina and the Labor Party of Australia in the Process of Economic and Political Development. *Comparative Politics* 3: 71–90.

Murillo, V.M. 1999. Recovering Political Dynamics: Teachers'Unions and the Decentralization of Education in Argentina and Mexico. *Journal of Inter-American Studies and World Affairs* 41: 31–57.

Parisi, A. 1999. *Formacion y trabajo: una incursion en las PYMEs de la ciudad de Córdoba en el contexto de la globalizacion*. Córdoba: Universidad Nacional de Córdoba.

Ranis, P. 2004. Rebellion, Class, and Labor in Argentine Society. *Working USA* 7 (4): 8.

Remmer, K. 1993. The Political Economy of Elections in Latin America, 1980–1991. *The American Political Science Review* 87: 393–407.

Sabatini, C.A. 1996. *Political Parties and Democratization in the Time of Economic Crisis and Reform: A Case Study of the Radical and Peronist Parties in Argentina, 1983–1995*.Unpublished PhD. Dissertation, University of Virginia,Charlottesville.

Saettone, F.M. 2006. La relación líder-partido en Argentina [The leader-party relationship in Argentina]. *Scripta Ethnologica* 28: 121–135.

Sanchez-Roman, J.A. 2007. De Las 'escuales artes y oficios' a la Universidad Obrero Nacional: estado, elites y educacion technica en Argentina, 1914–1955. *Cuadernos del Instituto Antonio de Nebrija* 10: 269–299.

Snow, P. 1963. Argentine Radicalism: 1957–1963. *Journal of Inter-American Studies* 5: 507–531.

Stokes, S. 1998. Constituency Influence and Representation. *Electoral Studies* 17: 351–367.

Tcach, C. 2006 [1991]. *Sabbatinismo y peronismo: partidos politicos en Córdoba 1943–1955* [Sabbatinism and Peronism: Political Parties in Córdoba 1943–1955]. Córdoba: Universidad Nacional de Córdoba.

CHAPTER 5

After Fordism: The Politics of Industrial Conflict Patterns in the Global South

The qualitative evidence from the comparative findings on Turkey and Argentina suggests that, as opposed to unitary systems—where political congruence between the central and local administration is high—federal systems are more likely to be characterized by partisan conflict between the federal and provincial administration. As we have seen, an ongoing partisan rivalry in Córdoba, Argentina has created a room for prolonged labor mobilization against post-Fordist reorganization of production. On the other hand, in unitary Turkey, emerging worker opposition to these measures were contained and eliminated swiftly under the auspices of local governors who rarely step out of the expectations of the central administration in Ankara. While these findings from the Turkish and Argentine context reveal the significance of political-institutional set up in understanding labor mobilization patterns, the small number of cases limit the explanatory framework in terms of its generalizability. How far do these findings travel beyond these two cases?

Going beyond Turkey and Argentina, the manufacturing industry elsewhere also witnessed the growing inflow of foreign capital and the burgeoning of local industries that supply semi-finished goods and raw materials to these companies. In most of these settings, the arrival of MNCs—as in the automobile industry—had a transformative effect on local economies (Ahlquist and Prakash 2008). This is because new technologies of surplus labor extraction implemented by these companies alter

© The Author(s) 2018
F. Apaydin, *Technology, Institutions and Labor*, International Political Economy Series, https://doi.org/10.1007/978-3-319-77104-5_5

the existing configurations of industrial relations and trigger new conflicts between business and labor (Robertson and Teitelbaum 2011). This chapter shows that the degree and intensity of this conflict-inducing effect not only varies across different political regimes, but also across democratic countries, which are previously reported to have a moderating effect on strikes (Robertson 2007). Following the principles of Rohlfing's (2008) case-based nested analysis, this chapter couches Turkey and Argentina in macro-level data to test the effect of political institutions on industrial conflict patterns in the developing world after Fordism. As we shall see, the results show that federal systems are indeed more conducive to prolonged labor mobilization in contrast to their unitary counterparts.[1] This is because federal systems accommodate multiple governments ruling over a single territory, which increases the likelihood of disagreements among politicians operating at the federal and subnational level. This enables labor unions to maintain their contentious position by means of exploiting rivalries in a multi-level political competition.

ORGANIZING POWER AND LABOR MOBILIZATION IN THE DEVELOPING WORLD

While some scholars suggest that federal systems lower political risk and facilitate greater FDI in less-democratic environments (Jensen and McGillivray 2005), prolonged labor mobilization instigated by the arrival of international capital introduces additional challenges. These findings speak to a growing body of scholarship that highlights how political institutions influence industrial conflict and development pathways (Gunderson and Melino 1990; Rubin and Smith 1991; Tuman 1994; Murillo 2001; Li and Resnick 2003; Murillo and Ronconi 2004; Crowley 2004; Hurst 2004; Vernby 2007; Pinto and Pinto 2008; Aleman 2009; Kim and Gandhi 2010; Biglaiser and Staats 2010; Robertson and Teitelbaum 2011; Lee et al. 2014). In that sense, moving the spotlight on institutional factors complements explanations based on shopfloor dynamics, macroeconomic factors and/or rational calculations of actors involved in an industrial strife.

In the developing world, struggles between private interest groups in the economic domain—such as industrial conflicts between unions and business organizations—can be politically decisive. Major strikes can make or break governments. In some cases, extended labor mobilization may have a domino effect, leading to revolutionary episodes[2] that result in regime change (Bellin 2013; Berman 2015). Moreover, in countries where production is characterized by the dominance of a select few sectors over others, an exclusive focus on the frequency of strikes may be misleading, especially if the majority of these interruptions take place in less-value-added industries and/or across sectors that employ a very small share of the workforce. Particularly across sectors of critical importance—such as those designated as locomotives of development—extended strikes may have a spillover effect in supplier industries. Thus, lengthy strikes in critical sectors may initiate a slow-down effect on the overall performance of the economy.

Relatedly, the duration of strife between business and labor has notable implications on the rate of capital accumulation and reinvestment, which has further repercussions on development policy-making and redistribution. A greater number of days lost in strikes may have a negative effect on productivity (McHugh 1991), product quality (Krueger and Mas 2004) and stock value of companies (Dinardo and Hallock 2002). Most notably, the disruption of economic activity for prolonged periods poses a warning sign to incoming investors, and may trigger capital flight if labor contention is extended over a longer time frame not only in democracies, but also in authoritarian regimes (Kim and Gandhi 2010, 647).

On the more positive end, prolonged labor mobilization in authoritarian contexts could empower workers to push for democratization. Historically, labor unions have either played or continue to play a notable role in democratization processes (Przeworski and Sprague 1986; Collier and Collier 1991; Rueschemeyer et al. 1992; Collier 1999; Silver 2003; Tilly 2004; Berman 2007). In that sense, the duration of strike activity offers important clues about civil liberties in democratizing settings as these incidents test the regime's limits for accommodating collective action.

Among existing explanations that problematize the length of business-labor strife, two key lines stand out. Among the students of labor economics, the role of firm-level dynamics such as the fulfillment of employee expectations (Ashenfelter and Johnson 1969), economic wellbeing of the workforce (Kennan 1980; Reder and Neumann 1980), level of firm profits (Teitelbaum 2007), information asymmetries between unions and firms (Kennan and Wilson 1989; Card 1990), and/or the type of firm ownership (Baah and Reilly 2009) stand out as micro-level factors that influence industrial conflict trajectories. Others in this school highlight broader factors such as the inflation rate (Owoye 1992), GDP per capita (Harrison and Stewart 1989), and unemployment rate (Ashenfelter and Johnson 1969) as predictors of industrial conflict duration in quantitative studies.

A second group coming from the tradition of industrial sociology seeks to go beyond economic variables and puts the emphasis on factors that affect the bargaining capacities and abilities of the unions. These include geographic distribution of labor in a given jurisdiction (Shorter and Tilly 1974), organizational capacity and size of the unions (Campolieti et al. 2005), difficulties among unions and workers to transmit information (Connel and Cohn 1995), degree of disagreement between the employer and the union (Ondrich and Schnell 1993), media attention (Flynn 2000), variation in industrial relations systems (Ortiz 1999), and sheer worker motivation to protect their former gains and avoid future losses (Brym et al. 2013).

Though these influential bodies of work predominantly highlight economic interests and organizational capacities, they also face several limitations. First, studies that exclusively focus on shopfloor and/or firm dynamics are very limited in their attempt to reach broader generalizations. Second, majority of existing studies that explore the dynamics behind prolonged labor mobilization lack a broad comparative cross-national focus, and tend to base their claims on either a single case or cases selected from advanced industrialized countries. Third, with only a few exceptions, a sizeable portion of these studies sidesteps the role of the political context in which these conflicts unfold.

Recent works on the political economy of industrial policy in the developing world offer important insights to fill in these empirical and theoretical gaps. Especially after the import-substitution-industrialization era, most governments in the developing world are increasingly enthusiastic about attracting and retaining foreign direct investment (FDI), hoping that this will facilitate job creation, capital accumulation and technology transfer on a faster pace (Jensen 2003; Blanton and Blanton 2012). As we have seen in previous chapters, this was indeed a key motivation behind the Turkish and Argentine attempts in prioritizing automobile industry as the locomotive of development. Policy-makers driven by this motivation exhibit a very low tolerance for prolonged industrial conflicts and seek to reduce and/or eliminate risks that may trigger capital flight. However, their capacity to intervene in ongoing conflicts is also constrained by a host of other factors, including rules of electoral competition (Vernby 2007), labor regulations (Kus and Ozel 2010) and institutional legacies (Cohen 1989; Cook 1998). While this framework puts the emphasis on institutional factors, unpacking the causal mechanism behind industrial conflict duration calls for a closer look into how political structures affect the capacities of firms and unions to negotiate. In that sense, a focus on the distribution of power among political actors—such as key veto players—provides a useful starting point.

Veto-Points Model

Veto players are individual or collective actors whose consent is required for reaching an agreement to initiate a change (Tsebelis 1995; 289; Tsebelis 2002). According to this framework, there are at least two major types of veto players in any given political system: institutional and partisan. In democratic regimes, institutional veto players refer to individuals or entities whose decision-making powers are formally specified in the constitution, such as the executive (e.g. president), legislature (e.g. parliament, upper chamber) and the judiciary. On the other hand, partisan veto players refer to elected parties in the government, which depends on the party system and the composition of incumbent coalitions (Tsebelis 1995, 304). Most importantly, the number of veto players involved in negotiations varies depending on at least four key factors: the administrative organization (e.g. federal vs. unitary), political system (presidential vs. parliamentary), electoral institutions (e.g. proportional vs. majoritarian) and the issue area in question (Tsebelis 1995, 307).

According to Tsebelis, when the majority of these players act on a common position, then they have sufficient capacity to challenge those in opposition and move away from the status quo. This framework predicts that the probability of moving away from the status quo decreases as the number of veto players increases. Under these circumstances, the likelihood of congruence and cohesion among political actors is lower. In the case of industrial conflicts, we should expect the resolution of disputes to last longer as the number of veto players increases. Thus:

H1a: The average duration of an industrial conflict is likely to be longer in political systems characterized by a greater number of veto points.

However, when special interest groups (such as unions and business organizations) are involved in negotiations, greater number of veto players may facilitate a faster move away from the status quo under some circumstances (Gehlbach and Malesky 2010). According to this model, policy change is especially likely if special interest groups need to compensate multiple veto players for the promotion of their narrow interests because higher costs attached to defending their stance becomes less attractive as an option. Based on these assumptions, I further test the following hypothesis:

H1b: The average duration of an industrial conflict is likely to be shorter in political systems with multiple veto points.

Multi-Level Government Model

The veto-players framework indeed provides notable insights to explain industrial disagreements. As the earlier findings on responses to technological change in the Turkish and Argentine cases reveal, the level at which these actors are situated (national vs. subnational) may also influence business-labor conflict pathways. This is important because in some developing settings, separation of powers induces even more intense political competition between national and subnational levels of government. These rivalries also affect the consolidation of industrial peace in local settings. During much of the 1990s, the arrival of multinational companies into the developing world triggered a process where the manufacturing sector experienced a radical reorganization of the shopfloor and employment policies were modified in favor of a more flexible framework (Murillo 2001; Anner 2011; Etchemendy 2011; Schrank 2011). In some cases, the negotiations around highly controversial issues went beyond peak business and labor associations, and involved political veto players, including members of the executive at local and national level who fiercely competed with each other on multiple fronts.

In an environment characterized by institutional instabilities, this rivalry may have a negative impact on the macro-economic performance, especially at times of economic re-adjustment under globalization pressures (Wibbels 2000, 687). Similarly, inter-jurisdictional competition in federal systems may have a corroding effect on the central government's capacity to reduce conflict and enhance welfare (Cai and Treisman 2004). On the industrial front, conflicts are more likely to remain unresolved in areas characterized by highly competitive non-consensual institutions (Crepaz 1996; Birchfield and Crepaz 1998). Overall, a politically competitive multi-government setting—where several veto players situated at different levels interact with each other concerning issues related to a common territory—may cause delays in the resolution of industrial conflicts. Based on these insights, we expect competition between political actors in federal systems operating at *different levels* of the government to have a prolonging effect on the duration of an industrial unrest. Thus:

> H2: *The average duration of an industrial conflict is likely to be longer in federal systems that accommodate multiple governments ruling over a single territory.*

Government Fractionalization Model

Further, when industrial policy readjustments are contested by workers in the developing world, I expect lower number of institutional and partisan veto players in unitary systems to increase the likelihood of an alignment among political actors. Often, the greater likelihood of an overlap among fewer actors prepares the ground for a quicker resolution of the dispute. Especially when the majority of ministers in the cabinet side with business—as in the case of Turkey—labor opposition may be more rapidly contained. Thus, workers are likely to yield in the face of proposed policy changes by abandoning their contentious position in relatively shorter period of time.

Though most unitary systems are characterized by a lower number of veto players, the number of these critical actors may also increase especially under coalition governments. When multiple political parties hold key positions in the executive, partisan rivalries in the government may delay concerted action among the involved parties, and unions may exploit this lack of agreement at the top, staying in resistance for longer periods. Thus:

> H3: *The average duration of an industrial conflict is likely to be longer as the number of partisan veto-players in a national government increases.*

DATA AND ESTIMATION STRATEGY

To test these hypotheses, I use an original unbalanced panel dataset with 459 observations on 37 countries (middle and lower-middle income)[3] with an average yearly FDI/GDP share above 0.001, covering the period between 1990 and 2012. These countries were included based on the availability of data for the key measure used in constructing the dependent variable: total number of workdays lost per worker due to industrial conflict in a given year. Countries with less than four observations were excluded from the sample. The period of coverage for each country varies between 4 and 23 years. We exclude advanced industrialized countries from the sample because the historical evolution of political and economic institutions across these settings is considerably different than the experience of those in the developing world (Hall and Soskice 2001; Streeck and Thelen 2005; Thelen 2012). Typically, the latter are characterized by greater institutional instabilities, regime breakdowns and diverse economic trajectories (Schneider and Karcher 2010; Schneider 2013; Acemoglu and Robinson 2013).

Dependent Variable: Industrial Conflict Duration

Following earlier studies (Teitelbaum 2007; Vernby 2007), I calculate the average duration of industrial conflict by dividing the total number of workdays lost due to industrial conflict in a given year by the total number of workers involved. The data is taken from the International Labor Organization (ILO) statistics database and covers the period between 1990 and 2012 for 37 countries. This measure allows us to focus on average workdays lost per worker across the countries included in the sample.

Independent Variable 1: Political Constraint Index (POLCON V)

In order to test H1a and H1b, I include a measure of political constraint for each country-year, developed by Henisz (2000). This indicator varies between 0 and 1, where a higher score points to a greater number of veto players in a given political system and vice versa.[4]

Independent Variable 2: Federalism Dummy

In order to test H2, I include a federalism dummy, which is a binary variable that is coded as 1 if the country is federal and 0 if unitary. Though this variable does not vary within cases, it varies *across* countries, which allows to assess its role in industrial conflict duration.

Independent Variable 3: Government Fractionalization (Govfrac)

In order to test H3, I also include a variable that measures the probability of partisan fractionalization in a given national government. This measure is taken from Beck et al.'s (2001) database on political institutions and calculates the probability that two deputies picked at random in a government will be of different parties.

Control Variables

In order to control for economic factors that are cited in earlier studies as probable culprits, I include unemployment rate,[5] inflation,[6] economic crisis,[7] share of FDI[8] and GDP/Capita per year[9]in the model. Also, following Beck and Katz (2011), I also include a one-year lagged dependent variable to partially address problems related to omitted variable bias. In addition to economic variables, I also control for political and institutional variables cited in earlier studies: the political system (presidential/ parliamentary),[10] the electoral system (majoritarian/proportional representation)[11] and labor rights.[12] Finally, I also control for regional effects by including a Latin America dummy[13] in the sample, given the longer history of contentious labor mobilization and concentration of federal systems in South America.

Estimation Strategy

Because the dataset is an unbalanced panel data, this imposes notable restrictions on the availability of models when estimating the coefficients. In particular, the likelihood of autocorrelation in this type of data eliminates simple ordinary least squares (OLS) as a reliable method. This is because OLS coefficient estimates are inevitably biased when sampling is non-random and unobserved errors are correlated with one of the independent variables.

Though Beck and Katz (1996) suggest using panel corrected standard errors in OLS estimation to avoid problems related to serial autocorrelation, this technique is not optimal since this solution largely applies to balanced datasets (Beck and Katz 2011) whereas the dataset is strongly unbalanced. Similarly, hazard function models—which are often used to estimate strike duration—are not feasible because the dependent variable is a continuous variable that measures average number of workdays lost per worker in a given year for the countries included in the sample. Others have used negative binomial regression models (with fixed effects) to overcome bias induced by contagion effects (Hausman et al. 1984), especially when estimating the number of days lost in strikes using count-data (Robertson 2007; Kim and Gandhi 2010). However, this model is also not the most suitable since the dependent variable is a continuous variable that measures average workdays lost per worker in a given year and not a count measure that varies between 8 and 40.[14] Finally, Fixed-Effects Vector Decomposition models, which estimate the effect of time-invariant models in three stages developed by Plümper and Troeger (2007) yield dramatic overconfidence in the estimates (Breusch et al. 2011; Greene 2011) due to errors in the calculation of standard errors. This procedure has been since disowned by the authors in a later study, yet the new technique that Plümper and Troeger (2011) develop as an alternative only applies to balanced panel data. Finally, since the federal dummy is not randomly assigned, treatment effect models are unfit for estimating the coefficients (Winship and Mare 1992). Under these circumstances—given the moderate time length and the number of countries involved in the panel—correlated random effects (CRE) model for unbalanced panel data (Bafumi and Gelman 2006; Wooldridge 2010) stands as the most reliable technique to estimate the coefficients for Hypothesis 2 and models that include federal dummy on the right hand side of the equation. Other models that exclude this variable were estimated using fixed effects.

Until very recently, CRE models were primarily applied to non-linear models, however, recent extensions of the Chamberlain-Mundlak approach by Bafumi and Gelman (2006) and Wooldridge (2010) and applications (Papke and Wooldridge 2008) offer a solution to the treatment of unobserved heterogeneity (correlation between individual effects and the error term) problem, especially when the independent variable of interest is time-invariant. Under these circumstances, recent CRE models have clear advantages over fixed-effects models. Often, estimating coefficients with fixed-effects models relies on very strong assumptions about the nature of the data, including stationarity and, in some cases, independence of serial autocorrelation (Wooldridge 2010). However, in practice, most unbalanced time-series cross-sectional data do not always conform to these high standards (Bell and Jones 2015).

CRE models for unbalanced panel data analysis provide an alternative solution to these problems starting with the assumption that sample selection is not systematically related to unobserved shocks, that is: there is no cross-group dependence (Wooldridge 2010, 2013). At the same time, the model does not restrict serial dependence in the data and allows selection and covariates to be correlated with unobserved heterogeneity in unbalanced panels (Wooldridge 2010). Though this may otherwise lead to biased estimates, CRE models reduce this by including mean values of variables that are not constant across time and space in the model as instrumental variables. Formulated this way, generalized least squares regression with random effects addresses a major source of bias in estimates and standard errors (Bafumi and Gelman 2006; Wooldridge 2010, 2013). In particular, this model allows for estimating coefficients when the key independent variable of interest is time-invariant.

The correlated random effects model used in this study is:

$$Y_{it} = \alpha + \beta_1 Y_{it-1} + \beta_2 X_{it} + \beta_3 \overline{X}_{it} + u_i + \varepsilon_{it} \tag{5.1}$$

where Y_{it} is the dependent variable in country i at time t; α is the intercept; Y_{it-1} is a one-year lagged dependent variable, X_{it} is a 1×K row vector whose components vary across i or i and t; $\overline{X}_{it}$ is the vector containing the means of all variables that vary over i and t; u_i is individual heterogeneity effects and ε_{it} is random error. While CRE model allows correlation between X_{it} and u_i, the assumption of strict exogeneity between X_{it} and ε_{it} must hold across all observations. This allows room for estimating coefficients of time-invariant variables—such as the federal dummy in the model—that would otherwise be absorbed by the intercept in fixed-effect models. It must be added that though recent CRE models offer notable advantages over fixed-effects models, the interpretation of the results still requires some caution because these models do not completely eliminate potential biases induced by omitted variables.

THE FINDINGS

Veto-Points Model

I first test whether a greater number of veto players in a given political system has any significant impact on the duration of strikes. Stepwise models in Table 5.1 show that POLCON V is not significant in any of the models. In other words, even though the direction of the relationship is negative, as predicted by H1b, greater number of veto points does not significantly increase or decrease the duration of an industrial conflict. Therefore, H1a and H1b are rejected.

However, introducing the federal dummy in the presence of theoretically informed controls in Model 3 reveals an interesting pattern: while the total number of veto players has no significant impact on the outcome,

Table 5.1   Veto-points model, dependent variable: industrial conflict duration

	(1)	*(2)*	*(3)*
Federal dummy			5.032***
			(1.636)
LA Dummy			0.151
			(1.377)
POLCONV	**−4.015**	**−5.723**	**−5.465**
	(6.912)	(8.192)	(8.835)
Strike duration(t-1)	0.146***	0.194***	0.195*
	(0.0428)	(0.0470)	(0.111)
Frequency of strikes(t-1)	−0.0448	−0.320**	−0.320**
	(0.0418)	(0.124)	(0.142)
Unemployment(t-1)	0.169	0.242	0.216
	(0.436)	(0.470)	(0.279)
Inflation rate(t-1)	−0.0110**	−0.0102**	−0.00960*
	(0.00427)	(0.00442)	(0.00529)
Crisis dummy	−4.267*	−4.305	−4.415**
	(2.361)	(2.642)	(1.905)
Imports	−0.278*	−0.233	−0.228
	(0.163)	(0.174)	(0.183)
FDI/GDP	120.8**	77.72	78.57**
	(56.52)	(61.29)	(33.07)
Parliamentary dummy		16.07	9.081
		(22.71)	(6.542)
Majoritarian dummy		5.298	5.263
		(7.806)	(4.983)
PR dummy		1.819	2.290
		(6.049)	(2.858)
ILO conventions		1.350	1.393
		(1.580)	(1.293)
(Mean) PolconV			8.230
			(9.102)
(Mean) Strike duration(t-1)			0.808***
			(0.127)
(Mean) Frequency of strikes(t-1)			0.799***
			(0.263)
(Mean) Unemployment(t-1)			−0.0310
			(0.351)
(Mean) Inflation rate(t-1)			0.0126**
			(0.00572)
(Mean) Crisis dummy			5.423
			(4.459)
(Mean) Imports			0.201

(*continued*)

Table 5.1 (continued)

	(1)	(2)	(3)
			(0.196)
(Mean) FDI/GDP			−98.96**
			(43.75)
(Mean) Parliamentary dummy			−6.341
			(7.359)
(Mean) Majoritarian dummy			−8.062
			(5.528)
(Mean) PR dummy			−4.270
			(3.279)
(Mean) ILO conventions			−0.451
			(1.609)
Constant	25.16***	11.10	−7.652**
	(8.411)	(14.54)	(3.388)
Fixed effects	Yes	Yes	No
Correlated random effects	No	No	Yes
Observations	454	397	397
R-squared	0.083	0.112	
Number of countries	36	31	31

Robust standard errors in parentheses; *** $p<0.01$, ** $p<0.05$, * $p<0.1$

strikes taking place in a multi-government setting are significantly longer. On average, federal systems prolong workdays lost per worker in an industrial conflict by about 5 days, which can be substantial in the context of developing settings with moderate GDP levels.

Multi-Level Government Model

In order to test H2, the models in Table 5.2 were also constructed in a stepwise manner, first introducing economic control variables, followed by the introduction of political and institutional controls. All four models in Table 5.2 reveal that federal countries are more likely to experience longer periods of industrial conflict (around 4.6 days) and the size of the effect is not substantially different than results reported in Model 3 in Table 5.1. The federal dummy coefficient is positively correlated with the dependent variable, and significant at $p < 0.05$ in models 1, 2 and 3. The significance of this variable further increases once I include one-year lagged frequency of strikes (defined as number of strikes per 1000 workers at time t

Table 5.2   Multi-level government model, dependent variable: industrial conflict duration

	(1)	(2)	(3)	(4)
Federal dummy	2.444**	4.513**	4.366**	4.693***
	(1.229)	(1.980)	(1.931)	(1.666)
LA dummy			1.321	0.109
			(1.845)	(1.343)
Strike duration(t-1)	0.143	0.175	0.175	0.199*
	(0.103)	(0.111)	(0.111)	(0.111)
Frequency of strikes(t-1)				−0.322**
				(0.141)
Unemployment(t-1)	−0.0244	0.201	0.204	0.215
	(0.259)	(0.277)	(0.276)	(0.285)
Inflation rate(t-1)	−0.0107*	−0.0101*	−0.00996*	−0.00947*
	(0.00562)	(0.00568)	(0.00578)	(0.00526)
Crisis dummy	−4.917**	−5.225**	−5.214**	−4.869**
	(2.007)	(2.199)	(2.198)	(2.154)
Imports	−0.305*	−0.242	−0.238	−0.225
	(0.167)	(0.177)	(0.178)	(0.182)
FDI/GDP	94.89	58.88*	62.20**	76.06**
	(64.46)	(31.06)	(31.19)	(31.07)
Parliamentary dummy		6.482	6.733	5.439
		(4.522)	(4.700)	(4.739)
Majoritarian dummy		7.368**	7.587**	5.248
		(3.728)	(3.744)	(4.890)
PR dummy		2.325	2.349	2.350
		(3.109)	(3.116)	(3.069)
ILO conventions		1.379	1.415	1.319
		(1.181)	(1.217)	(1.254)
(Mean) strike duration(t-1)	0.946***	0.926***	0.916***	0.806***
	(0.105)	(0.120)	(0.122)	(0.121)
(Mean) frequency of strikes (t-1)				0.850***
				(0.247)
(Mean) unemployment(t-1)	0.141	0.00380	0.0353	−0.113
	(0.280)	(0.319)	(0.328)	(0.331)
(Mean) inflation rate(t-1)	0.0157*	0.0125	0.0128*	0.0125**
	(0.00953)	(0.00768)	(0.00720)	(0.00614)
(Mean) crisis dummy	5.023	2.425	3.552	5.300
	(4.176)	(5.005)	(5.086)	(4.646)
(Mean) imports (%)	0.320*	0.243	0.245	0.191
	(0.180)	(0.191)	(0.191)	(0.193)
(Mean) FDI/GDP	−119.6	−51.05	−68.07	−99.44**

(*continued*)

Table 5.2 (continued)

	(1)	(2)	(3)	(4)
	(86.56)	(49.53)	(47.23)	(45.27)
(Mean) Parliamentary		−3.486	−3.337	−1.970
		(5.380)	(5.461)	(5.345)
(Mean) Majoritarian		−8.477*	−8.477*	−7.681
		(4.715)	(4.705)	(5.430)
(Mean) PR		−4.022	−4.016	−4.452
		(3.659)	(3.636)	(3.516)
(Mean) ILO conventions		0.101	−0.110	−0.0588
		(1.576)	(1.707)	(1.608)
Constant	−3.836	−8.632**	−9.332**	−6.839**
	(3.323)	(3.733)	(3.963)	(3.210)
Correlated random effects	Yes	Yes	Yes	Yes
Observations	459	400	400	397
Number of countries	37	31	31	31

Robust standard errors in parentheses; ***p<0.01, **p<0.05, *p<0.1

in country i) in Model 4. Based on these findings on Tables 5.1 and 5.2, I am unable to reject H2.

The results also reveal an interesting relationship between macro-economic factors and conflict duration. First, higher inflation rates and the presence of an economic crisis both have a negative effect on the outcome, and the size of these effects is very similar across different models. While the effect of inflation is weakly significant at $p < 0.1$, economic crisis seems to have a stronger effect on reducing the duration of conflict at $p < 0.05$. On the other hand, unemployment is not a significant predictor of strike duration in any of these models. This suggests that decision to continue with strikes may be driven by another variable other than fears associated with losing one's job. Second, there is a positive and significant relationship between the share of FDI and conflict duration: 1% increase in the share of FDI in GDP leads to an increase in the workdays lost per worker between 0.58 and 0.76 days in Table 5.2 (see Models 2, 3 and 4). This finding is in line with earlier observations, and there is support in favor of arguments that suggest greater industrial conflict following the arrival of foreign investors (Robertson and Teitelbaum 2011). Interestingly, the frequency of strikes has a negative effect on the outcome across all the models: the greater the number of strikes per 1000 workers, the shorter the conflict. This suggests that frequent strikes may prevent the build-up of industrial tension by allowing workers to communicate their demands and may have a moderate effect on lowering the prospects of prolonged mobilization.

On the political-institutional front, majoritarian systems have a positive effect on the dependent variable in Models 2 and 3, and this relationship is significant in the context of developing countries, at $p<0.05$. This finding is in line with earlier observations that suggest higher frequency of labor disputes and workdays lost in single-member-district systems. According to this line of argument, majoritarian systems provide incentives to unions to strike with greater frequency especially right before the elections, because the incumbent party will be more responsive to labor demands in a highly competitive electoral environment. However, the significance of this variable disappears once the frequency of strikes is introduced in Model 4. Thus, the findings expose the limits of this argument and caution against the broader generalizability of this claim. Additionally, whether a given political system is presidential or parliamentary has no significant impact on the dependent variable, suggesting that political competition at the national level has no meaningful effect on the outcome.

Surprisingly, however, the institutional framework of labor rights protections in a given country does not play a significant role in the average duration of industrial conflict. While earlier research finds a positive relationship between protective labor market institutions and social pacts committed to maintaining peaceful exchanges between labor, business organizations and politicians (Aleman 2009), greater institutional commitment to internationally binding labor regulations does not significantly increase the maneuvering capacity of workers in a protest. Put differently, an enhanced framework of labor rights does not automatically translate into a capacity to bargain for longer periods. These findings suggest that resources available to unions and favorable political opportunities may play a more effective role in predicting the duration of worker mobilization.

Government Fractionalization Model

The results on Table 5.3 include models that test: is greater probability of partisan division in the national government a significant predictor of strike duration? The findings in all models lead us to reject H3: *Govfrac* is not significant in the presence of relevant controls in any of the models.

Table 5.3 Government fractionalization model, dependent variable: industrial conflict duration

	(1)	(2)	(3)
Federal dummy			**4.810***
			(1.707)
LA dummy			−0.127
			(1.440)
Govfract	**−7.052**	**−6.814**	**−6.404**
	(5.357)	(5.779)	(5.511)
Strike duration(t-1)	0.141***	0.192***	0.192*
	(0.0429)	(0.0469)	(0.112)
Frequency of strikes(t-1)	−0.0455	−0.330***	−0.327**
	(0.0417)	(0.124)	(0.142)
Unemployment(t-1)	0.161	0.243	0.219
	(0.435)	(0.469)	(0.279)
Inflation rate(t-1)	−0.0119***	−0.0111**	−0.0102**
	(0.00430)	(0.00447)	(0.00501)
Crisis dummy	−4.171*	−4.520*	−4.583**
	(2.322)	(2.553)	(2.189)
Imports	−0.305*	−0.251	−0.237
	(0.163)	(0.174)	(0.183)
FDI/GDP	110.5*	65.21	72.09**
	(56.67)	(61.30)	(31.41)
Parliamentary dummy		14.43	5.237
		(22.37)	(5.398)
Majoritarian dummy		3.657	4.059
		(7.889)	(5.908)
PR dummy		2.072	2.492
		(6.040)	(3.183)
ILO conventions		0.937	1.009
		(1.598)	(1.316)
(Mean) Govfrac			9.791
			(6.456)
(Mean) strike duration(t-1)			0.819***
			(0.126)
(Mean) frequency of strikes (t-1)			0.766***
			(0.260)
(Mean) unemployment(t-1)			−0.0806
			(0.340)
(Mean) inflation rate(t-1)			0.0119**
			(0.00588)
(Mean) crisis dummy			3.328
			(4.960)

(continued)

Table 5.3 (continued)

	(1)	*(2)*	*(3)*
(Mean) imports (%)			0.205
			(0.194)
(Mean) FDI/GDP			−83.86*
			(45.84)
(Mean) Parliamentary			−2.251
			(6.008)
(Mean) Majoritarian			−6.669
			(6.444)
(Mean) PR			−4.764
			(3.733)
(Mean) ILO conventions			0.610
			(1.747)
Constant	26.65***	14.33	−7.854**
	(8.255)	(14.91)	(3.323)
Fixed effects	Yes	Yes	No
Correlated random effects	No	No	Yes
Observations	455	397	397
R-squared	0.086	0.114	–
Number of countries	37	31	31

Robust standard errors in parentheses; ***$p<0.01$, **$p<0.05$, *$p<0.1$

Interpreting this outcome together with the results in Table 5.1, I argue that the sheer number of veto players does not have a significant impact on the increase of workdays lost per worker. This is quite surprising and exposes the limitations of models that highlight this variable as significant, especially in the context of middle and lower-middle income economies. Moreover, Model 4 in the final column further reveals that federalism dummy is significant at $p<0.01$ even in the presence of *Govfrac*, suggesting that partisan rivalries between multiple governments may play a more prominent role in industrial conflict duration outcomes. The size of this effect is similar to those reported in Tables 5.1 and 5.2.

Other controls included in the models exhibit consistency with the results reported in Tables 5.1 and 5.2, with a few exceptions. First, inflation rate turns out to be an even more significant predictor at $p<0.05$, though the magnitude of its effect on reducing conflict duration is still relatively small. Second, an economic crisis also reduces the duration of an industrial conflict between 4.2 and 4.6 workdays lost per worker. The presence of FDI, on the other hand, also has a conflict-prolonging effect

(1% increase leading to 0.72 days lost in Model 3) at $p<0.05$. In line with earlier observations, whether a given political system is presidential or parliamentary has no significant impact and neither majoritarian nor proportional representation system appears to have any significant relationship with the dependent variable.

These findings suggest that political fractionalization at the national level may not necessarily bar politicians from reconciling in the face of prolonged labor protests. This could be due to at least two reasons. First, veto players in national platforms may be more likely to work together toward the resolution of industrial disputes because they are able to communicate more frequently. Second, national level politicians may be more likely to have shared interests to keep FDI in country unless they are strongly opposed to foreign capital investment due to ideological commitments.

CONCLUSION

This chapter tested a series of hypotheses derived from the two case studies and existing debates on industrial conflict duration. The findings confirm that the duration of industrial conflict in developing areas is contingent on political factors beyond daily shopfloor interactions between the managers and employees. Most importantly, the territorial organization of political power in the developing world is a significant predictor of industrial conflict pathways. Specifically, there is a positive relationship between prolonged strikes and federal systems, suggesting that industrial conflicts taking place in a multi-government setting may be more difficult to resolve in a shorter time frame due to political disagreements between federal and local politicians. The results are robust under different models that include theoretically informed control variables. These findings also resonate with earlier research that finds a positive and significant association between labor mobilization and elite political competition (Robertson 2007). Overall, by revealing the role of a formerly underemphasized variable—the system of government—this study further complements the findings based on the small-N comparison by highlighting political institutions as *explanans* of labor mobilization.

Across much of the developing world including Turkey and Argentina, production has been increasingly reorganized around regional clusters after the 1990s. This was most prominently the case in the manufacturing industry, where incoming FDIs constituted nodes of localized production and suppliers were situated around a production belt immediately surrounding the factories. This had at least three prominent effects on worker mobilization patterns. First, the geographic distribution of organized labor was characterized by a concentration of union activity around regional production centers (Perulli 1993). Second, industrial conflicts erupting in these areas often had spillover effects, adding to the workdays lost in strikes, work stoppages and walkouts (Lee 2003). Third, and most significantly, industrial conflicts associated with the arrival of FDIs increasingly became more local in character, bargaining took place increasingly at the firm or enterprise level, and centered around demands associated with reorganization of production (such as contestation over shopfloor rotations, working hours and rotating shifts) (Rutherford and Gertler 2002).

In multi-level government settings, such as in Argentina, prolonged industrial disputes turn into bargaining chips especially at times of center-periphery rivalries and elite-level conflicts between the federal and local politicians. As we have seen in the case of Córdoba, local governors may contribute to the prolongation of labor unrest by inaction, and thereby use these incidents either to resist federal demands that run against their political interest or push forward local agendas that are not supported by the center.

Second, the study of how multi-level political competition influences strike duration would benefit greatly from a systematic identification of the issue areas that intensify political rivalries among the elites. As the Turkish and Argentine cases reveal, national governments in developing economies serve as midwives of FDIs and facilitate the arrival of foreign investors. These politicians are very sensitive to unresolved labor disputes and seek to end industrial conflicts in order to avoid capital flight. In doing so, they have to work with local politicians to move swiftly. However, especially in federal settings, political disputes over sensitive issue areas such as fiscal reform, decentralization and electoral competition offer workers new opportunities to voice their demands persistently. In Argentina, labor mobilization around changing work conditions at a multinational automobile producer lingered for months (Atzeni 2009) as the local and federal government fought over other political priorities including terms of fiscal and administrative decentralization and the federal education bill

(Falleti 2010). In this particular case, federal and local politicians from rival parties were distracted by partisan concerns, and mobilized workers found an opportunity to resist even more fiercely to have their demands fulfilled.

Third, it should be stressed that the generalizability of these findings is limited to middle and lower-middle income countries. Advanced industrialized countries present a more complex picture: while some suggest that federal systems like the USA and Canada score exceptionally high on workdays lost to industrial conflict (Gunderson and Melino 1990), others find that Germany is characterized by shorter and lesser frequency of strikes (Dribbusch 2007). While the German anomaly may be explained by a highly institutionalized collective bargaining and vocational education system in a corporatist setting, extending these arguments to apply to advanced industrialized countries requires further tests.

Further results from qualitative studies on automobile sector development in other federal settings such as Mexico offer evidence on the broader implications of political institutions on development.[15] For example, Carrillo (2004) notes that multinational companies based in Ciudad Juarez in the Chihuahua province of Mexico-were loosely connected to the local politicians (Carrillo 2004, 150). As a result, though the producers invested in technological and industrial upgrading on their own account, this did not guarantee success for a greater number of automobile supplier firms to compete effectively in international export markets (Carrillo 2004, 149).[16] Martin's (2006) study on automobile industry in Mexico echoes these findings. Across the auto-parts producers in maquiladoras, working conditions have gradually deteriorated and employees have been subject to rising social costs, let alone any systematic investment in skills (Kopinak 2005; Martin 2006).

To be sure, the significance of political institutions in the transformation of Mexican automobile industry from Fordism to post-Fordism is not limited to production in auto-parts producers based in maquiladoras only. In a study that focuses on the beginnings of this transformation during the 1980s, Carrillo (1995) compares three Ford plants based in different states in Mexico, and finds that the implementation of post-Fordist training modules and practices showed a notable variation across factories based in Hermosillo (Sonora), Cuautitlan (State of

Mexico), and San Lorenzo (Chihuahua). While the transition in Hermosillo was relatively smooth in the absence of a major political conflict during the 1980s/early 1990s, Ford workers in Cuautitlan opposed and resisted the implementation of flexible production techniques in a state that went through a major intra-partisan conflict during the late 1980s (Carrillo 1995; 95; Armbruster 1998). While the workers in Hermosillo plant were exposed to routinized trainings on a regular basis with the collaboration of the union, participation in similar trainings at the Cuautitlan factory was significantly low (Carrillo 1995, 95). Though Carrillo's comparison does not pay systematic attention to partisan dynamics in this analysis, others scholars such as Ward and Rodriguez (1999) reveal that State of Mexico province was a hotbed of partisan conflict and polarization during the late 1980s under Salinas, where the governor Mario Ramon Beteta from PRI was forced to resign on the grounds that he was not loyal to the party and the president (Ward and Rodriguez 1999, 676). Clearly, assessing the link between transition to post-Fordism, labor mobilization patterns and partisan conflict across subnational political units in Mexico requires a more systematic comparison with an in-depth analysis of multiple cases, however, these outcomes in a federal country offers further substantiation in support of the key finding of this study.

The quantitative results also introduce areas of further research to unpack the precise mechanism that undergirds these relationship patterns. The comparative findings from the Turkish and Argentine cases reveal that the presence or absence of a vocational education system that serves as an effective transmission belt for communicating business expectations to future blue-collars is one influential strategy to contain labor mobilization. Future research needs to focus on the role of vocational education in developing countries, going beyond assessing the number of technical students and the number of students involved in these institutions. An important aspect that begs closer inquiry is a cross-national, comparative curricular analysis: the content of what these young minds are exposed to in their early training is an important predictor of their behavior as professional employees (Apaydin 2017).

Though a relatively faster elimination of conflict is likely to consolidate industrial peace, this does not unconditionally generate employee empowerment. Indeed, shopfloor rearrangements and innovations on the management front generate additional barriers to the diffusion of solidarity among the workers especially when protests are cut short (Atzeni 2009). One consequence is a decline in active participation in the union (Nichols and Sugur 2004). At times of conflict, workers rarely seek help from the union, abandon collective action platforms and prefer to negotiate directly with their supervisors. This may have distinct implications on the political participation patterns of unionized workers, and eventually lead to distinct patterns of unionism, political incorporation of labor and development outcomes (Cebolla-Boado and Ortiz 2014).

APPENDIX

Below is the table summarizing descriptive statistics for the dataset used in the analysis (Table 5.4).

Table 5.4   Descriptive statistics

	N	Mean	SD	Min	Max
Strike duration (t−1)	547	17.351	28.16	0.0027	205.779
Federal dummy	571	0.249	0.433	0	1
POLCON V	568	0.473	0.272	0	1
Govfrac	571	0.248	0.289	0	0.893
LA dummy	571	0.392	0.489	0	1
Frequency of strikes (t−1)	546	6.671	23.58	0.0111	500
Unemployment (t−1)	540	9.853	6.129	0.900	31.50
Inflation (t−1)	546	62.36	433.0	−1.167	7482
Crisis dummy	546	0.449	0.498	0	1
FDI/GDP	564	0.0266	0.0336	−0.198	0.398
Parliamentary dummy	501	0.345	0.476	0	1
Imports %	564	39.38	22.51	6.962	152.8
Majoritarian	543	0.593	0.492	0	1
PR	541	0.701	0.458	0	1
ILO conventions	571	3.478	1.487	0	7

NOTES

1. According to existing approaches, strike duration is classified as long if the median duration is longer than 20 days. Strikes with an average duration of five days or less are classified as short (Baah and Reilly 2009, 461–462).
2. A revolutionary episode is "a period of rupture within an established political order that involves a mass siege of an established government by its own population with the aims of displacing the incumbent regime and substantially altering the political or social order, irrespective of whether oppositions actually succeed in displacing incumbent regimes" (Beissinger 2014, 10–11).
3. These countries are Argentina, Belarus, Brazil, Botswana, Chile, Costa Rica, Algeria, Ecuador, Egypt, Guyana, Hungary, Indonesia, India, Jamaica, Sri Lanka, Morocco, Mexico, Mauritius, Malaysia, Namibia, Nigeria, Nicaragua, Pakistan, Panama, Peru, Philippines, Papua New Guinea, Romania, El Salvador, Suriname, Swaziland, Thailand, Tunisia, Turkey, Ukraine, South Africa, Zambia.
4. For an overview of how **POLCON V** is calculated, see the codebook available for download at http://www-management.wharton.upenn.edu/henisz/.
5. **Unemployment rate** is an ILO estimate and refers to the percentage of unemployed who are available and actively seeking for employment within the total labor force. The data is taken from the World Bank and covers the period between 1990 and 2012.
6. **Inflation** is measured as the yearly percentage increase in the consumer price index (calculated as the annual percentage change in the cost to the average consumer of acquiring a basket of goods and services in a given year). The data is taken from the World Bank and covers the period between 1990 and 2012.
7. **Crisis Dummy**: This is coded as 1 if the country-year is experiencing a major economic crisis and 0 if otherwise. It is calculated based on information included in the Reinhardt and Rogoff (2011) database on economic crises and World Bank/IMF indicators on banking crises (Laeven and Valencia 2012).
8. **Share of FDI as a percentage of GDP** is calculated by dividing total flow of FDI investments in USD by GDP in USD for a given country/year. The data is taken from the World Bank and covers the period between 1990 and 2012.
9. **GDP/Capita** is calculated by dividing gross domestic product by the mid-year population, and is in current USD. The data is taken from the World Bank and covers the period between 1990 and 2012.
10. **Political System:** Countries are coded as presidential (0) or parliamentary (1) for a given year based on information in Beck et al.'s (2001) database on political institutions at the World Bank.

11. **Electoral System**: The data on whether electoral rules in a given country/ year follow majoritarian and/or proportional representation are taken from Beck et al.'s (2001) database on political institutions at the World Bank.
12. **ILO Conventions:** In order to control for institutional framework that regulates labor rights, I coded the number of relevant ILO conventions that have been ratified and in force in a given year for each country based on the information available on ILO NATLEX database. A greater commitment to protecting labor rights may prolong worker protests and increase the average number of workdays lost per worker.
13. **Latin America Dummy**: I also control for regional effects by including a Latin America dummy in the sample, given the longer history of contentious labor mobilization and concentration of federal systems in South America.
14. On the optimum number of counts when modeling using negative binomial regression models, see Hilbe 2007.
15. For a discussion of multiple varieties of populist legacies in Mexico in comparative perspective, see Gibson 1997; Knight 1998; Murillo 2001; Snyder 2001. For an overview of populism and populist legacies in Brazil see French 1989; Perruci and Sanderson 1989; Panizza 2000.
16. In terms of training, technicians, engineers, and managers in auto-parts producers were the ones who were exposed to new techniques, and the blue-collars were not embedded in a network of coordinated vocational education schemes (Carrillo 2004, 150).

BIBLIOGRAPHY

Acemoglu, D., and J. Robinson. 2013. *Why Nations Fail?* New York: Crown Business.

Ahlquist, J., and A. Prakash. 2008. The Influence of Foreign Direct Investment on Contracting Confidence in Developing Countries. *Regulation & Governance* 2 (3): 316–339.

Aleman, J. 2009. The Politics of Tripartite Cooperation in New Democracies: A Multi-level Analysis. *International Political Science Review* 30 (2): 141–162.

Anner, Mark. 2011. *Solidarity Transformed: Labor Responses to Globalization and Crisis in Latin America*. Ithaca: ILR Press, an Imprint of Cornell University Press.

Apaydin, F. 2017. Uneasy Discipline: Training Workers After Fordism in Turkey and Argentina. *Studies in Political Economy* 98 (2): 151–174.

Armbruster, R. 1998. Cross-Border Labor Organizing in Garment and Automobile Industries: The Phillips van Heusen and Ford Cuautitlan Cases. *Journal of World Systems Research* 4: 20–51.

Ashenfelter, O., and G. Johnson. 1969. Bargaining Theory, Trade Unions and Industrial Strike Activity. *The American Economic Review* 59 (1): 35–49.

Atzeni, M. 2009. Searching for Injustice and Finding Solidarity? A Contribution to the Mobilisation Theory Debate. *Industrial Relations Journal* 40: 5–16.

Baah, A.Y., and B. Reilly. 2009. An Empirical Analysis of Strike Durations in Ghana from 1980 to 2004. *Labour* 23 (3): 459–479.

Bafumi, J., and A. Gelman. 2006. *Fitting Multi-Level Models When Predictors and Group Effects Correlate*. Paper Presented at the 2006 Midwest Political Science Association Meeting, Chicago.

Beck, N., and J. Katz. 1996. Nuisance vs. Substance: Specifying and Estimating Time-Series Cross Section Models. *Political Analysis* 6 (1): 1–36.

———. 2011. Modeling Dynamics in Time Series Cross-Section Political Economy Data. *Annual Review of Political Science* 14: 331–352.

Beck, T., G. Clarke, A. Groff, P. Keefer, and P. Walsh. 2001. New Tools in Comparative Political Economy: The Database of Political Institutions. *World Bank Economic Review* 15 (1): 165–176.

Beissinger, M.R. 2014. *The Changing Face of Revolution, 1900–2012*. Paper Presented at the Comparative Workshop on Mass Protests, London School of Economics, June 13–14.

Bell, A., and K. Jones. 2015. Explaining Fixed Effects: Random Effects Modeling of Times Series Cross Sectional and Panel Data. *Political Science Research and Methods* 3 (1): 133–153.

Bellin, E. 2013. Drivers of Democracy: Lessons from Tunisia. *Brandeis University Crown Center for Middle East Studies*, Middle East Brief, No. 75.

Berman, S. 2007. Lessons from Europe. *Journal of Democracy* 18 (January): 28–41.

Berman, C. 2015. *The Durability of Revolutionary Protest Coalitions? Bridging Revolutionary Mobilization and Post-Revolutionary Politics*. Paper presented at Middle East Studies Association Meeting, Boulder.

Biglaiser, G., and J. Staats. 2010. Do Political Institutions Affect Foreign Direct Investment? A Survey of U.S. Corporations in Latin America. *Political Research Quarterly* 63 (3): 508–522.

Birchfield, V., and M. Crepaz. 1998. The Impact of Constitutional Structures and Collective and Competitive Veto Points on Income Inequality in Industrialized Democracies. *European Journal of Political Research* 34: 175–200.

Blanton, R., and S. Blanton. 2012. Labor Rights and Foreign Direct Investment: Is There a Race to the Bottom? *International Interactions* 38 (3): 267–294.

Breusch, T., M.B. Ward, H.T.M. Nguyen, and T. Kompas. 2011. FEVD: Just IV or Just Mistaken? *Political Analysis* 19 (2): 165–169.

Brym, R., L.B. Bauer, and M. McIvor. 2013. Is Industrial Unrest Reviving in Canada? Strike Duration in the Early Twenty-First Century. *Canadian Review of Sociology/Revue canadienne de sociologie* 50 (2): 227–238.

Cai, H., and D. Treisman. 2004. State Corroding Federalism. *Journal of Public Economics* 88: 819–843.

Campolieti, M., R. Hebdon, and D. Hyatt. 2005. Strike Incidence and Strike Duration: Some New Evidence from Ontario. *ILR Review* 58 (4): 610–630.

Card, D. 1990. Strikes and Wages: A Test of an Asymmetric Information Model. *The Quarterly Journal of Economics* 105 (3): 625–659.

Carrillo, J. 1995. Flexible Production in the Auto Sector: Industrial Reorganization at Ford Mexico. *World Development* 23 (1): 87–101.

———. 2004. Transnational Strategies and Regional Development: The Case of GM and Delphi in Mexico. *Industry & Innovation* 11: 127–153.

Cebolla-Boado, H., and L. Ortiz. 2014. Extra-Representational Types of Political Participation and Models of Trade Unionism: ACross-Country Comparison. *Socio-Economic Review* 12: 747–778.

Cohen, Youssef. 1989. *The Manipulation of Consent: The State and Working-Class Consciousness in Brazil*. Pittsburgh: University of Pittsburgh Press.

Collier, R.B. 1999. *Paths Toward Democracy*. New York: Cambridge University Press.

Collier, R.B., and D. Collier. 1991. *Shaping the Political Arena*. Notre Dame: University of Notre Dame Press.

Connel, C., and S. Cohn. 1995. Learning from Other People's Actions: Environmental Variations and Diffusion in French Coal Mining Strikes. *American Journal of Sociology* 101: 366–403.

Cook, Maria Lorena. 1998. Toward Flexible Industrial Relations? Neo-Liberalism, Democracy, and Labor Reform in Latin America. *Industrial Relations: A Journal of Economy and Society* 37 (3): 311–336.

Crepaz, M.M.L. 1996. Consensus vs. Majoritarian Democracy: Political Institutions and Their Impact on Macroeconomic Performance and Industrial Disputes. *Comparative Political Studies* 29: 4–26.

Crowley, S. 2004. Explaining Labor Weakness in Post-Communist Europe: Historical Legacies and Comparative Perspective. *East European Politics & Societies* 18 (3): 394–429.

Dinardo, J., and K.F. Hallock. 2002. When Unions "Mattered": The Impact of Strikes on Financial Markets, 1925–1937. *ILR Review* 55 (2): 219–233.

Dribbusch, H. 2007. Industrial Action in a Low-Strike Country: Strikes in Germany 1968–2005. In *Strikes Around the World*, ed. S. van der Velden, H. Dribbusch, D. Lyddon, and K. Vandaele, 1968–2005. Amsterdam: Aksant Publishers.

Etchemendy, S. 2011. *Models of Economic Liberalization: Business, Workers, and Compensation in Latin America, Spain and Portugal*. New York: Cambridge University Press.

Falleti, T.G. 2010. *Decentralization and Subnational Politics in Latin America*. New York: Cambridge University Press.

Flynn, F.J. 2000. No News Is Good News: The Relationship Between Media Attention and Strike Duration. *Industrial Relations: A Journal of Economy and Society* 39 (1): 139–160.

French, J.D. 1989. Industrial Workers and the Birth of the Populist Republic in Brazil, 1945–1946. *Latin American Perspectives* 16: 5–27.

Gehlbach, S., and E. Malesky. 2010. The Contribution of Veto-players to Economic Reform. *Journal of Politics* 72 (4): 957–975.

Gibson, E.L. 1997. The Populist Road to Market Reform: Policy and Electoral Coalitions in Mexico and Argentina. *World Politics* 49: 339–370.

Greene, W. 2011. Fixed Effects Vector Decomposition: A Magical Solution to the Problem of Time-Invariant Variables in Fixed Effects Models? *Political Analysis* 19 (2): 135–146.

Gunderson, M., and A. Melino. 1990. The Effects of Public Policy on Strike Duration. *Journal of Labor Economics* 8 (3): 295–316.

Hall, P.A., and D. Soskice. 2001. *Varieties of Capitalism: The Institutional Foundations of Comparative Advantage*. Oxford: Oxford University Press.

Harrison, A., and M. Stewart. 1989. Cyclical Fluctuations in Strike Durations. *American Economic Review* 79 (4): 827–841.

Hausman, J., B.H. Hall, and Z. Griliches. 1984. Econometric Models for Count Data with an Application to the Patents-R&D Relationship. *Econometrica* 52 (4): 909–938.

Henisz, W. 2000. The Institutional Environment for Economic Growth. *Economics and Politics* 12 (1): 1–31.

Hilbe, J.M. 2007. *Negative Binomial Regression*. New York: Cambridge University Press.

Hurst, W. 2004. Understanding Contentious Collective Action by Chinese Laid-Off Workers: The Importance of Regional Political Economy. *Studies in Comparative International Development* 39: 94–120.

Jensen, N. 2003. Democratic Governance and Multinational Corporations: Political Regimes and Inflows of Foreign Direct Investment. *International Organization* 57 (3): 587–616.

Jensen, N., and F. McGillivray. 2005. Federal Institutions and Multinational Investors: Federalism, Government Credibility, and Foreign Direct Investment. *International Interactions* 31 (4): 303–325.

Kennan, J. 1980. Pareto Optimality and the Economics of Strike Duration. *Journal of Labor Research* 1 (1): 77–94.

Kennan, J., and R. Wilson. 1989. Strategic Bargaining Models and Interpretation of Strike Data. *Journal of Applied Econometrics* 4 (S1): S87–S130.

Kim, W., and J. Gandhi. 2010. Coopting Workers Under Dictatorship. *The Journal of Politics* 72 (03): 646–658.

Knight, A. 1998. Populism and Neopopulism in Latin America, Especially Mexico. *Journal of Latin American Studies* 30: 223–248.

Kopinak, K., ed. 2005. *The Social Costs of Industrial Growth in Northern Mexico.* Boulder: Lynne Reiner.

Krueger, A., and A. Mas. 2004. Strikes, Scabs, and Tread Separations: Labor Strife and the Production of Defective Bridgestone/Firestone Tires. *Journal of Political Economy* 112: 253–289.

Kus, B., and I. Ozel. 2010. United We Restrain, Divided We Rule: Neoliberal Reforms and Labor Unions in Turkey and Mexico.*European Journal of Turkish Studies. Social Sciences on Contemporary Turkey* 11,October 21. http://ejts. revues.org/4291.

Laeven, L., and F. Valencia. 2012. *Systemic Banking Crises: A New Database.* IMF Working Paper WP/08/224.

Lee, Y. 2003. Lean Production Systems, Labor Unions, and Greenfield Locations of the Korean New Auto Assembly Plants and Their Suppliers. *Economic Geography* 79 (3): 321–339.

Lee, H., G. Biglaiser, and J. Staats. 2014. The Effects of Political Risk on Different Entry Modes of Foreign Direct Investment. *International Interactions* 40 (5): 683–710.

Li, Q., and A. Resnick. 2003. Reversal of Fortunes: Democracy, Property Rights and Foreign Direct Investment Inflows in Developing Countries. *International Organization* 57 (1): 175–211.

Martin, S.B. 2006. *Global Sourcing Dynamics, Inequality, and 'Decent Work' in Auto Parts: Mexico Through the Brazilian Looking Glass,* Working Paper Series, No. 2006–08, Graduate Program in International Affairs. NYC: The New School.

McHugh, R. 1991. Productivity Effects of Strikes in Struck and Nonstruck Industries. *Industrial and Labor Relations Review* 44 (4): 722–732.

Murillo, M.V.. 2001. *Labor Unions, Partisan Coalitions, and Market Reforms in Latin America.* Cambridge: Cambridge University Press.

Murillo, M.V., and L. Ronconi. 2004. Teachers' Strikes in Argentina: Partisan Alignments and Public-Sector Labor Relations. *Studies in Comparative International Development* 39 (1): 77–98.

Nichols, T., and N. Sugur. 2004. *Global Management, Local Labor: Turkish Workers and Modern Industry.* Basingstoke: Palgrave Macmillan.

Ondrich, J.I., and J.F. Schnell. 1993. Strike Duration and the Degree of Disagreement. *Industrial Relations: A Journal of Economy and Society* 32 (3): 412–431.

Ortiz, L. 1999. Unions' Responses to Teamwork: Differences at National and Workplace Levels. *European Journal of Industrial Relations* 5 (1): 49–69.

Owoye, O. 1992. Incomes Policies, Inflation and Strikes in Nigeria, 1950–1985: An Empirical Investigation. *Applied Economics* 24 (6): 587–592.

Panizza, F. 2000. Neopopulism and Its Limits in Collor's Brazil. *Bulletin of Latin American Research.* 19: 177–192.

Papke, L.E., and J.M. Wooldridge. 2008. Panel Data Methods for Fractional Response Variables with an Application to Test Pass Rates. *Journal of Econometrics* 145 (1–2): 121–133.

Perruci, G., and S.E. Sanderson. 1989. Presidential Succession, Economic Crisis and Populist Resurgence in Brazil. *Studies in Comparative International Development* 24: 30–50.

Perulli, P. 1993. Towards a Regionalization of Industrial Relations. *International Journal of Urban And Regional Research* 17 (1): 98–113.

Pinto, P.M., and S.M. Pinto. 2008. The Politics of Investment Partisanship and the Sectoral Allocation of Foreign Direct Investment. *Economics and Politics* 20: 216–254.

Plümper, T., and V.E. Troeger. 2007. Efficient Estimation of Time-Invariant and Rarely Changing Variables in Finite Sample Panel Analyses with Unit Fixed Effects. *Political Analysis* 15 (2): 124–139.

———. 2011. Fixed-Effects Vector Decomposition: Properties, Reliability, and Instruments. *Political Analysis* 19 (2): 147–164.

Przeworski, A., and J. Sprague. 1986. *Paper Stones: A History of Electoral Socialism*. Chicago: University of Chicago Press.

Reder, M.W., and G.R. Neumann. 1980. Conflict and Contract: The Case of Strikes. *Journal of Political Economy* 88 (5): 867–886.

Reinhardt, C., and K. Rogoff. 2011. From Financial Crash to Debt Crisis. *American Economic Review* 101 (5): 1676–1706.

Robertson, G.B. 2007. Strikes and Labor Organization in Hybrid Regimes. *American Political Science Review* 101 (4): 781–798.

Robertson, G.B., and E. Teitelbaum. 2011. Foreign Direct Investment, Regime Type, and Labor Protest in Developing Countries. *American Journal of Political Science* 55 (3): 665–677.

Rohlfing, I. 2008. What You See and What You Get: Pitfalls and Principles of Nested Analysis in Comparative Research. *Comparative Political Studies* 41 (11): 1492–1514.

Rubin, B.A., and B.T. Smith. 1991. Strike Durations in the United States. *Sociological Quarterly* 32 (1): 85–101.

Rueschemeyer, D., E. Huber Stephens, and J. Stephens. 1992. *Capitalist Development and Democracy*. Chicago: University of Chicago Press.

Rutherford, T.D., and M.S. Gertler. 2002. Labour in 'Lean' Times: Geography, Scale and the National Trajectories of Workplace Change. *Transactions of the Institute of British Geographers* 27: 195–212.

Schneider, B.R. 2013. *Hierarchical Capitalism in Latin America: Business, Labor, and the Challenges of Equitable Development*. New York: Cambridge University Press.

Schneider, B.R., and S. Karcher. 2010. Complementarities and Continuities in the Political Economy of Labor Markets in Latin America. *Socio-Economic Review* 8 (4): 623–651.

Schrank, A. 2011. Co-producing Workplace Transformation: The Dominican Republic in Comparative Perspective. *Socio-Economic Review* 9: 419–445.

Shorter, E., and C. Tilly. 1974. *Strikes in France*. Cambridge: Cambridge University Press.

Silver, B. 2003. *Forces of Labor*. New York: Cambridge University Press.

Snyder, R. 2001. *Politics After Neoliberalism*. Cambridge: Cambridge University Press.

Streeck, W., and K. Thelen. 2005. *Beyond Continuity: Institutional Change in Advanced Political Economies*. Oxford: Oxford University Press.

Teitelbaum, E. 2007. In the Grip of a Green Giant: How the Rural Sector Tamed Organized Labor in India. *Comparative Political Studies* 40 (6): 638–664.

Thelen, K. 2012. Varieties of Capitalism: Trajectories of Liberalization and the New Politics of Social Solidarity. *Annual Review of Political Science*. 15: 137–159.

Tilly, C. 2004. *Contention and Democracy in Europe, 1650–2000*. New York: Cambridge University Press.

Tsebelis, G. 1995. Decision Making in Political Systems: Veto Players in Presidentialism, Parliamentarism, Multicameralism and Multipartyism. *British Journal of Political Science* 25 (03): 289–325.

———. 2002. *Veto Players: How Political Institutions Work*. Princeton: Princeton University Press.

Tuman, J.P. 1994. Organized Labor Under Military Rule: The Nigerian Labor Movement, 1985–1992. *Studies in Comparative International Development* 29 (3): 26–44.

Vernby, K. 2007. Strikes Are More Common in Countries with Majoritarian Electoral Systems. *Public Choice* 132: 65–84.

Ward, P.M., and V.I. Rodriguez. 1999. New-Federalism, Intra-Governmental Relations and Co-governance in Mexico. *Journal of Latin American Studies* 31: 673–710.

Wibbels, E. 2000. Federalism and the Politics of Macroeconomic Policy and Performance. *American Journal of Political Science* 44 (4): 687–702.

Winship, C., and R.D. Mare. 1992. Models for Sample Selection Bias. *Annual Review of Sociology* 18: 327–350.

Wooldridge, J. 2010. *Correlated Random Effects Models with Unbalanced Panels*, Working Paper.

———. 2013. *Correlated Random Effects Models with Unbalanced Panels*. Lecture Notes. IZA Summer School in Labor Economics. May 13–19.

CHAPTER 6

Conclusion: Technological Change, Institutions and Labor in Developing Contexts

The qualitative findings on post-Fordist transformations in Bursa, Turkey and Córdoba, Argentina and the quantitative findings based on a broader set of cases both illustrate that political institutions are influential in shaping labor responses to novel forms of surplus extraction in developing contexts. As we have seen, the arrival of new technologies in Turkey and Argentina introduced further challenges to surplus extraction and capital accumulation in the manufacturing sector. During the 1990s, FIAT's Bursa and Córdoba plants—both embedded in a densely connected local network of auto-parts providers—introduced the same guidelines and procedures issued by the company headquarters in Italy. In both cases, workers were required to complete a greater number of tasks in lesser time, sustain top-level performance when rotated across different units, collaborate with their peers frequently on cost-cutting and quality improvement, be flexible in the face of production reorganization and refrain from demanding pay-rise in return for their extra efforts. Despite these shared expectations on the corporate end in Bursa and Córdoba, the duration of worker resistance in the face of mounting tasks and diminishing wages showed notable variation: FIAT's Córdoba workers in Argentina opposed the imposed changes for a much longer period between 1996 and 1997, demonstrated little interest in quality improvement workshops, contested the proposal schemes and questioned rotation across different workstations. On the other hand, FIAT management in Bursa did not experience a major problem with

185
F. Apaydin, *Technology, Institutions and Labor*, International Political Economy Series, https://doi.org/10.1007/978-3-319-77104-5_6

getting the workers on board: there, a major industrial conflict triggered by the transformation of production in 1998 surprisingly cooled off in a relatively shorter period of time, and workers were much faster in adapting to novel practices. During this process, the reorganization of production driven by the principle of flexibility and intellectual participation by the workers demanded a more routinized and continuous vocational training scheme that extended beyond the factory, requiring coordination between vocational schools, training centers and the unions.

Very importantly, the arrival of new production technologies brought politics to the forefront in these areas. Across Bursa and Córdoba, new production systems created not only new incentives but also generated significant challenges that put politicians to a test, as each struggled to stay and excel in their career by turning limitations into new opportunities. While Córdoba governors in federal Argentina were motivated by electoral interests, sought to retain their incumbent status and therefore prioritized their partisan commitments against the federal government's policy imposition, the appointed governors in unitary Turkey worked toward fulfilling the expectations of their superiors in Ankara to secure promotion (Apaydin 2012).

As we have seen, labor unrest triggered by new industrial practices exhibited notable discrepancies ranging from outright rejection to enthusiastic approval of these new techniques even across different factories of the same corporation located in these two countries. This is because the reorganization of production along lean technologies generates ground-shaking effects by transforming surplus extraction, capital accumulation and reinvestment, and worker response to these upheavals is contingent on the political context in which they operate. As multinational automobile companies introduce new techniques on the shopfloor, local producers that supply goods and services to the MNCs are increasingly compelled to adopt similar strategies. This is because lean production not only calls for the reorganization of shopfloor along the principles of just-in-time production and total quality control, but also the development of new relations with the suppliers (Humphrey 1995: 150).

Thus, when new methods inspired by Toyotism hit the Turkish shores, politicians in Ankara government under the rule of center-right wing governments were highly sensitive to firm demands in favor of creating a new worker profile. To that end, politicians and their appointed bureaucrats vowed to contain and quickly eliminate any labor unrest. Such a level of political commitment to meet business demands was further bolstered in the absence of a multi-level political competition under a unitary system.

A unitary system of government formally eliminates administrative, fiscal and political autonomy of provincial units. In most circumstances, provincial governors are not elected but appointed, have no fiscal autonomy to raise taxes and do not work with an elected local legislature. Political competition for the legislative and executive positions exclusively occurs at the national level. Thus, local governors hold limited or no powers to influence legislation and the implementation of labor law.

This institutional set-up minimizes the political rivalries between the central and local government because appointed governors in unitary systems—like those in Bursa—are often in the status of career bureaucrats and formally accountable to the central government.[1] Though governors may have political aspirations, the realization of their political goals depends on the extent to which they demonstrate a satisfactory performance to their superiors. As evident in the case of Bursa, appointed governors—whose careers are tied to decisions made in the Ministry of the Interior—rarely challenged the expectations of the government in Ankara. While some suggest that the picture may become more complex when a coalition government is at power, this has not been the case in Bursa.[2]

On the other hand, in federal Argentina, technological change in production systems aggrandized partisan preferences in the process of setting up of economic reform coalitions. There, local politicians were far from passively yielding to the demands of multinational producers who were in alliance with their federal counterparts. Rather, they were more sensitive to political opportunities and negotiated accordingly. Importantly, a multi-government setting increased the likelihood of political conflicts between the provincial units and the center. This was especially visible at a time when contested economic liberalization reforms were implemented under President Carlos Menem—a politician known for his wholehearted commitment to the neoliberal principles of the Washington Consensus. Most of the reforms pushed forward by the Menem government met staunch resistance from the provincial governments, including those in Córdoba. In this tense environment, suppressing and eliminating labor opposition and mobilizing resources to upgrade vocational programs were not immediate priorities. While politicians in Bursa mobilized resources to overhaul the vocational education and training programs, their counterparts in Córdoba were compelled to focus on other pressing agendas that posed immediate threats to their political careers. Under these circumstances, FIAT workers found an opportunity to repeatedly voice their demands.

In that sense, federalism empowered societal groups in provincial units to contest, negotiate and/or oppose policy proposals of the federal government. Unlike their appointed counterparts in unitary systems, provincial governors rarely act as mere transmission belts for policies formulated at the center. With the advent of a new production regime, partisan identities in federal systems gained salience at the subnational level, in part because policy proposals to undertake economic reforms were highly polarizing. In settings where bi-partisan rivalry dominated the scene, (e.g. Córdoba), partisan polarization created within party cracks, and aggravated competition between different political wings of the same party, pushing these groups to seek alliances with competing business organizations and labor unions.[3]

Relatedly, these findings also overlap with studies that highlight political dynamics of adapting to new growth-oriented approaches (Sellers 2002). Especially in automobile regions that produce for export markets (most notably, affordable cars for middle and lower-middle income group customers), the consolidation of these adjustments calls for establishing stronger partnerships to keep up with customer-oriented production, specialization and enhancing product variety (Weiss 1995).

Additionally, the paired analysis of Bursa and Córdoba around a single MNC, FIAT, reveals that the local political context in which factories of MNCs are based plays a notable role on the surplus extraction and capital accumulation patterns across these production centers. Comparative evidence from the two FIAT factories further show the limitations of explanations that highlight individual, firm or union interests as key explanatory variables behind variation in post-Fordist transitions. Even though the management of both factories strictly adhered to the new guidelines imposed by the central headquarters in Italy (e.g. as a part of the FIAT 178 project), the response of workers to these schemes have been notably different in federal and unitary systems.

Going beyond labor responses, a glance at capitalist development trajectories in Latin America and the Middle East reveals that there is significant subnational variation in industrial development outcomes, especially in federal systems (Richards and Waterbury 1996; Henry and Springborg 2001; Acosta and Gasparini 2007; Gezici and Hewings 2007; Vos and Ocampo 2009). In particular, surplus extraction and capital accumulation patterns also differ across local political units, competitiveness of local firms varies, and industrial development policy shows significant divergence across industrial zones. In Argentina, industrial production is largely concentrated across provinces in the middle-belt, but skill formation policies across the automobile regions (e.g. Córdoba) differ quite substantially from its counterparts elsewhere despite the arguably homogenizing pressures of globalization introduced by multinational investors.

As discussed earlier, existing analytical frameworks (Kang 2002; Royo 2008; Schneider 2009) that attempt to conceptualize capitalist development beyond advanced industrialized countries remain silent in the face of local differences in industrial development across the Global South. Most of these studies take national economies as the key unit of analysis without problematizing subnational variation in industrial development, and conceptualize new varieties of capitalism based on a comparison of macro-level political and economic institutions. As such, they run the risk of missing the nuances, and possibly distort the validity of their claims with concept stretching.[4] In developing settings, going beyond national varieties of capitalism approach is a crucial first step because territorial organization of political power and institutions matter in economic policy implementation and capital accumulation.

The findings of this book raise a number of important follow-up questions. First, how well does the argument travel to other economic sectors? Does the arrival of new technologies unfold similarly across the manufacturing sector beyond automobiles? If not, how should we account for this? Second, how do post-Fordist transitions affect surplus extraction and capital accumulation practices in the informal sector? Developing countries like Turkey and Argentina are included among economies with increasing number of workers with no formal contract. How do political institutions shape the responses of informal labor in face of rapidly changing production technologies? The rest of this chapter discusses these questions to situate the findings in a broader perspective.

Skill Formation and Labor Response Beyond Automobiles

As discussed in Chap. 2, automobile production is technology-intense, creates new jobs for first and second tier parts producers beyond the main plant, and the post-Fordist techniques require an effective combination of manual and intellectual labor across a flexible labor force. However, the use of these techniques is not limited to automobile production only: within the past few decades, disruptive technological advances spread to other

industries, and company managers switched to using new versions of quality improvement methods, exposing the workforce to routinized trainings
on the shopfloor. For many of these companies, the formation of a flexible,
competitive and committed worker-base has become an essential priority,
especially for those who produce goods and services for export markets.
Therefore, across many industrial zones, managers needed support from
local administrators in order to craft a vocational training system that would
sustain these goals in the long run, and discipline the workers.

One of the sectors that followed a similar route is household appliances
industry. Just like automobiles, producing quality refrigerators, washing
machines, microwaves, TV and music sets, and similar electronic goods
along just-in-time principles requires a well-trained workforce. In many
ways, the reorganization of production at these factories mimics that in
automobile production.[5] Besides manual labor, the managers of these
firms strive to maximize intellectual participation of their employees
through proposal systems, quality improvement techniques (i.e. Kaizen,
5S, TQM), and they frequently rotate workers to develop flexible skills.

In Turkey, the production of household electronic goods is increasingly
concentrated in two provinces: Kocaeli (Gebze Organized Industrial
District) and Tekirdag (Cerkezkoy Organized Industrial District). Just like
in Bursa, the governors in both provinces have concentrated their efforts
on expanding the investment opportunities available to the domestic and
multinational producers and succeeded in attracting more FDI within the
last decade. During this process, vocational education council in both
provinces worked toward linking schools and apprentice centers with the
producers, and encouraged labor unions to undertake similar training
activities with an emphasis on post-Fordist skills. As a result, the number
of vocational schools expanded substantially, and the curricula of these
departments were upgraded in collaboration with firms that settled in
these provinces.[6] The substantive focus of these schools were upgraded to
create new tracks to meet the needs of companies, with an exclusive focus
on electrical processes and electronics studies. In both cases, a political
institutional setting under a unitary system facilitated the consolidation of
a routinized training scheme that exposed workers to multiple rounds of
behavioral training beyond the factory.

In sectors that rely much less on the intellectual participation of the
workers, such as textiles and apparel, the picture is quite different. Though
a flexible work environment is increasingly common in textile and apparel
production, the workers are often repeating the same task—whether it is

spinning, weaving, printing, cutting or assembling—which requires swift movement of the hands to specialize in the assigned task (Eraydin and Erendil 1999).[7] Even though producers occasionally seek trained workers for positions that require specialized knowledge and expertise, the majority of the employees in big factories are trained on the job, often with very low expectations on intellectual participation to improve the surplus extraction process. But more importantly, a sizeable portion of production in this sector—especially apparel—relies on subcontracting and putting out, which imposes further complications on coordinating flexible training modules.[8] This does not mean quality-related concerns are undervalued, however. Just like automobiles, apparel and textile production in Turkey is largely export-oriented, and producers are increasingly pressured to improve the quality standards of their goods in international markets. However, unlike multinational automobile companies with production sites in developing economies, multinational textile and apparel giants work more extensively with domestic partners and/or subcontractors, and usually no longer manufacture finished apparel goods on site themselves (Collins 2003; Cammett 2007).[9] Therefore they are less involved in negotiations on improving work conditions, and have very little input on skill formation-related debates.

In contrast to the automobile sector, politicians are less sensitive to training strategies in textile and apparel production and appear reluctant to take part in crafting policies specifically tailored to address the needs of these workers. This is because of several reasons. First, unlike automobiles, the life cycle of clothing apparel goods is very short in the market, with some firms launching between eight to twelve different lines per year (Cammett 2007: 41). This puts an enormous pressure on the workers to work around the clock, and leaves little time to think about production process improvement and routinized workforce training. Second, though textile and apparel production occupies a sizeable portion of exports, its value added is relatively low in contrast to automobiles. Moreover, unlike the automobile sector, the majority of the employees in textiles are women, who are categorized as a vulnerable group in labor market especially in the developing economies (Benton 1990; Beneria and Roldan 1987; Pessar 1994). Because the wages are significantly lower due to gender bias, producers do not feel compelled to pursue other means to keep these workers under control: low wages, absence of benefit schemes and permanent job insecurity are the primary mechanisms for avoiding disruptive labor mobilization. In short, not all manufacturing industries have a similar experience with post-Fordist techniques; and the resulting policies, practices and institutions vary depending on the organization of work and surplus extraction techniques used on the shopfloor.

Empirically, earlier studies on the textile industry in Istanbul offer some supporting evidence in favor of this observation. Since the beginning of 2000s, textile and apparel goods production skyrocketed in Istanbul, and occupied a leading place in the manufacturing sector (Ocakci 2001). During the 1990s, most of the newcomers—in particular, the small and medium sized enterprises—have often lacked political connections to advance their business plans with skilled workers (Riddle and Gillespie 2003) and therefore focused on recruiting employees that are less likely to mobilize, can work fast and perform intricate sewing and cutting work efficiently. Most of these enterprises largely employ women who hold no vocational diploma or certificate (Ocakci 2001) and are not unionized.[10]

Moreover, the older textile producers who have been organized under TGSD—the sectoral business organization of textile and apparel producers—were neglected by the politicians during the period of economic liberalization. Particularly after the 1994 economic crisis, when the leaders of this organization went from door to door in Istanbul and then in Ankara, DYP politicians were mostly aloof to the demands of notable producers in Istanbul.[11] Though these businessmen also faced a challenge of improving the quality of the goods, these efforts remained uncoordinated in the absence of government support, and a large portion of apparel production in Istanbul was carried by the growing informal sector, with poorly educated workers cutting and sewing pieces of fabric for long hours in sweatshops in return for low wages.

This brings us to the question of how post-Fordist transitions affect the informal sector. How are workers without any job security or access to benefits affected by major technological changes in the economy? To what extent do political institutions shape labor mobilization and collective action patterns of these workers, if any?

POLITICAL INSTITUTIONS, INFORMAL LABOR AND THE MANUFACTURING INDUSTRY

Informal sector refers to a complex web of economic activities and transactions where the state "neither provides protection nor receives a cut" (Centeno and Portes 2006), and therefore "the relationship between the informal economy and the state is, by definition, one of inevitable conflict" (Centeno and Portes 2006: 30).[12] Despite this inherent strife, developing economies have tolerated the informal sector because it largely acts as a protective cushion by creating alternative opportunities for the unemployed. In developing contexts like Turkey and Argentina, the informal sector has been growing at an unprecedented speed especially after privatizations and rising unemployment (Patroni 2004). This process gained further momentum after a switch to an export-oriented industrialization model. During this process, the coming of a neoliberal age has also altered the conditions of employment in the manufacturing sector across most informal producers (Castells and Portes 1989; Pérez Sáinz 1995; Itzigsohn 2000; Centeno and Portes 2006): working conditions have become more precarious (i.e. without job and workplace security, health and retirement benefits), with longer hours and lower pay in the absence of basic workplace health and security measures.[13] At the same time, manufacturing in the informal sector is highly unstandardized. In particular, informal microenterprises in developing areas are either engaged in subsistence production or deliver to low income consumers who do not share the same preference on product quality and sophistication (Itzigsohn 2000: 148–149).[14]

Unlike the formal sector, workers in the informal domain are largely unorganized and often lack resources to get together and voice their demands. However, the organizational capacity of these workers to mobilize is also contingent on the political institutional context in which they operate. Initial observations from Argentina reveal that informal industry workers are more likely to overcome barriers to collective action and resource limitations in a federal setting, especially when politicians see attractive opportunities through appealing to these groups. During the 2000s, this was the preferred route by President Nestor Kirchner and President Christina Fernandez de Kirchner: as the Peronist movement sought new ways to enhance its populist appeal in the aftermath of the 2000 economic crisis, informal labor organizations found new opportunities to voice their discontent, even though their mobilization did not give way to an effective political incorporation (Etchemendy and Collier 2007). On the other hand, the ability of similar movements to become politically visible was very limited in unitary Turkey and any attempt at collective action by these groups was quickly contained and/or suppressed.

As I have shown in previous chapters, when national politicians are committed to ensure the global competitiveness of selected industries, other producers who are not considered as strategically important get scant attention from the policy makers. Perhaps one implication of this exclusion is the sharply rising level of inequality. As the recent evidence from other countries in the Global South reveals, there is a positive correlation between the expansion of informal sector and the increasing rates of inequality (Rosser Jr. et al. 2000; Chong and Gradstein 2007) accompanied by spatial segregation in the form of mushrooming gated communities (Coy 2006), gentrification (Güzey 2009), and similar urban transformation projects. Likewise, in Córdoba, the expansion of informal sector in manufacturing industry during the 1990s coincided with fast-rising income inequality indicators (Rivero and Michel 2007; Valdes 2009).

THE TRADE-OFF: ECONOMIC DEVELOPMENT OR DEMOCRACY?

While worker consent to new business practices is likely to establish industrial peace and increase surplus extraction via enhanced productivity, this seemingly frictionless arrangement yields questionable results in terms of employee empowerment and sustainable worker consent. Recent research on worker response to post-Fordist rearrangements suggest that while these techniques can motivate employees, in the absence of political controls over the workers, shopfloor games are "difficult to master and offer few rewards for sustained participation" (Sallaz 2015). To be sure, workers resort to a variety of strategies to maximize their dignity in the workplace, and this includes means to avoid direct abuse, tactics for creating an individual space to exercise autonomy (Hodson 1996: 722) and individual strategies to develop friendly co-worker relationships (Hodson 1996: 724). Yet, increasing competition under post-Fordist rearrangements generates additional barriers to the diffusion of solidarity among the workers (Nichols et al. 2002a, b).

One consequence of this is a decline in organized forms of resistance (Nichols and Sugur 2004). At times of conflict, the immediate response of these workers is to use conflict-resolution techniques rather than seeking union assistance. Under these circumstances, workers are increasingly atomized under post-Fordist schemes and associate their survival with firm survival, especially at times of crisis. With labor solidarity gradually dissolving, unions lose their relevance and legitimacy in the eyes of rank-and-file workers (Lee and Guloglu 2014). This may widen existing rifts among the working class (Kaya 2008) and has further implications not only on future efforts to sustain worker consent, but also on rank-and-file participation in civil platforms to take collective action in democratizing settings.

The capacity of labor unions to mobilize and voice their demands in the Global South have further implications on development and democratic consolidation (Collier and Collier 1991; Rueschemeyer et al. 1992; Heller 2000). Elsewhere in the world, the political incorporation of labor unions not only enabled them to mobilize in the face of insecurities generated by capitalist development, but also empowered them to democratically negotiate the terms of capitalist transformation (Heller 2000).[15] Though the transition from ISI to an export-oriented production threatened union power in both Turkey and Argentina, majority of labor unions in the latter—including those organized in the automobile industry—found new opportunities to strengthen their position in return for partisan political support for Carlos Menem during the 1990s (Levitsky 2003; Murillo 2001). During this period, the changing political landscape under a neoliberal reform agenda and a highly disputed set of decentralization measures (Falleti 2010) further increased the political salience of labor unions. As we have seen, provincial branches of unions in the metalworking industry exploited the political conflicts between the federal and provincial governments. During the 2000s, labor unions continued to play an important role under the Kirchner governments as the PJ government saw new opportunities in the political reincorporation of labor. While the cooptation of labor movements to further partisan political ends carry important risks for unions to advance their independent agenda (Selwyn 2012), the political incorporation of labor simultaneously enabled unions to be highly relevant actors in the consolidation of Argentine democracy.

This stands in stark contrast to the experience of their Turkish counterparts where no such institutionalized political competition between the central government and the appointed governors exist. Under businessfriendly governments, progressive metalworking unions—already in a weaker position due to absence of political incorporation, rapid loss of membership and anti-unionist policies of right-wing coalition governments (Nichols and Sugur 2004)—were unable to resist the combined pressures of business and local government in favor of a Toyotist turn. This has contributed to the weakening of labor unions as membership rates rapidly decreased over the last three decades. Currently, labor unions hardly stand as relevant political actors in Turkey and union density is the lowest among OECD countries. While the macro-economic performance indicators of Turkey stand far better than those in Argentina, Turkey is certainly not making much progress toward democratization in the absence of a powerful and progressive labor movement.

CONCLUSION

Political institutions and the territorial organization of political power influence surplus extraction, skill formation and labor responses to technological change. In the case of Bursa, a unitary setting encouraged faster capital accumulation through a systematic embedding of post-Fordist skill formation policies beyond the factory. At the same time, this left relatively little room for incorporating the demands of those producers who were clearly not among the winners. In particular, textile producers in Bursa were left out of these schemes. Gradually, the volume of textile and apparel production in Bursa experienced a downturn, and insecurity about the future development of the industry dominated the scene (Akgungör 2006). In that sense, an exclusive emphasis on the development of automobile sector makes Bursa highly vulnerable to economic crises and fluctuations in global automobile supply and demand cycles. For example, after the 2001 crisis, the factory management had to halt production for extended periods, sent workers on compulsory unpaid vacations, and eventually laid off large groups of workers between 2001 and 2002 (Ozkan 2003).[16]

On the other hand, the experience of Córdoba after the 2001 crisis and the elections that followed provide some positive signs on how partisan polarizations somewhat subsided under the newly elected governors José Manuel de la Sota and Juan Schiaretti, both from PJ. During the 2000s, the new governments under PJ leaders in Cordoba mirrored their counterparts in Buenos Aires and followed a policy of incorporation, inviting representatives of producers from multiple sectors in common platforms, and initiated a series of collaborative vocational education and training programs not only in support of main automobile producers like FIAT and Renault, but also for the first and second tier parts suppliers.[17] Despite this lack of political friction between the provincial and federal administration, the vocational education and training system is still far from resembling that in Bursa, though there are some signs of improved coordination among business organizations, labor unions and politicians in the local government.[18] On the other hand, the composition of economic landscape seems more diversified in Córdoba, with the current government paying a balanced attention to the agro-industry, software, mining, construction and services.[19]

The relationship between central politicians and their local counterparts hold the key to understand how labor responses to new production technologies unfold on the ground. This may have significant implications on the competitiveness of local industry in export markets, and influence future development trajectories in the long run. At the same time, the scope and intensity of labor mobilization holds important clues on workers' capacity to mobilize and influence political debates. Very importantly, the degree of labor mobilization in democratizing settings signals important information on the prospects of democratic consolidation.

At the same time, the post-1990s experiences of Bursa and Córdoba present new puzzles and open up a new agenda of research for further exploration, especially with respect to the long-term impact of political institutions on developmental outcomes. A first line of inquiry needs to unpack the diffusion of robotics and artificial intelligence systems in the Global South. Current debates on the rise of automated production systems largely focus on its implications in advanced industrialized countries with very little discussion on the arrival of these systems in developing contexts. How do governments, businesses and unions respond to these changes? Do political institutions enable or constrain the maneuvering capacity of labor to defend its interests in similar ways?

A related area of inquiry that begs further attention is worker responses to the rise of electric cars. Though the sale volume of these vehicles is currently not very high, recent advancements in battery life, growing government subsidies and the increasing availability of recharging zones are expected to boost the sales of electric automobiles and transform the landscape as we know it. This shift from fossil fuel-based cars to renewables-driven technology subsequently calls for a revamping of existing training systems and reorganization of production. Together with the arrival of robotics on the shopfloor and recent improvements on self-driving cars, the automobile workers face yet another round of challenges to keep their jobs. New research on the politics of skill formation and labor mobilization needs to engage these puzzles introduced by similar developments more carefully in detail.

Labor movements in developing areas face multiple challenges today. Their organizational resources are dwindling, union density rates are falling, employment security is declining and new technologies demand workers to constantly reinvent themselves to keep their jobs. While transnational networks may empower isolated unions through sharing of information and learning new tactics, a comparative focus on the domestic institutional context could further enhance labor repertoires of action. In that sense, this study offers useful clues not only to the students of comparative politics and development studies but also to policy practitioners and labor leaders.

It is my hope that the findings are especially relevant in the face of increasing use of robotics and artificial intelligence systems in automobile production and other industries. These developments call for a careful analysis of how political institutions influence labor responses to contemporary technological innovations in advanced industrialized countries as well.

NOTES

1. See law no. 5542, article 4.
2. Earlier studies on Turkey suggest that when a coalition partner dominates decision-making processes on economic policy, it adopts a more exclusionary position to the detriment of other coalition partners' constituencies (Kemahlioglu 2008).
3. Existing studies on the impact of party systems on development in semi-peripheral contexts offers further insights that support this observation. Though most of these scholars derive their conclusions from cross-national comparative analysis, their findings reveal that partisan competition plays a notable role in economic policy-making under externally induced challenges (Roberts and Wibbels 1999; Frye 2002). For example, looking at post-communist countries, Frye finds that political polarization between ex-communists and anti-communists had a devastating effect on capitalist economic growth in these countries (Frye 2002: 309).
4. For example, Schneider and Soskice (2009) argue that the concept of *Hierarchized Market Economies*, where firms and big conglomerates dominate decision-making on economic development processes, best characterizes capitalist development in Latin American countries. They suggest that the roots of this *business penetration* into politics lie in the electoral system (Majoritarian for presidential elections and proportional representation for the legislature). However, this account misses a few important points. First, it assumes that politicians are always susceptible to external pressures from businesses, and tacitly act in favor of big conglomerate interests without opposing them. Yet, existing studies (e.g. Dominguez 1996; Gibson 1997; Corrales 2000; Murillo 2001, 2002, 2009; Calvo and Murillo 2004) reveal that this is not always the case and show that politicians and partisan choices of the actors create significant biases, which are influential in setting the course of market reforms. Second, the same electoral institutions yield very different outcomes at the subnational level: local politicians are not always easily influenced by powerful business actors—as the case of Cordoba reveals. In other words, firms are not always able to *buy* local politicians. Finally, the concept of hierarchical market economies does not pay enough attention to historical legacies that shape contemporary trajecto-

ries of capitalist development. For an extended critique on this point, see Schrank 2009.

5. See Nichols and Sugur (2004) for a comparison of production processes across the automobile and white-goods industry, based on cases from Turkey.

6. For a study on how curricula at a vocational school in Kocaeli were updated, see Aytac and Deniz (2005). The governors in both provinces have increasingly taken direct initiative to start vocational education and apprentice training programs within the past decade. See "[Tekirdag'da] Mesleki Egitim Kurslari Basliyor" (Vocational Education Programs Take a Start in Tekirdag), *Devrim*, 18 March 2010, accessed at http://www.devrimgazetesi.com.tr/haberdetay.asp?ID=4966; "Issizlige Kocaeli Modeli" (Kocaeli Model Against Unemployment) *Gebze Gazetesi*, http://www.gebzegazetesi.com/haber_detay.asp?haberID=2848&haber-issizlige-kocaeli-modeli, accessed on 1 April 2010.

7. Particularly in the textile manufacturing, even though the processes of spinning, weaving and finishing are relatively complex and capital intensive (Cammett 2007: 27), workers' proposal systems are much less in use, because workers are required to concentrate more on speed and rapid completion of a garment. For an overview of production in a textile factory shopfloor based in the USA, see Collins 2003.

8. In contrast to textiles, apparel production is labor-intensive, relying on low wage labor, requires minimal start-up capital and few specialized skills (Cammett 2007: 27–28).

9. For example Liz Claiborne is a typical case of an apparel firm with off-shore factories worldwide: in a sense, it is a global apparel firm without a single chimney in the USA. See Collins 2003.

10. In a research on textile workers in Istanbul Eraydin and Erendil (1999) find that "on average women employed in the Istanbul clothing industry are young (54% were below the age of 25) and poorly educated (64% reported that they had not proceeded beyond primary school)" (Eraydin and Erendil 1999: 264).

11. See Jale Ozgenturk, "Turkiye'de Krizler Hep Ayni...Konusulanlar da" (In Turkey Crises are All the Same... And the conversations), *Referans*, 22 November 2008. Accessible at http://www.referansgazetesi.com/haber. aspx?YZR_KOD=38&HBR_KOD=111135.

12. It should be noted that Itzigsohn (2000) draws a distinction between two major types where economic actors in the informal sector avoid regulations. First dimension refers to shying away from registration and taxation. Second dimension of informality includes producers that evade labor market regulations such as minimum wage, social security, job and employment security and provision of retirement benefits (Itzigsohn 2000: 11).

My use of the term "informal sector" covers both, but particularly refers to the producers that fall in the latter category, because the second dimension is a clear indication of how these firms/producers extract surplus labor value in production, which is a major point of distinction from the techniques used for the same purpose in the formal sector.

13. Some researchers (Henley et al. 2009) argue that not everyone who falls under the informal sector are subject to insecure work conditions, which may also allow workers better employment opportunities through self-employment and choice over hours of work (see for example Cohen and House 1996; Maloney 2004; Marcoullier et al. 1997; Saavedra and Chong, 1999).

14. Itzigsohn argues that the variation in informal production across semi-peripheral economies is largely shaped by "regulatory regimes," which refer to the general institutional context in which markets are regulated. According to this argument, "it is not the amount of state intervention that matters but the general institutional context in which market regulation takes place" (Itzigsohn 2000: 83). My explanation does not disregard variation in the historical evolution of regulatory regimes but complements this explanation by pointing out how the political organization of power can indeed play a significant role at times of game-changing technological innovations.

15. For example, Heller (2000) finds that in Kerala, India, the long-term legacy of social mobilization and organized social movements enabled labor unions to push for political and economic inclusion, where organized class interests and strong state institutions led to the institutionalization of class conflicts and class compromises across agrarian and industrial sectors (Heller 2000: 3). According to Heller, following this political and economic inclusion under a democratic framework, the social mobilization of subordinate classes in the face of capitalist development challenges served as a key engine of development.

16. Moreover, the dominant position of union leadership over the rank-and-file in TURKMETAL generated significant problems at times of worker lay-offs. In particular, the workers who lost their jobs protested the union leadership for their undemocratic practices and sued the company for turning a blind eye to their mistreatment. This reveals that overlapping partisan preferences at the top, which includes politicians, business organizations and union leaders may not always yield outcomes favorable to democratic participation for the rank-and-file. Interview #40, Labor Lawyer, 1 November 2007, Bursa, Turkey. Other experts also highlight problems generated by the autarchic governance structure in Turkmetal. Interview#37, Sociologist, September 2007, Eskisehir, Turkey and Interview #29, Sociologist, 8 October 2007, Cardiff, UK.

17. Interview #34, 5 August 2008, Córdoba, Argentina; and Interview#56, 1 July 2008, Córdoba, Argentina. An official at CIM also noted that the cooperation with local government on vocational training has increased steadily after 2002. Interview #24, 17 July 2008, Córdoba, Argentina. In an interview, the representative of SMATA-Córdoba also highlighted growing cooperation with the local government on training. Interview#5, 27 June 2008 and 3 July 2008, Córdoba, Argentina.
18. Interview #28, Argentina, 30 July 2008, Córdoba, Argentina.
19. See "Produccion Córdoba" Informe de Gestion: 2003–2007, Córdoba: Ministerio de Produccion y Trabajo.

BIBLIOGRAPHY

Acosta, P., and L. Gasparini. 2007. Capital Accumulation, Trade Liberalization, and Rising Wage Inequality: The Case of Argentina. *Economic Development and Cultural Change* 55 (4): 793–812.

Akgungör, S. 2006. Geographic Concentrations in Turkey's Manufacturing Industry: Identifying Regional Highpoint Clusters. *European Planning Studies* 14: 169–197.

Apaydin, F. 2012. Partisan Preferences and Skill Formation Policies: New Evidence from Turkey and Argentina. *World Development* 40 (8): 1522–1533.

Aytac, A., and V. Deniz. 2005. Quality Function Deployment in Education: A Curriculum Review. *Quality and Quantity* 39: 507–514.

Beneria, L., and M. Roldan. 1987. *The Crossroads of Class and Gender: Industrial Homework, Subcontracting and Household Dynamics in Mexico City.* Chicago: University of Chicago Press.

Benton, L. 1990. *Invisible Factories: The Informal Economy and Industrial Development in Spain.* Albany: State University of New York Press.

Calvo, E., and M.V. Murillo. 2004. Who Delivers? Partisan Clients in the Argentine Electoral Market. *American Journal of Political Science* 48: 742–757.

Cammett, M. 2007. *Globalization and Business Politics in Arab North Africa.* New York: Cambridge University Press.

Castells, M., and A. Portes. 1989. World Underneath: The Origins, Dynamics, and Effects of the Informal Economy. In *The Informal Economy: Studies in Advanced and Less Industrialized Countries,* ed. A. Portes, M. Castells, and L. Benton. Baltimore: Johns Hopkins University Press.

Centeno, M., and A. Portes. 2006. The Informal Economy in the Shadow of the State. In *Out of the Shadows: Political Action and the Informal Economy in Latin America,* ed. P. Fernández-Kelly and J. Shefner. University Park: Pennsylvania State University Press.

Chong, A., and M. Gradstein. 2007. Inequality and Informality. *Journal of Public Economics* 91: 159–179.

Cohen, B., and W.J. House. 1996. Labor Market Choices, Earnings and Informal Networks in Khartoum, Sudan. *Economic Development and Cultural Change* 44: 589–618.

Collier, R.B. 1999. *Paths Toward Democracy*. New York: Cambridge University Press.

Collier, R.B., and D. Collier. 1991. *Shaping the Political Arena*. Notre Dame: University of Notre Dame Press.

Collins, J.L. 2003. *Threads: Gender, Labor and Power in Global Apparel industry*. Chicago: University of Chicago Press.

Corrales, J. 2000. Presidents, Ruling Parties, and Party Rules: A Theory on the Politics of Economic Reform in Latin America. *Comparative Politics* 32: 127–149.

Coy, M. 2006. Gated Communities and Urban Fragmentation in Latin America: The Brazilian Experience. *GeoJournal* 66: 121–132.

Dominguez, J.I. 1996. *Technopols: Freeing Politics and Markets in Latin America in the 1990s*. University Park: Pennsylvania State University Press.

Eraydin, A., and A. Erendil. 1999. The Role of Female Labour in Industrial Restructuring: New Production Processes and Labour Market Relations in the Istanbul Clothing Industry. *Gender, Place & Culture* 6: 259–272.

Etchemendy, S., and R.B. Collier. 2007. Down But Not Out: Union Resurgence and Segmented Neocorporatism in Argentina (2003–2007). *Politics and Society* 35 (3): 363–401.

Falleti, T. 2010. *Decentralization and Subnational Politics in Latin America*. New York: Cambridge University Press.

Frye, T. 2002. The Perils of Polarization: Economic Performance in the Postcommunist World. *World Politics* 54: 308–337.

Gezici, F., and G. Hewings. 2007. Spatial Analysis of Regional Inequalities in Turkey. *European Planning Studies* 15: 383–403.

Gibson, E.L. 1997. The Populist Road to Market Reform: Policy and Electoral Coalitions in Mexico and Argentina. *World Politics* 49: 339–370.

Güzey, O. 2009. Urban Regenation and Increased Competitive Power: Ankara in an Era of Globalization. *Cities* 26: 27–37.

Heller, P. 2000. *The Labor of Development: Workers and the Transformation of Capitalism in Kerala, India*. Ithaca: Cornell University Press.

Henley, A., R. Arabsheibani, and F. Carneiro. 2009. On Defining and Measuring the Informal Sector: Evidence from Brazil. *World Development* 37: 992–1003.

Henry, C.M., and R. Springborg. 2001. *Globalization and the Politics of Development in the Middle East*. New York: Cambridge University Press.

Hodson, R. 1996. Dignity in the Workplace Under Participative Management: Alienation and Freedom Revisited. *American Sociological Review* 1: 719–738.

Humphrey, J. 1995. Industrial Reorganization in Developing Countries: From Models to Trajectories. *World Development* 23 (1): 149–162.

Itzigsohn, J. 2000. *Developing Poverty: The State, Labor Market Deregulation and the Informal Economy in Costa Rica and the Dominican Republic*. University Park: Pennsylvania State University Press.

Kang, D.C. 2002. *Crony Capitalism: Corruption and Development in South Korea and the Philippines*. Cambridge, MA: Cambridge University Press.

Kaya, Yunus. 2008. Proletarianization with Polarization: Industrialization, Globalization, and Social Class in Turkey, 1980–2005. *Research in Social Stratification and Mobility* 26: 161–181.

Kemahlioglu, O. 2008. Particularistic Distribution of Investment Subsidies Under Coalition Governments: The Case of Turkey. *Comparative Politics* 40: 189–207.

Lee, Eul-Teo, and Tuncay Guloglu. 2014. Prejudice Against Labor Unions and Effects on Membership. In *Labor and Employment Relations in a Globalized World, Contributions to Economics*, ed. T. Dereli et al. Cham: Springer International Publishing.

Levitsky, S. 2003. *Transforming Labor Based Parties in Latin America: Argentine Peronism in Comparative Perspective*. Cambridge: Cambridge University Press.

Maloney, W.F. 2004. Informality Revisited. *World Development* 32: 1159–1178.

Marcoullier, D., V. Ruiz de Casilla, and C. Woodruff. 1997. Formal Measures of the Informal-Sector Wage Gap in Mexico, El Salvador, and Peru. *Economic Development and Cultural Change* 45: 367–392.

Murillo, M.V. 2001. *Labor Unions, Partisan Coalitions, and Market Reforms in Latin America*. Cambridge: Cambridge University Press.

———. 2002. Political Bias in Policy Convergence: Privatization Choices in Latin America. *World Politics* 54: 462–493.

———. 2009. *Political Competition, Partisanship, and Policy Making in Latin American Public Utilities*. Cambridge: Cambridge University Press.

Nichols, T., and N. Sugur. 2004. *Global Management, Local Labor: Turkish Workers and Modern Industry*. Basingstoke: PalgraveMacmillan.

Nichols, T., N. Sugur, and E. Demir. 2002a. Globalised Management and Local Labour: The Case of the White-Goods Industry in Turkey. *Industrial Relations Journal* 33: 68–85.

———. 2002b. Beyond Cheap Labor: Trade Unions and Development in the Turkish Metal Industry. *The Sociological Review* 50: 23–47.

Ocakci, M. 2001. Commuting to the Istanbul Historical Core: The Case of Industrial Employees. *European Planning Studies* 9: 117–127.

Ozkan, S. 2003. More Global than Ever, as Local as Always: Internationalization and Shop-Floor Transformation at Oyak-Renault and Tofas-FIAT in Turkey. *Actes Gerpisa* 36: 143–160.

Patroni, V. 2004. Disciplining Labour, Producing Poverty: Neoliberal Structural Reforms and Political Conflict in Argentina. In *Neoliberalism in Crisis, Accumulation, and Rosa Luxemburg's Legacy*, Research in Political Economy, vol. 21, 91–119. Bingley : Emerald Group Publishing Limited.

Pérez Sáinz, J.P. 1995. Globalizacion y neoinformalidad en America Latina [Globalization and Neo-Informality in Latin America]. *Nueva Sociedad* 135: 36–41.

Pessar, P.R. 1994. Sweatshop Workers and Domestic Ideologies: Dominican Women in New York's Apparel Industry. *International Journal of Urban and Regional Research* 18: 127–142.

Richards, A., and J. Waterbury. 1996. *A Political Economy of the Middle East*. Boulder: Westview.

Riddle, L.A., and K. Gillespie. 2003. Information Sources for New Ventures in the Turkish Clothing Export Industry. *Small Business Economics* 20 (1): 105–120.

Rivero, A., and D. Michel. 2007. El indice coincidente mensual de la actividad económica de Córdoba [The Monthly Coincidental Index of Economic Activity in Córdoba]. *Revista de Economía y Estadística* 45: 31–73.

Roberts, K.M., and E. Wibbels. 1999. Party Systems and Electoral Volatility in Latin America: A Test of Economic, Institutional, and Structural Explanations. *American Political Science Review* 93: 575–590.

Rosser, B., Jr., M.V. Rosser, and E. Ahmed. 2000. Income Inequality and the Informal Economy in Transition Economies. *Journal of Comparative Economics* 28: 156–171.

Royo, S. 2008. *Varieties of Capitalism in Spain: Remaking the Spanish Economy for the New Century*. London: Palgrave Macmillan.

Rueschemeyer, D., E. Huber Stephens, and J. Stephens. 1992. *Capitalist Development and Democracy*. Chicago: University of Chicago Press.

Saavedra, J., and A. Chong. 1999. Structural Reform, Institutions and Earnings: Evidence from the Formal and Informal Sectors in Urban Peru. *Journal of Development Studies* 35: 95–116.

Sallaz, J.J. 2015. Permanent Pedagogy: How Post-Fordist Firms Generate Effort But Not Consent. *Work and Occupations* 42 (1): 3–34.

Schneider, B.R. 2009. Hierarchical Market Economies and Varieties of Capitalism in Latin America. *Journal of Latin American Studies* 41: 553–575.

Schneider, B.R., and D. Soskice. 2009. Inequality in Developed Countries and Latin America: Coordinated, Liberal and Hierarchical Systems. *Economy and Society* 38: 17–52.

Schrank, A. 2009. Understanding Latin American Political Economy: Varieties of Capitalism or Fiscal Sociology? *Economy and Society* 38: 53–61.

Sellers, J.M. 2002. *Governing from Below: Urban Regions and the Global Economy*. Cambridge, MA: Cambridge University Press.

Selwyn, B. 2012. *Workers, State and Development in Brazil: Powers of Labour, Chains of Value*. Manchester: Manchester University Press.

Valdes, E. 2009. Segregacion residencial: una aproximacion desde los mercados de trabajo en la Ciudad de Córdoba [Residential Segregation: An Approach from the Labour Markets in the City of Córdoba]. Mimeo: VI Encuentro Interdisciplinario de Ciencias Sociales y Humanas.

Vos, R., and J.A. Ocampo. 2009. *Uneven Economic Development.* New York: Orient Longman Private Limited, Zed Books Ltd and Third World Network.

Weiss, L. 1995. Governed Interdependence: Rethinking the Government-Business Relationship in East Asia. *The Pacific Review* 8: 589–616.

APPENDIX

PRIMARY SOURCES AND LIST OF INTERVIEWS

Newspapers

- Cumhuriyet, 1990–2000
- Evrensel, 1996–2001 [Published as Emek in 1997 and 1998]
- La Voz del Interior, 1990–2000
- Milliyet, 1999–2000

Original Documents
- FIAT Auto Córdoba Worker Training Notes 2007
- FIAT Auto Isvor Presentations, 1995, 1996
- Bursa Vocational Education Council Meeting Minutes, 1991–2004

Reports
- Prominent Industrial Sectors in the Cities [Illerde One Cikan Sanayi Sektorleri], Basbakanlik DPT Publications, August 2006.
- Fifth Five-Year Development Plan, Ankara, Turkey [Besinci bes yil-lik kalkinma plani]. 1984.
- Sixth Five-Year Development Plan, Ankara, Turkey [Altinci bes yil-lik kalkinma plani]. 1989.

© The Author(s) 2018   207
F. Apaydin, *Technology, Institutions and Labor*, International Political
Economy Series, https://doi.org/10.1007/978-3-319-77104-5

- Eight Five-Year Development Program, Secondary Education, General Education, Vocational Education, Technical Education, Private Advisory Committee Report. [Sekizinci Bes Yillik Kalkinma Plani, Ortaogretim, Genel Egitim, Meslek Egitimi, Teknik Egitim, Ozel Istisare Kurulu Raporu]. 2001.
- National Ministry of Education, Total Quality System in Technical Education (MEB Teknik Egitimde Toplam Kalite Yonetimi) MEB: Ankara. 2001.
- Produccion Córdoba: Informe de Gestion: 2003–2007 [Production in Córdoba: Report on Management: 2003–2007]. Córdoba: Ministerio de Produccion y Trabajo. 2008.
- Report on the Follow-up project of Vocational and Technical School Graduates [Mesleki ve Teknik Egitim Kurumlari mezunlarinin izlenmesi projesi raporu]. Ministry of Education (Milli Egitim Bakanligi) Ankara. 2007.

Worker Training Questionnaires

FIAT Bursa (50).
FIAT Córdoba (40)

List of Interviews

Interview ID	Position	Date	Location
#1	Former Government Official	24 July 2008	Córdoba, Argentina
#2	Manager, FIAT Córdoba	5 May 2008	Córdoba, Argentina
#3	Manager, FIAT Bursa	30 January 2008	Bursa, Turkey
#4	Former Ministry of Education Istanbul Office Member	12 January 2009	Ankara, Turkey
#5	Former Training Secretary of SMATA-Córdoba	27 June 2008 and 3 July 2008	Córdoba, Argentina
#6	Training Office, FIAT Bursa	21 November 2007 and 26 December 2007	Bursa, Turkey
#7	Former Manager, FIAT, Argentina	17 June 2008	Córdoba, Argentina
#8	Former Government Official	1 August 2008	Córdoba, Argentina
#9	Birlesik Metal Training Office	5 December 2007	Istanbul, Turkey
#10	Manager, Delphi Automotive	21 November 2007	Bursa, Turkey
#11	Former Manager, FIAT-Bursa	29 November 2007	Istanbul, Turkey
#12	Manager, FIAT-Bursa	21 November 2007	Bursa, Turkey
#13	Vice Directorate of Ministry of Education	24 March 2008	Istanbul, Turkey
#14	Director, Apprentice Training Center, Istanbul	23 January 2008	Istanbul, Turkey
#15	Leadership, SMATA-Córdoba	27 June 2008	Córdoba, Argentina
#16	Leadership, Turkmetal Istanbul	14 November 2007	Istanbul, Turkey
#17	Manager, FIAT Córdoba	8 July 2008	Córdoba, Argentina
#18	Former FIAT Worker and Shopfloor Leader	8 August 2008	Córdoba, Argentina
#19	Former Government Member	19 July 2008	Córdoba, Argentina
#20	Former FIAT worker	1 November 2007	Bursa, Turkey
#21	Leadership,Birlesik-Metal	4 December 2008	Istanbul, Turkey
#22	Former Turk-Is Representative	8 January 2009	Istanbul, Turkey

(*continued*)

(continued)

Interview ID	Position	Date	Location
#23	Former FIAT Worker	3 November 2007	Bursa, Turkey
#24	CIM Training Secretariat	17 July 2008	Córdoba, Argentina
#25	Turk-Is Confederation Regional Representative	10 January 2009	Bursa, Turkey
#26	Smata Córdoba-Secretariat of Training	9 June 2008	Córdoba, Argentina
#27	Former Government Official	8 August 2008	Córdoba, Argentina
#28	Rep. for the Agency for the Economic Development of Córdoba	30 July 2008	Córdoba, Argentina
#29	Expert Sociologist, Cardiff University	8 October 2007	Cardiff, UK
#30	Federal Ministry of Labor, Department of Training	6 June 2008	Buenos Aires, Argentina
#31	Former Government Member	7 August 2008	Córdoba, Argentina
#32	Former Government Member	30 June 2008	Córdoba, Argentina
#33	Engineer, Delphi Automotive	18 December 2007	Istanbul, Turkey
#34	Provincial Secretariat of Labor	5 August 2008	Córdoba, Argentina
#35	UIC Training Secretariat	7 July 2008	Córdoba, Argentina
#36	Director, Federal Ministry of Labor and Social Security	11 August 2008	Buenos Aires, Argentina
#37	Expert Sociologist	September 2007	Eskisehir, Turkey
#38	Former Turkmetal Bursa Branch Leader	2 November 2007	Bursa, Turkey
#39	Principal's Office, Tophane Vocational and Technical High School	12 January 2009	Bursa, Turkey
#40	Labor Lawyer	1 November 2007	Bursa, Turkey
#41	Officer, Bursa Ministry of Education	15 January 2008	Bursa, Turkey
#42	TurkmetalShopfloor Representative	25 February 2008	Istanbul, Turkey

(*continued*)

(continued)

Interview ID	Position	Date	Location
#43	Former TurkmetalShopfloor Representative	7 September 2007	Gebze, Kocaeli, Turkey
#44	Former Manager, Delphi Automotive	15 November 2007	Istanbul, Turkey
#45	Former Manager, Delphi Automotive	20 March 2008	Istanbul, Turkey
#46	FIAT worker	29 April 2008	Córdoba Argentina
#47	FIAT worker	14 June 2008	Córdoba Argentina
#48	FIAT worker	18 June 2008	Córdoba Argentina
#49	FIAT worker	28 January 2008	Bursa, Turkey
#50	Delphi worker	28 February 2008	Istanbul, Turkey
#51	Delphi worker	25 February 2008	Istanbul, Turkey
#52	Delphi worker	26 March 2008	Istanbul, Turkey
#53	Delphi worker	25 February 2008	Istanbul, Turkey
#54	Leadership, UOM-Córdoba	15 July 2008	Córdoba Argentina
#55	Former Consultant to the Minister of Labor	21 July 2008	Córdoba Argentina
#56	Secretariat, Vocational Training Office	1 July 2008	Córdoba Argentina
#57	Federal Ministry of Labor and Social Security Office in Córdoba Coordinator	24 June 2008	Córdoba Argentina

Index[1]

---

[1] Note: Page numbers followed by 'n' refer to notes.

© The Author(s) 2018   213
F. Apaydin, *Technology, Institutions and Labor*, International Political
Economy Series, https://doi.org/10.1007/978-3-319-77104-5